Microsoft Whiteboard Basics

A Beginner's Guide

Kiet Huynh

Table of Contents

Introduction

What is Microsoft Whiteboard?

In the ever-evolving world of digital collaboration, finding tools that enhance both creativity and productivity is crucial. One such tool that has become increasingly popular in both educational and business settings is Microsoft Whiteboard. But what exactly is Microsoft Whiteboard, and why has it become such a valuable asset for teams and individuals alike? This section explores what Microsoft Whiteboard is, its core features, and how it can transform the way you collaborate and brainstorm.

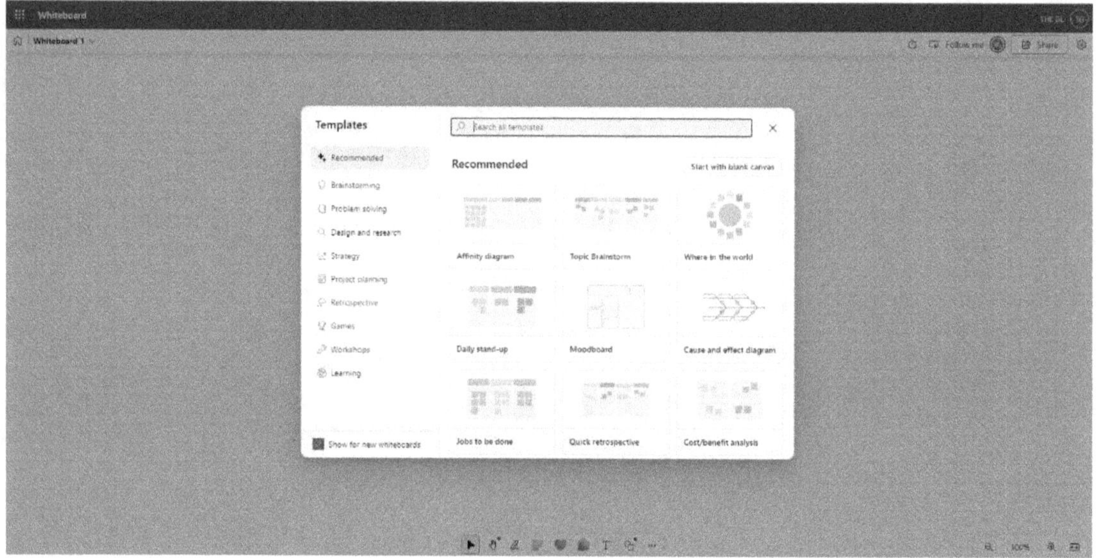

1.1 A Visual Collaboration Platform

At its core, Microsoft Whiteboard is a cloud-based digital whiteboarding application. It provides users with an infinite canvas where they can visually express their ideas, organize thoughts, and collaborate in real time. Designed to mimic the traditional whiteboard used in classrooms and meeting rooms, this digital alternative offers far more functionality and flexibility, thanks to its seamless integration with the Microsoft 365 suite of tools.

The app is available across multiple platforms, including Windows, iOS, Android, and web browsers. This cross-platform availability ensures that users can access their whiteboards and collaborate with others anytime, anywhere, from virtually any device. Microsoft Whiteboard allows for an enhanced collaborative experience, as multiple users can draw, write, and manipulate objects on the canvas simultaneously, all in real time.

1.2 Key Features of Microsoft Whiteboard

Infinite Canvas

One of the standout features of Microsoft Whiteboard is its infinite canvas. Unlike a physical whiteboard that is limited by size, the digital canvas in Microsoft Whiteboard expands as you add more content. This enables users to explore ideas without feeling restricted by space, which is particularly useful for brainstorming sessions, mind mapping, and large project planning.

Drawing and Inking Tools

Microsoft Whiteboard comes equipped with a wide variety of drawing tools, including pens, highlighters, and an eraser. The drawing tools are pressure-sensitive, providing a natural and intuitive drawing experience, especially when used with a stylus or touchscreen device. Users can choose from different colors and adjust the thickness of their lines, allowing for precise control when sketching diagrams, flowcharts, or annotations.

Text, Sticky Notes, and Shapes

In addition to freehand drawing, Microsoft Whiteboard allows users to insert text boxes, sticky notes, and pre-made shapes. These features make it easy to organize information and categorize ideas. For example, you might use sticky notes to jot down quick thoughts during a brainstorming session, then organize those notes into categories by dragging them into position. Pre-made shapes, such as squares, circles, and arrows, are useful for creating clean and professional-looking diagrams.

Real-Time Collaboration

Perhaps the most powerful feature of Microsoft Whiteboard is its real-time collaboration capability. Users can invite others to their whiteboard, enabling simultaneous participation. This makes Microsoft Whiteboard an ideal tool for remote teams, as everyone can contribute their ideas, draw, and comment on the same board regardless of their location. Collaboration can be further enhanced through its integration with Microsoft Teams, allowing for direct communication while working on the whiteboard.

Templates for Productivity

To help users get started quickly, Microsoft Whiteboard includes a range of templates. These templates are designed for common tasks such as brainstorming, project planning, and teaching. Instead of starting from scratch, users can choose a template that matches their needs, customize it, and get to work immediately. Templates provide structure and help ensure that collaborative sessions remain focused and productive.

Cloud Integration

Since Microsoft Whiteboard is part of the Microsoft 365 ecosystem, it offers deep integration with other Microsoft services such as OneDrive and SharePoint. Whiteboards are automatically saved to the cloud, which means users never have to worry about losing their work. Additionally, they can easily share whiteboards with others via Microsoft Teams, email, or by generating a shareable link.

1.3 How Microsoft Whiteboard Transforms Collaboration

Microsoft Whiteboard redefines the way teams collaborate by breaking down the barriers of time, distance, and physical limitations. Whether you're brainstorming ideas with colleagues in the same office or collaborating with remote teams spread across the globe, the tool facilitates an open, fluid, and visually engaging way of working together.

Enhancing Creativity in Brainstorming Sessions

Traditional whiteboards often fall short in capturing the full extent of a team's brainstorming capabilities. Microsoft Whiteboard, on the other hand, fosters creativity by providing an unlimited space to explore ideas without erasing previous thoughts. You can easily branch off into different concepts, create mind maps, and use sticky notes or color coding to organize ideas.

Furthermore, because multiple people can work on the whiteboard at the same time, participants are no longer passive observers. Each person can actively contribute, whether by drawing, adding notes, or manipulating content. This leads to a richer, more inclusive brainstorming session where every voice is heard.

Visualizing Complex Concepts and Ideas

Microsoft Whiteboard is an excellent tool for visual learners. Complex ideas and data can be represented visually, making them easier to understand and digest. Whether you're diagramming workflows, outlining strategies, or solving problems, the ability to draw connections between ideas using lines, shapes, and images allows for a more effective and dynamic representation of concepts.

In a business environment, this can be particularly valuable during project planning sessions. For example, using Microsoft Whiteboard, a project manager can create a Gantt chart or workflow diagram in real time, with team members contributing their input on deadlines and tasks. This shared visual space ensures everyone is on the same page and aligned with the project's goals.

Integrating with Other Microsoft Tools

One of the most significant advantages of using Microsoft Whiteboard is how seamlessly it integrates with other Microsoft 365 tools. For instance, while conducting a meeting via Microsoft Teams, participants can open a shared whiteboard directly within the meeting window, enabling real-time collaboration without switching between apps. Similarly, content from Word, Excel, and PowerPoint can be easily integrated into the whiteboard, allowing for collaborative editing and visual augmentation.

For educators, the integration with OneNote and PowerPoint is particularly useful. Teachers can create engaging, interactive lessons by embedding whiteboards into their presentations or note-taking applications. This makes classroom activities more interactive and provides students with a space to visually engage with the material.

1.4 Microsoft Whiteboard Use Cases

In Education

Microsoft Whiteboard has proven to be a valuable tool in both traditional and virtual classrooms. Teachers can use it to explain complex concepts, conduct interactive lessons, and encourage student participation. For example, in a mathematics lesson, an educator can draw diagrams, plot equations, and highlight key points directly on the whiteboard, with students contributing their answers or annotations in real time. Additionally, with students being able to join the whiteboard from any device, the tool is ideal for distance learning or hybrid classroom setups.

In Business

For business professionals, Microsoft Whiteboard offers an efficient way to conduct meetings, plan projects, and collaborate on ideas. In project management, for instance, whiteboards can be used to break down tasks, assign responsibilities, and track progress visually. With its real-time collaboration features, it enables teams working across different locations to stay aligned and engaged.

Brainstorming sessions, often the heart of creative work in marketing and product development, are another key use case for businesses. The infinite canvas, along with sticky notes and templates, makes ideation a more structured yet creative process, helping to turn abstract ideas into actionable plans.

In Creative and Design Industries

Microsoft Whiteboard's drawing tools and infinite canvas are well-suited for creative industries, such as advertising, design, and architecture. Designers can sketch concepts, collaborate on wireframes, and even storyboard ideas for projects. The ability to collaborate with others in real time—be it team members or clients—adds value by streamlining the creative process and reducing feedback loops.

For example, an advertising agency might use Microsoft Whiteboard during a client meeting to sketch out initial concepts for a campaign. The client can then add comments or make suggestions directly on the board, leading to more effective communication and faster decision-making.

1.5 Accessibility and Inclusivity

Microsoft Whiteboard also supports inclusivity by offering features that cater to diverse user needs. For example, the app supports multiple input methods, including touch, stylus, and keyboard, making it accessible to individuals with different preferences or physical limitations. The integration of assistive technologies such as screen readers also ensures that visually impaired users can navigate and interact with the content on the whiteboard.

Additionally, because Microsoft Whiteboard is available across multiple platforms, it provides access to a broader range of users, regardless of the device they are using. This cross-platform compatibility ensures that no one is excluded from collaboration, whether they're working on a desktop, tablet, or mobile device.

Conclusion

Microsoft Whiteboard is more than just a digital replacement for traditional whiteboards; it's a dynamic and versatile tool that enhances collaboration, boosts creativity, and simplifies complex tasks. Its integration with the Microsoft 365 ecosystem, combined with its powerful real-time collaboration features, makes it an essential tool for businesses, educators, and creative professionals alike.

In the next sections of this guide, we will dive deeper into how you can use Microsoft Whiteboard to its fullest potential, starting with a detailed look at how to navigate the interface and use its most fundamental features.

Why Use Microsoft Whiteboard?

Microsoft Whiteboard offers a versatile and dynamic platform for visual collaboration, making it an essential tool for teams, educators, and individuals who need to think, plan, and communicate ideas visually. Its flexibility and ease of use allow users to brainstorm, organize, and share ideas in ways that go beyond traditional tools like word processors or presentation software. Here are several reasons why Microsoft Whiteboard stands out as a valuable tool.

2.1 Seamless Collaboration

One of the most compelling reasons to use Microsoft Whiteboard is its ability to foster real-time collaboration. In today's world, where remote work and virtual teams have become the norm, the ability to work together across different locations is crucial. Microsoft Whiteboard allows multiple users to collaborate on the same canvas, no matter where they are. This means that whether you're working from home, in an office, or on the go, you and your team can brainstorm, plan, and draw up ideas together, with everyone contributing in real time.

The collaboration features of Microsoft Whiteboard are integrated with Microsoft Teams, making it even easier to bring colleagues together. You can open a Whiteboard directly within a Teams meeting, share it with all participants, and begin working on ideas as if everyone were in the same room. Each participant can add their input, be it through text, images, or drawings, allowing for an interactive, engaging experience that enhances productivity and creativity.

Additionally, collaboration isn't limited to just team members with Microsoft accounts. You can invite guests to your Whiteboard, offering them the opportunity to contribute without requiring them to have specific software or subscriptions. This makes Microsoft Whiteboard a great tool for working with clients, partners, or stakeholders who may not be part of your organization.

2.2 Creative Brainstorming and Ideation

Microsoft Whiteboard excels in facilitating creative brainstorming sessions. The platform provides an expansive digital canvas where users can jot down ideas, sketch out concepts, and visually organize thoughts. Unlike traditional brainstorming tools, Whiteboard offers unlimited space, allowing ideas to flow naturally without the constraints of a physical board or limited screen space.

Its drawing tools, such as the pen and highlighter, make it easy to sketch and annotate, providing a free-form environment where ideas can evolve. You can start with rough sketches, which can later be refined into more polished visuals, enabling a process of iterative development. The inclusion of sticky notes and text boxes allows for structured thinking when necessary, and users can categorize and group ideas as they develop.

The ability to import images and PDFs further enhances the brainstorming process. Teams can analyze visual data, diagrams, or charts and collaborate directly on them. For example, product teams can import mockups or wireframes and annotate them with feedback and suggestions, making Microsoft Whiteboard a versatile platform for ideation and creative thinking.

2.3 Visual Learning and Conceptualization

For those who learn and process information visually, Microsoft Whiteboard is an indispensable tool. It enables users to present information in a way that is easy to comprehend and visually engaging. By combining text, images, shapes, and drawings, complex ideas can be broken down and represented in simpler forms. For educators and trainers, this makes Microsoft Whiteboard an ideal platform for teaching and explaining abstract concepts.

Visual learners can benefit from the platform's flexibility in how content is displayed. For example, teachers can create visual mind maps to illustrate relationships between different concepts, helping students better understand and retain information. Similarly, professionals can use Whiteboard for concept mapping, outlining workflows, or presenting project timelines in ways that are easy to follow and comprehend.

The use of templates in Microsoft Whiteboard further simplifies the conceptualization process. For instance, the built-in brainstorming and project planning templates provide ready-made structures that can help guide discussions and ensure that key elements are not overlooked. These templates can be customized to suit specific needs, saving time and ensuring consistency in the presentation of information.

2.4 Efficient Meeting Tool

Incorporating Microsoft Whiteboard into meetings, whether virtual or in person, can significantly enhance the productivity and engagement of participants. Whiteboards are traditionally used to jot down key points during discussions, but with Microsoft Whiteboard, this process is brought into the digital age. You can create a shared space where meeting participants can add notes, ideas, or drawings in real time, ensuring that everyone is engaged and contributing.

A key advantage of using Whiteboard in meetings is that it allows participants to express ideas visually. Rather than just discussing ideas verbally or through text-based tools like chats, team members can quickly sketch out ideas or highlight important details on a shared canvas. This makes meetings more dynamic, as users are not constrained by the limitations of traditional meeting formats.

Additionally, the use of Microsoft Whiteboard in meetings helps in maintaining focus and accountability. Action points, decisions, and next steps can be noted on the board, providing a visual summary that all participants can refer to after the meeting. The board can be saved and shared with participants, ensuring that no important details are lost. This visual record of the meeting can be invaluable for follow-up tasks and ongoing projects.

2.5 Integration with the Microsoft Ecosystem

Another reason why Microsoft Whiteboard is a powerful tool is its seamless integration with other Microsoft products, particularly within the Microsoft 365 ecosystem. For users who already rely on Microsoft tools such as Word, Excel, PowerPoint, and Teams, Whiteboard enhances the overall workflow by acting as a natural extension of these applications.

For example, users can embed Whiteboards into PowerPoint presentations or export ideas from a Whiteboard session into Word documents. This flexibility allows for a smooth transition between brainstorming sessions and formal documentation. Integration with Microsoft Teams enables Whiteboard to become a core component of meetings, allowing team members to brainstorm and plan in real time within the same ecosystem they use for communication and file sharing.

Beyond meetings, the integration with OneNote allows users to embed Whiteboards in their notes or even use them as part of a digital notebook for capturing creative ideas. By being able to move content effortlessly between different Microsoft applications, users can enhance productivity, collaboration, and creativity.

2.6 Easy to Use and Accessible

One of the primary reasons why Microsoft Whiteboard is becoming a go-to tool for many organizations is its user-friendly interface. Whether you're a tech-savvy user or someone new to digital collaboration tools, Microsoft Whiteboard is designed to be intuitive and easy to use. The interface is clean, with all the necessary tools accessible from a simple toolbar. Users can quickly get started with little to no training, making it an excellent tool for all skill levels.

Moreover, Microsoft Whiteboard is accessible across multiple devices, including desktops, tablets, and smartphones. This makes it easy to pick up where you left off, no matter which device you are using. The mobile app offers similar functionality to the desktop version, allowing users to sketch, write, and collaborate while on the go. This cross-platform accessibility ensures that your ideas and collaborative efforts are always within reach, regardless of the device you're using.

2.7 Unlimited Canvas for Big Ideas

Microsoft Whiteboard offers an unlimited digital canvas, allowing users to expand their workspace as their ideas grow. Unlike traditional whiteboards, where space is limited, the digital canvas in Microsoft Whiteboard provides endless room for ideas, drawings, and notes. This makes it ideal for brainstorming sessions, project planning, or mapping out complex concepts that require more room than a physical whiteboard can offer.

The ability to zoom in and out of the canvas gives users a bird's-eye view of their entire board, helping them see the big picture while also being able to focus on specific details. This expansive workspace is especially beneficial for large teams or projects, where multiple ideas and components need to be organized in a single space.

2.8 Time-Saving Templates and Tools

Microsoft Whiteboard offers a variety of templates and tools that make it easier to get started and save time on repetitive tasks. Whether you're planning a project, brainstorming ideas, or organizing a meeting, Whiteboard provides ready-made templates to help you kickstart the process. These templates ensure that important elements are not missed and help structure discussions or plans more effectively.

For example, the Kanban board template allows teams to manage tasks visually, while the SWOT analysis template is perfect for strategy sessions. These templates can be customized to suit specific needs, making Microsoft Whiteboard adaptable to different types of projects and workflows.

2.9 Enhanced Creativity and Engagement

Lastly, Microsoft Whiteboard promotes creativity by offering a digital space where users can experiment with ideas without the fear of making mistakes. The ability to erase, undo, and redo actions encourages users to think outside the box and try new things. It fosters an environment of exploration and experimentation, making it a powerful tool for both individual creativity and collaborative innovation.

In an educational setting, for example, students can engage with the material in a more interactive and hands-on way. Teachers can present lessons visually, and students can contribute to discussions by drawing or writing on the shared Whiteboard. This active participation leads to greater engagement and retention of information.

In summary, Microsoft Whiteboard offers a unique blend of functionality, flexibility, and creativity that sets it apart from other collaboration tools. Its ability to bring teams together, support creative thinking, and integrate with the Microsoft ecosystem makes it an essential tool for modern workplaces and educational environments. Whether you're brainstorming new ideas, planning a project, or teaching a concept, Microsoft Whiteboard offers the tools you need to visualize and communicate effectively.

Who This Book is For

Microsoft Whiteboard is a versatile tool, designed with a wide range of users in mind. Whether you're an individual working on creative projects, a teacher organizing a virtual classroom, or part of a business team collaborating remotely, Microsoft Whiteboard can support your workflow in unique and meaningful ways. This book is tailored to a diverse audience, ensuring that regardless of your background, you'll be able to harness the full potential of the software to improve creativity, collaboration, and productivity.

3.1. Educators and Teachers

In recent years, technology has transformed the way education is delivered, and Microsoft Whiteboard has emerged as a powerful tool for educators. Teachers looking to engage their students, particularly in a virtual or hybrid setting, will find this book especially helpful. Microsoft Whiteboard's intuitive interface allows teachers to create interactive lessons where students can participate in real-time, no matter where they are.

With features like drawing tools, text boxes, and sticky notes, educators can visually present complex concepts, facilitate group work, and create collaborative environments. For example, in a mathematics class, a teacher can sketch out a problem on the Whiteboard, and students can actively participate by adding their own annotations or solutions. In a literature or social studies class, group discussions can be organized using sticky notes, with each student contributing their ideas to a shared Whiteboard.

This book will walk you through the steps of setting up your whiteboard, sharing it with students, and using the various features that make lesson delivery smooth and interactive. From engaging brainstorming sessions to organizing classroom activities, Microsoft Whiteboard can significantly enhance your teaching methods, whether in-person or online. You'll also learn how to integrate Microsoft Whiteboard with other Microsoft 365 tools like OneNote and Teams, to further enhance the learning experience.

3.2. Business Professionals and Remote Teams

In today's globalized world, the need for effective remote collaboration is greater than ever, and Microsoft Whiteboard has proven to be a vital tool for business professionals and remote teams. Whether you are managing a small team or leading a large-scale project, this book will guide you through using Whiteboard to foster creativity, collaboration, and organization.

Business professionals can use Microsoft Whiteboard for brainstorming sessions, planning projects, and even conducting meetings in a more visual and engaging manner. Imagine a marketing team brainstorming a new campaign. Team members can easily draw diagrams, add sticky notes with ideas, and even insert images or files to flesh out the project. Each team member, regardless of location, can contribute in real-time, making the brainstorming process faster and more dynamic.

This book is designed for professionals looking to improve their team's productivity through seamless collaboration. You will learn how to share whiteboards with team members, manage permissions, and keep your whiteboards organized for future reference. We will also cover advanced features, such as integrating Whiteboard with Microsoft Teams, allowing you to present and collaborate during video meetings without needing to switch between platforms.

By the end of this guide, you will be equipped with the skills to use Microsoft Whiteboard in various business scenarios, from ideation and strategy sessions to detailed project planning and feedback collection.

3.3. Students and Learners

Students, whether in high school, college, or higher education, can benefit immensely from Microsoft Whiteboard. As an interactive, cloud-based tool, it offers a digital space for taking notes, brainstorming, organizing ideas, and collaborating with peers on group projects.

In this book, students will discover how to make the most of Microsoft Whiteboard's diverse set of tools to aid in their studies. For instance, during study sessions, a student can create a mind map to break down complex concepts, such as the branches of government in a political science course or the components of a chemical reaction in a science class. With the ability to insert images and files, students can enrich their Whiteboard with relevant resources, such as diagrams or textbook pages, making it a one-stop hub for study material.

Additionally, students working on group projects can use Microsoft Whiteboard to collaborate in real-time, no matter where their peers are located. This book will show students how to invite others to their whiteboards, assign specific tasks using sticky notes, and visually track progress throughout the project. You'll also learn about integrating

Whiteboard with OneDrive, making it easy to access your projects across devices and share your work with classmates or instructors.

This guide will also address specific tips and tricks for organizing study sessions, keeping track of deadlines, and visualizing complex topics, ensuring that students at all levels can benefit from Microsoft Whiteboard's features.

3.4. Freelancers and Creative Professionals

If you're a freelancer or creative professional, you probably value flexibility and adaptability in your tools. Whether you're a graphic designer, writer, architect, or consultant, Microsoft Whiteboard can help you bring your ideas to life. The visual nature of the platform makes it an ideal space for sketching out ideas, planning projects, and collaborating with clients or other freelancers.

For designers and artists, Microsoft Whiteboard offers the flexibility to create rough sketches and wireframes quickly. Whether you're designing a website, an app interface, or even a physical product, the drawing tools allow you to translate your ideas onto the screen. You can also import images and use them as part of your brainstorming process. This book will guide you through setting up your creative workspace, adjusting drawing tools to fit your needs, and sharing your designs with clients or collaborators for feedback.

Writers and content creators can also use Microsoft Whiteboard to organize their ideas. Whether you're drafting a novel, writing a blog post, or creating content for a brand, the ability to use sticky notes and text boxes allows you to break down your project into manageable pieces. For instance, a freelance writer can create a content outline, visually map out different sections, and move ideas around until they form a cohesive narrative.

As you progress through this book, you'll learn how to maximize Microsoft Whiteboard's flexibility for your specific creative needs. Whether you're collaborating with others or working on solo projects, this tool will help you stay organized, creative, and productive.

3.5. Project Managers and Team Leaders

For project managers, Microsoft Whiteboard is an invaluable tool that simplifies the complex nature of overseeing multiple tasks and teams. As a project manager, you're responsible for planning, delegating, and tracking the progress of various initiatives. This book will show you how to use Whiteboard to streamline these processes, making it easier to keep your projects on track.

Project managers can use Microsoft Whiteboard to create dynamic project roadmaps, visualize tasks, and assign responsibilities to team members. Imagine leading a software development project. You can create a detailed timeline on the Whiteboard, adding sticky notes to represent different tasks and assigning each task to a team member. As the project progresses, you can adjust the board to reflect any changes, ensuring that everyone stays informed about deadlines and progress.

Whiteboard's collaborative features are particularly useful for project managers working with remote teams. This book will cover how to use Whiteboard during virtual meetings to present updates, discuss challenges, and brainstorm solutions with team members in real-time. By the end of this guide, you'll have a clear understanding of how to use Microsoft Whiteboard to plan and manage projects efficiently, while keeping your team engaged and aligned with project goals.

3.6. Entrepreneurs and Small Business Owners

If you're an entrepreneur or small business owner, you understand the importance of adaptability and creativity in running a successful venture. Microsoft Whiteboard is an excellent tool for visualizing business plans, brainstorming new ideas, and working collaboratively with partners or employees.

This book will show you how to use Microsoft Whiteboard to map out your business strategy, create detailed plans for marketing or product development, and track your progress. Whether you're planning the launch of a new product or organizing the logistics of your operations, Whiteboard provides a flexible space where you can lay out your ideas visually and collaborate with others to refine them.

Entrepreneurs can use Whiteboard to conduct SWOT analyses, visualizing the strengths, weaknesses, opportunities, and threats facing their businesses. You can also use the tool to create timelines, chart financial projections, and brainstorm marketing strategies. This guide will walk you through practical examples of how to leverage Microsoft Whiteboard to enhance your business operations, from planning to execution.

3.7. Nonprofit Organizations and Social Impact Groups

Nonprofit organizations and social impact groups often rely on collaboration and creativity to achieve their goals, and Microsoft Whiteboard is the perfect tool to support those efforts. Whether you're planning an event, organizing a fundraising campaign, or brainstorming new initiatives, Microsoft Whiteboard can help your team stay aligned and focused on your mission.

Nonprofit leaders can use Microsoft Whiteboard to visualize project plans, map out goals, and assign tasks to team members. During virtual meetings, Whiteboard can facilitate real-time collaboration, allowing everyone to contribute ideas and feedback. This book will show you how to integrate Whiteboard into your nonprofit's workflow, making your team's efforts more organized and effective.

From grant writing and donor engagement strategies to volunteer coordination, this book will demonstrate how nonprofit organizations can leverage Microsoft Whiteboard to improve communication, collaboration, and strategic planning.

In summary, "Microsoft Whiteboard Basics: A Beginner's Guide" is designed for a wide variety of users, each with their own unique needs and goals. Whether you're an educator, a student, a creative professional, or a project manager, this book will help you unlock the potential of Microsoft Whiteboard, empowering you to enhance your work processes and collaborate more effectively with others.

CHAPTER I
Getting Started with Microsoft Whiteboard

1.1 Introduction to the Interface

Microsoft Whiteboard provides a versatile, intuitive, and user-friendly interface that allows individuals and teams to collaborate seamlessly on various tasks. Whether you're brainstorming ideas, teaching a class, managing a project, or just jotting down notes, Microsoft Whiteboard offers a digital space that mimics the traditional whiteboard experience while providing enhanced tools and features. This chapter will help you get familiar with the essential components of the Microsoft Whiteboard interface, so you can quickly get started and make the most of its capabilities.

The interface of Microsoft Whiteboard is designed to be minimalistic but powerful, offering users an organized space to focus on collaboration without feeling overwhelmed. In this section, we will explore the different elements that make up the interface, focusing on the toolbar, workspace, and essential navigation techniques that will help you create and organize your first whiteboard efficiently.

1.1.1 Navigating the Toolbar

The toolbar is the command center of Microsoft Whiteboard, providing quick access to a variety of tools that allow you to customize, draw, annotate, and manage your content. Positioned at the bottom or side of the screen (depending on your device or layout settings), the toolbar is designed for easy access and efficient use. Let's dive into the main elements of the toolbar and explore how each tool can assist you in your whiteboard experience.

A. The Drawing Tools

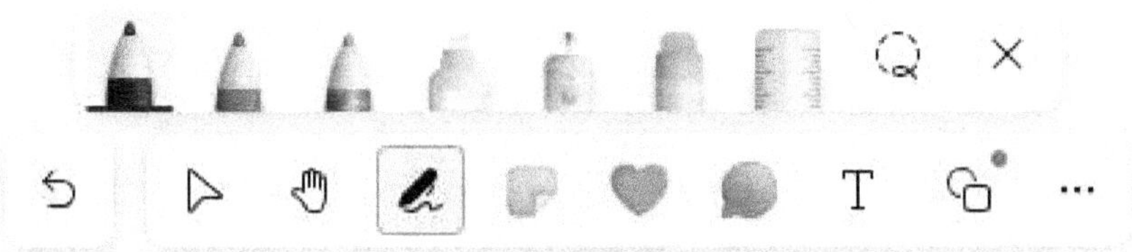

At the core of Microsoft Whiteboard is the ability to draw and annotate freely, just like on a physical whiteboard. The drawing tools are typically found as the first set of icons on the toolbar, enabling you to sketch, highlight, or write with different levels of precision.

- *Pen Tool:* The pen tool allows you to draw freehand on the canvas. You can select from different pen colors and sizes to suit your needs. The pen is perfect for quick sketches, handwritten notes, or marking up documents and diagrams.

- *Highlighter:* The highlighter tool lets you emphasize key points or ideas by applying a transparent layer of color over your content. It's ideal for drawing attention to specific sections of text or images on your whiteboard.

- *Color and Thickness Selector:* Next to the pen and highlighter, you'll find options to adjust the color and thickness of your lines. Microsoft Whiteboard provides a wide range of colors to personalize your drawings and notes. You can also adjust the pen's thickness to create finer or bolder lines, depending on the level of detail you need.

- *Custom Pens:* Microsoft Whiteboard also allows you to save custom pen settings. For instance, if you frequently use a specific color and thickness, you can create and save a custom pen to avoid having to adjust the settings each time.

B. Eraser Tool

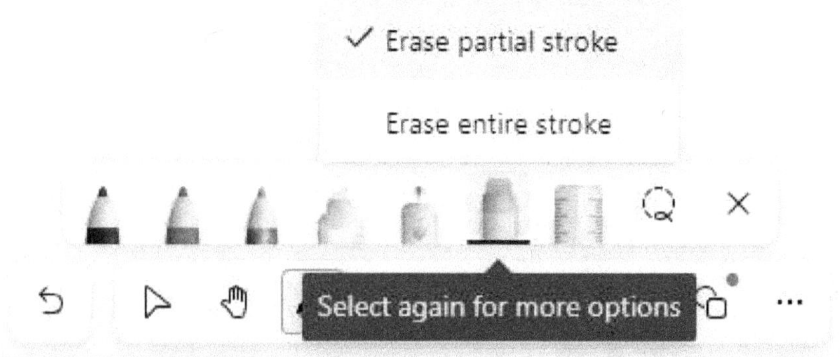

Mistakes are inevitable when you're drawing or writing freehand, and the eraser tool allows you to remove any unwanted marks on the whiteboard quickly and easily. The eraser comes in two forms:

- *Stroke Eraser:* This eraser removes entire strokes in one go. When you activate the eraser tool, you can click or tap on any stroke (e.g., a drawn line or a written word), and it will disappear entirely.

- *Partial Eraser:* In some versions of Microsoft Whiteboard, you may also have access to a partial eraser. This tool allows you to erase only parts of a stroke, offering more precision if you want to remove only a section of your drawing without affecting the entire line.

C. Undo and Redo Buttons

Located alongside the drawing tools, the Undo and Redo buttons provide quick access to correct mistakes or revert changes. Whether you've accidentally erased something or want to bring back a previously deleted stroke, these buttons give you complete control over the flow of your work.

- *Undo:* Removes the last action you performed, whether it was drawing, typing, or pasting an object.

- *Redo:* Re-applies the last action you undid, which can be useful if you change your mind.

D. Lasso Select Tool

The Lasso Select Tool is a powerful feature that lets you select multiple objects or elements on the whiteboard at once. This is particularly useful when you want to move or manipulate large sections of content, such as grouping sticky notes, text, and drawings together. To use the Lasso tool, simply draw a freeform shape around the content you wish to select. Once selected, you can resize, move, or group the elements as needed.

E. Sticky Notes and Text

In addition to freehand drawing, Microsoft Whiteboard offers the ability to add sticky notes and text boxes to your board. These tools are ideal for capturing key ideas, comments, or structured information that require more precision than hand-drawn notes.

- *Sticky Notes:* Sticky notes are great for brainstorming sessions or for creating quick, movable ideas on your whiteboard. You can change the color of the sticky note to help organize your ideas visually.

- *Text Tool:* The text tool allows you to add typed text to the whiteboard. This is particularly useful when clarity is important, or when you're collaborating with others who may find typed text easier to read than handwritten notes.

F. Image and Document Importing

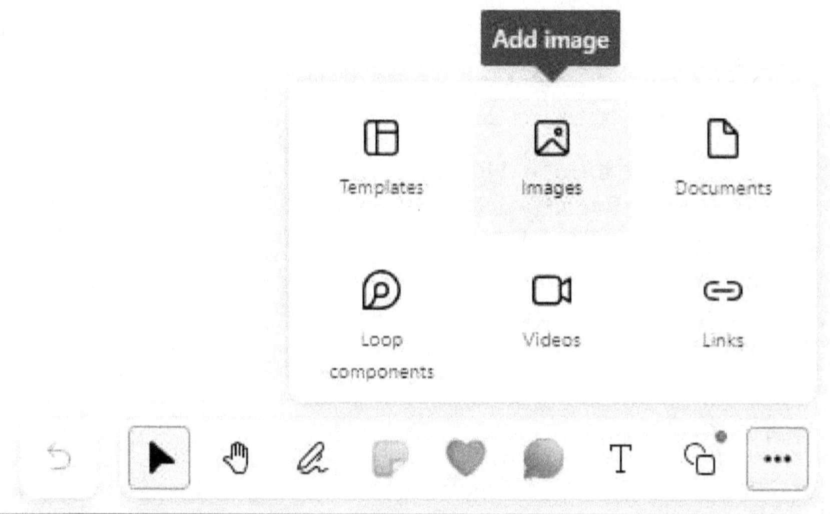

One of the standout features of Microsoft Whiteboard is its ability to integrate images and documents into your workspace. This feature enhances the collaborative experience by allowing users to work on visual or data-driven projects.

- *Insert Image:* You can easily add images to your whiteboard by either uploading them from your device or searching for images online. Once inserted, images can be resized, moved, or annotated.

- *Insert Document:* Microsoft Whiteboard allows you to upload PDFs and other documents, enabling collaboration and annotation directly on these files. This feature is especially useful for reviewing and marking up presentations, reports, or educational materials.

G. Shapes and Tables

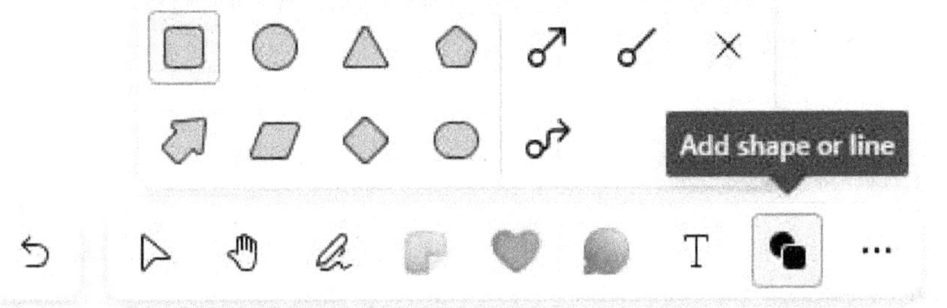

For those who need more structure on their whiteboard, Microsoft Whiteboard includes a variety of shapes and tables that can be used to organize ideas or data.

- *Shape Tool:* The shape tool lets you insert geometric shapes like circles, squares, triangles, and arrows. These shapes can be used to create flowcharts, diagrams, or structured layouts.

- *Table Tool:* Microsoft Whiteboard also offers a table tool, which allows you to organize data or information in rows and columns. You can quickly create grids for tracking tasks, organizing information, or building frameworks.

H. Templates

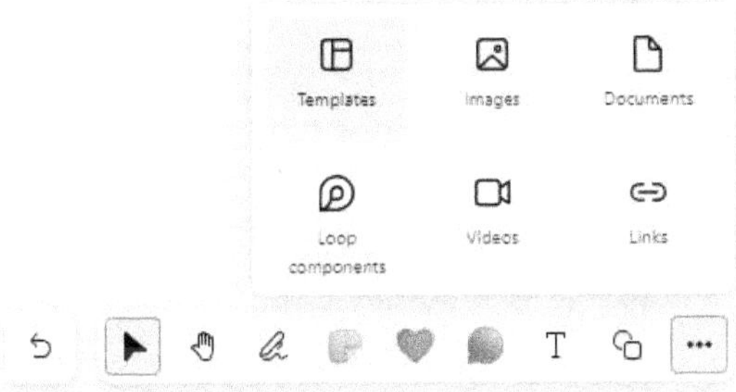

Microsoft Whiteboard provides several pre-made templates designed for common tasks such as brainstorming, project planning, and learning activities. These templates are customizable and can help streamline your workflow by providing structured layouts that fit your specific needs.

- *Brainstorming Templates:* Pre-built templates for brainstorming sessions help to organize ideas more efficiently, with spaces for team input and idea categorization.

- *Kanban and Task Planning Templates:* These are ideal for managing workflows, tracking project progress, and assigning tasks visually.

I. Collaboration Features

Microsoft Whiteboard is built with collaboration in mind. Several tools within the toolbar are dedicated to enhancing teamwork and ensuring that everyone's input is captured in real-time.

- *Sharing Options:* You can share your whiteboard with others via a unique link or invite collaborators via email. You can also set different permission levels, allowing collaborators to either view or edit the whiteboard.

- *Real-Time Collaboration:* As your team members join the whiteboard, you can see their inputs in real-time. Whether they are drawing, typing, or adding images, the changes will appear instantly on your screen.

- *Follow Mode:* In some cases, it may be helpful to lead your team through a particular section of the whiteboard. The Follow mode allows you to guide your collaborators through the board, focusing their attention on specific areas as you move around.

J. Reactions and Tags

Another unique feature of the toolbar is the ability to add reactions or tags to the whiteboard. These tools are useful for providing feedback or categorizing content during collaborative sessions.

- *Reactions:* You can add thumbs-up or thumbs-down icons, hearts, and other simple reactions to indicate approval or highlight important points on the board.

- *Tags:* Tags allow you to categorize content visually, making it easier to navigate and organize the whiteboard during group projects or brainstorming sessions.

Navigating the toolbar is essential to mastering Microsoft Whiteboard. By familiarizing yourself with these tools, you can enhance your productivity, creativity, and collaboration efforts, ensuring that every whiteboard session is efficient and impactful. As we proceed through the book, you will learn how to apply these tools in practical situations, maximizing your whiteboard experience.

1.1.2 Understanding the Workspace

The Microsoft Whiteboard workspace is where all the action happens. It serves as your canvas, where you can brainstorm ideas, collaborate with others, and visually represent information. Understanding the layout and functionality of this workspace is essential to becoming proficient in using Microsoft Whiteboard. In this section, we will explore the key elements of the workspace, how to navigate through it, and how you can maximize its potential for your projects.

The Infinite Canvas

One of the defining features of Microsoft Whiteboard is its infinite canvas. Unlike physical whiteboards or even many digital whiteboards that have a limited space, the infinite canvas of Microsoft Whiteboard allows you to keep expanding as much as you need. Whether you are working on a simple sketch or an elaborate mind map, you'll never run out of room. This endless space gives you the freedom to think and create without the constraints of a fixed border.

However, with great flexibility comes the need for effective navigation. When working on large whiteboards with many elements, it's important to know how to move around the canvas seamlessly. You can do this by using several tools available within the interface:

- *Panning:* You can pan through the canvas by holding down your mouse button or touchpad and dragging the board in the direction you want to move. On touch devices, you can achieve the same effect by simply swiping with two fingers. This feature allows you to easily move from one part of your whiteboard to another without getting lost in the expansive space.

- *Zooming:* Microsoft Whiteboard supports zoom functionality, which is vital when dealing with detailed work or larger whiteboards. You can zoom in and out using the scroll wheel on your mouse, the pinch-to-zoom feature on touch devices, or by using the zoom control buttons on the toolbar. Zooming is particularly useful when you need to get a close look at specific areas or zoom out for an overview of the entire project.

Layers and Grouping Content

Microsoft Whiteboard's workspace offers the ability to work with multiple layers of content. Although it doesn't operate with traditional layers like Photoshop, you can conceptually treat different elements (drawings, text, shapes, images, etc.) as being on various layers. This capability allows you to overlap content and create complex diagrams or structures, especially in group projects where multiple people are adding elements simultaneously.

- *Grouping content:* If you have several items that belong together (e.g., text, shapes, and images that form a section of your presentation), you can group them. By selecting multiple elements (click and drag to select), you can group them together, making it easier to move or resize the entire group as a unit. This is particularly useful when working on collaborative projects where organization and clarity are key.

Tools and the Workspace

Microsoft Whiteboard integrates various tools directly into the workspace to make it easier for you to visualize your thoughts. These tools include drawing pens, shapes, sticky notes, text boxes, and images. Here's a breakdown of how these tools interact with the workspace:

- *Pens and Highlighters:* Drawing directly on the canvas is one of the most intuitive ways to interact with the Whiteboard. With a variety of pen and highlighter options, you can sketch diagrams, write notes, or annotate on top of existing elements. The ability to change the thickness and color of the pens allows for a greater level of customization.

- *Sticky Notes and Text Boxes:* Adding sticky notes or text boxes allows for more structured text entry. These elements can be dragged, resized, and arranged anywhere on the canvas. Sticky notes are especially useful in brainstorming sessions or when organizing thoughts into clusters.

- *Shapes and Lines:* Shapes such as circles, squares, and arrows can be added to the canvas to create flowcharts, diagrams, or to emphasize certain elements. These shapes can be resized and rotated to suit your design. The snap-to-grid feature ensures that your shapes are aligned perfectly, giving your work a polished look.

- *Images and Files:* You can insert images directly into your whiteboard, making it easy to incorporate visual references, charts, or diagrams. Additionally, Microsoft Whiteboard allows for PDF and other file imports, which can be annotated or referenced during collaboration sessions. This feature transforms the whiteboard from just a sketching tool to a comprehensive workspace that integrates various media types.

Organizational Tools

A large whiteboard can quickly become chaotic if it's not well-organized, especially when multiple people are working on it at once. To maintain order in your workspace, Microsoft Whiteboard offers several *organizational tools:*

- *Grid Lines and Ruler:* The gridlines on the workspace help ensure that everything is aligned. If you need precise alignment, the ruler tool allows you to draw straight lines at any angle. You can rotate the ruler and use it as a guide for drawing or positioning elements. This is especially useful for creating structured layouts or diagrams.

- *Content Snap:* Whiteboard features content snapping, which automatically aligns objects, such as shapes or sticky notes, with one another. As you drag an element around the canvas, it will snap into alignment with other nearby elements, making it easier to create structured, organized content without manually adjusting every piece.

- *Lasso Select:* The lasso tool allows you to select multiple items by drawing a freeform shape around them. This is useful when you need to move or delete several elements at once or when you want to group them together.

Multi-User Collaboration and Workspace Management

One of the strongest features of Microsoft Whiteboard is its real-time collaboration. Multiple users can work on the same whiteboard simultaneously, making it a powerful tool for group projects, remote team meetings, or virtual brainstorming sessions.

- *Real-time Updates:* As each user adds, edits, or moves elements on the whiteboard, these changes are reflected in real-time for everyone involved. This instant feedback fosters a sense of collaborative effort, similar to working on a physical whiteboard together.

- *Color-Coding Users:* Each user can be assigned a color for their contributions, making it easy to see who added what. This feature is particularly useful in larger teams or when reviewing the whiteboard after a session, as you can track individual contributions and comments.

- *Follow Mode:* When multiple users are working on the same whiteboard, it's easy to lose track of where everyone is or what changes are being made. The Follow Mode feature allows users to follow another participant's view of the whiteboard. For example, if one person is presenting or leading a discussion, others can follow their screen, ensuring everyone stays on the same page (or section of the whiteboard).

Workflow Integration

Microsoft Whiteboard doesn't exist in a vacuum. It integrates seamlessly with other tools in the Microsoft 365 ecosystem, enhancing your workflow across various platforms:

- *Integration with Microsoft Teams*: Whiteboard is fully integrated into Microsoft Teams, allowing you to open and share your whiteboard directly during a Teams meeting. This makes it easy to brainstorm or share ideas in real-time without leaving the meeting interface. After the meeting, the whiteboard remains accessible, so team members can continue collaborating asynchronously.

- *Integration with OneNote and Outlook:* You can also export your whiteboards to OneNote or send them via Outlook. This is useful for archiving whiteboards, sharing them with people who didn't attend the session, or incorporating them into meeting notes.

Customizing Your Workspace

One of the great things about Microsoft Whiteboard is its flexibility in adapting to different users' needs. You can *customize* the workspace to match your workflow and preferences.

- *Background Options:* Microsoft Whiteboard allows you to change the background of the canvas. You can choose from different colors or grid options (e.g., ruled lines, dotted grids) depending on the task you're working on. These background options can help you create more structured designs or simply make the workspace more visually appealing.

- *Content Accessibility:* To ensure that your whiteboard is accessible to all users, you can enable or disable certain accessibility features, such as high contrast mode, which makes the content easier to view for people with visual impairments.

In summary, understanding the workspace in Microsoft Whiteboard is key to unlocking its full potential. The infinite canvas, combined with powerful drawing, text, and organizational tools, gives you the freedom to create, collaborate, and visualize your ideas in a structured and efficient way. By mastering the navigation, tools, and customization options available, you can create whiteboards that are not only functional but also visually engaging and well-organized. Whether you are working alone or in a team, the Microsoft Whiteboard workspace adapts to meet your needs, making it an essential tool for modern collaboration

1.1.3 Creating Your First Whiteboard

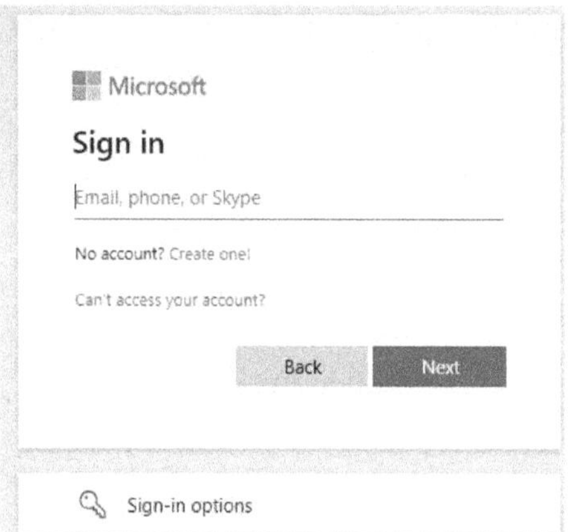

Now that you're familiar with the toolbar and workspace in Microsoft Whiteboard, it's time to dive into creating your very first whiteboard. Whether you're brainstorming ideas, collaborating with a team, or visualizing concepts, the whiteboard is your digital canvas where you can draw, write, add notes, and even import images or files. This section will guide you step by step through creating a new whiteboard, understanding how to use its essential tools, and personalizing it to suit your needs.

Getting Started: Creating a Blank Whiteboard

To create your first whiteboard in Microsoft Whiteboard, follow these simple steps:

1. Open Microsoft Whiteboard:

Begin by launching Microsoft Whiteboard from your desktop, web browser, or mobile app, depending on which platform you prefer. If you're using the desktop app, you can find it in the Start Menu on Windows or via a shortcut you may have created. Alternatively, you can open it through the Microsoft Whiteboard web app by navigating to whiteboard.microsoft.com.

2. Sign In to Your Account:

You will be prompted to sign in with your Microsoft account. This could be a personal account, work account, or school account. Once signed in, your whiteboards will sync across all devices, allowing you to pick up where you left off from any platform.

3. Create a New Whiteboard:

After signing in, you'll see the dashboard displaying all your existing whiteboards. To create a new one, click on the "Create New Whiteboard" button. This will open a blank whiteboard where you can start your project.

4. Naming Your Whiteboard:

It's a good idea to name your whiteboard, especially if you plan to create multiple boards over time. To name your whiteboard, click on the "Untitled Whiteboard" text at the top and give it a relevant name, such as "Project Ideas" or "Team Meeting Notes." This makes it easier to organize and find later.

Understanding the Blank Canvas

Once your new whiteboard is open, you'll be greeted by a blank, infinite canvas. Unlike traditional whiteboards or digital drawing apps, Microsoft Whiteboard offers an endless space that you can navigate and expand as needed. This infinite canvas is ideal for brainstorming sessions, large projects, or ongoing collaborative efforts where you don't want to feel restricted by space.

Let's break down some of the key elements and features of the blank canvas:

1. Canvas Navigation:

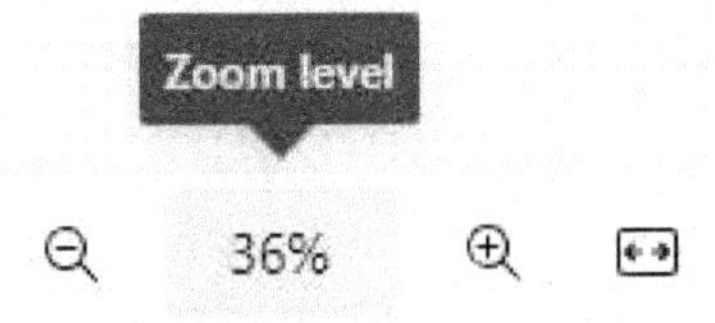

To move around the canvas, you can simply click and drag with your mouse (or your finger if you're on a touch-enabled device). You can zoom in and out using your mouse's scroll wheel or by pinching on a touch device. This functionality allows you to zoom into specific details or zoom out to see the big picture, which is incredibly useful during complex projects.

2. Grid and Guidelines:

By default, the whiteboard appears as a plain, blank space. However, if you prefer more structure, you can enable gridlines or guidelines by clicking on the Settings icon (gear icon) in the toolbar and selecting "Grid" or "Guidelines." This feature can help you align objects or draw more precisely.

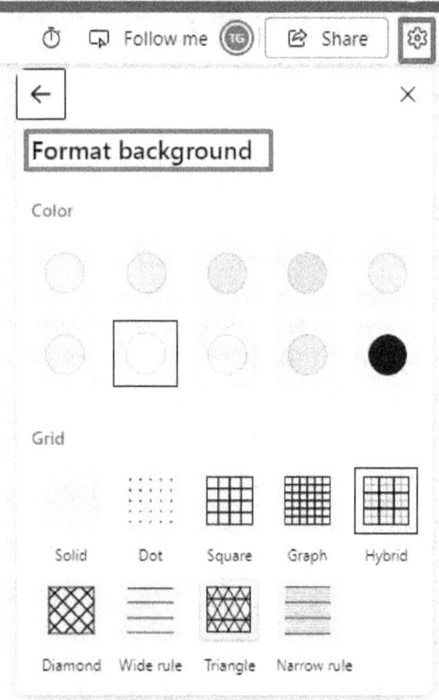

3. Canvas Background:

You can also customize the background of your whiteboard to make it more visually appealing or functional. Click on the Settings icon and choose "Canvas Background" to select different colors or patterns. You can use a grid background for technical drawings, a ruled background for note-taking, or a custom color that matches your project's theme.

Using Basic Tools to Create Content

Now that you've set up your whiteboard, it's time to start adding content. Microsoft Whiteboard provides several essential tools that you can use to draw, write, add shapes, and more. Let's explore how to use these tools to begin building your whiteboard content.

1. Drawing and Writing with the Pen Tool:

One of the most fundamental tools in Microsoft Whiteboard is the Pen tool, which allows you to draw freehand on the canvas. Here's how you can use it:

- Select the Pen Tool from the toolbar. You'll see several pen options with different colors and thicknesses. Choose the pen that suits your needs.

- Click and drag on the canvas to draw. If you're using a touch device or stylus, you can also write directly on the screen.

- You can adjust the pen's color and thickness by clicking on the pen icon again and selecting from the available options. This flexibility allows you to create different line styles for various elements of your whiteboard.

The Pen tool is especially useful for brainstorming sessions, quick sketches, or writing notes directly on the board.

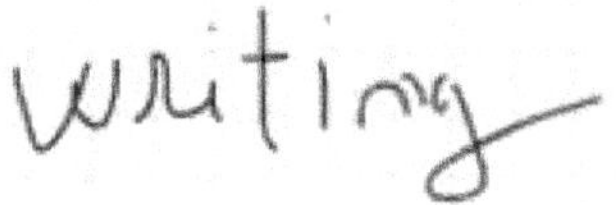

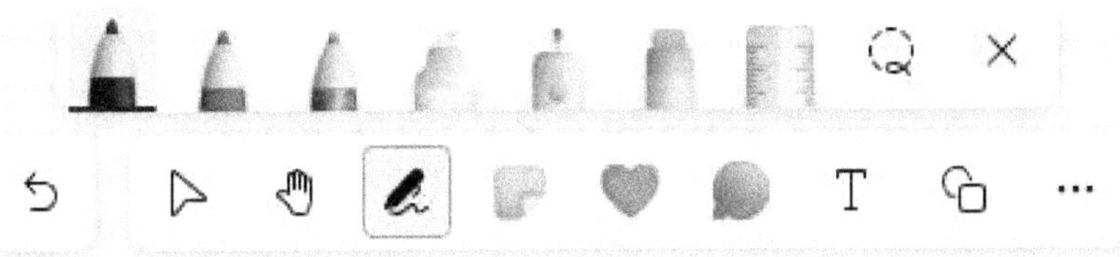

2. Using the Eraser Tool:

Mistakes are inevitable, but they're easy to fix with the Eraser tool. Simply click on the Eraser Tool in the toolbar and drag it over the areas you want to erase. You can also adjust the size of the eraser to cover larger or smaller sections of your drawing.

If you need to undo an action, use the Undo button (curved arrow icon) in the toolbar, or press Ctrl+Z on your keyboard. There's also a Redo button if you change your mind.

3. Adding Text Boxes:

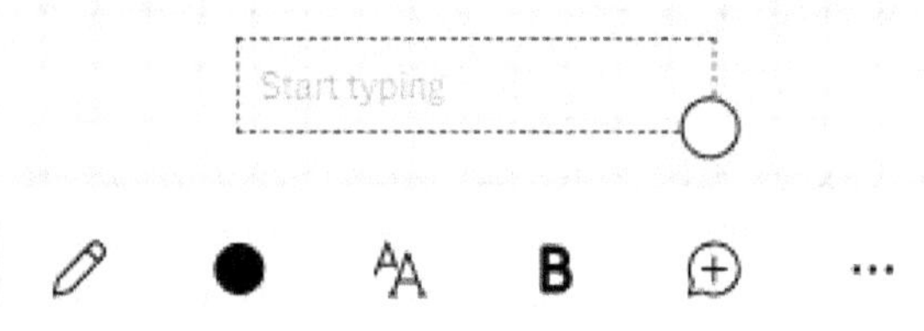

Text is a crucial part of any whiteboard, especially if you want to include notes or explanations alongside your visuals. To add a text box:

- Select the Text Tool from the toolbar (it looks like a capital "A").

- Click anywhere on the canvas to create a text box, then start typing.

- You can resize, move, and format your text box as needed by clicking on it and using the options that appear, such as adjusting the font size or alignment.

Text boxes are helpful for organizing ideas, labeling diagrams, or adding instructions to your whiteboard.

4. Using Sticky Notes:

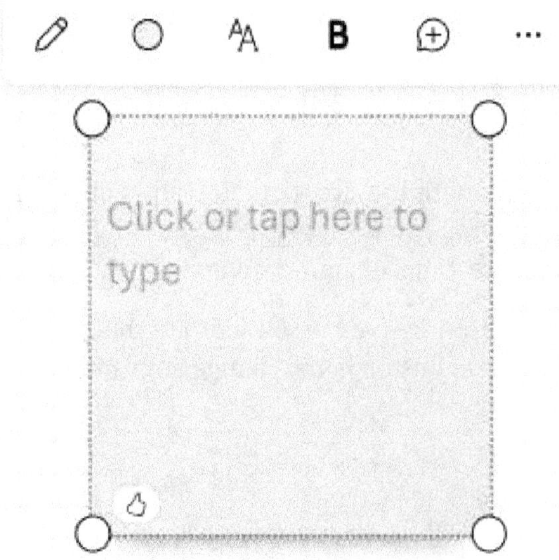

Sticky notes are a fantastic way to quickly jot down ideas or comments without cluttering your whiteboard. To add a sticky note:

- Click the Sticky Note Tool in the toolbar (it looks like a small note).

- Choose a color for your sticky note, then click on the canvas to place it.

- Start typing your note. Like text boxes, sticky notes can be moved, resized, and edited at any time.

Sticky notes are commonly used during brainstorming sessions or collaborative meetings to capture thoughts and feedback from participants.

5. Inserting Images and Files:

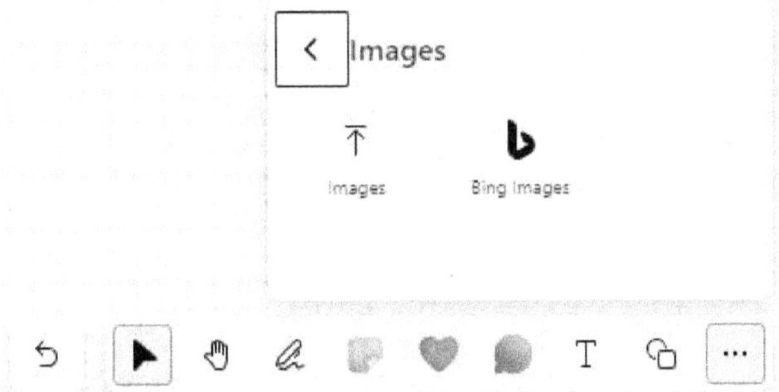

Microsoft Whiteboard allows you to insert images and documents directly into your whiteboard. This feature is incredibly useful if you're working on a project that requires visual references or documentation.

- To add an image, click the Insert Image tool in the toolbar and select an image from your device or search online.

- You can also insert PDFs or other files by selecting the Insert Document option. This allows you to attach relevant project files and even annotate them directly on the whiteboard.

Once inserted, images and documents can be resized, rotated, and moved to fit into your overall whiteboard layout.

Personalizing Your Whiteboard

Microsoft Whiteboard offers various ways to personalize your canvas, allowing you to tailor it to your specific needs and preferences. Here are a few personalization tips:

1. Organizing Your Whiteboard:

As you add content, it's important to keep your whiteboard organized, especially if you're dealing with complex projects or collaborating with others. Use the Select Tool to group related elements together, and consider creating sections for different topics or ideas. You can also add headers or labels to help clarify the structure of your whiteboard.

2. Color Coding:

Color coding is a simple yet effective way to categorize information visually. You can use different colors for pens, sticky notes, or shapes to distinguish between various themes, tasks, or ideas. For example, you might use blue for personal tasks and green for team-related tasks. This technique makes it easier to navigate and understand your whiteboard at a glance.

3. Using Shapes and Diagrams:

Microsoft Whiteboard includes a variety of shapes and diagram templates that you can use to add structure to your ideas. You can create flowcharts, Venn diagrams, mind maps, and more. Simply select the Shape Tool from the toolbar and choose the shape that fits your needs.

Shapes can be resized, moved, and edited, just like other whiteboard elements, making it easy to integrate them into your design.

Saving and Accessing Your Whiteboard

As you work on your whiteboard, Microsoft Whiteboard automatically saves your progress to the cloud. This ensures that your work is never lost and that you can access it from any device. To access a saved whiteboard, simply go back to the dashboard and select the whiteboard you want to open. You can also export your whiteboard as an image or PDF to share with others outside the Microsoft ecosystem.

Conclusion

Creating your first whiteboard in Microsoft Whiteboard is a straightforward process, but with its powerful tools and customization options, you can turn a blank canvas into a dynamic, collaborative workspace. From drawing and writing to inserting images and documents, the possibilities are endless. With this basic knowledge, you're now ready to explore more advanced features and make the most out of Microsoft Whiteboard's potential. Whether you're working solo or with a team, the whiteboard will become an indispensable tool for organizing your thoughts and communicating visually.

1.2 Setting Up Your Whiteboard

Before you begin using Microsoft Whiteboard to collaborate, create, or brainstorm, it's essential to ensure that you have your whiteboard environment set up correctly. Whether you're using Whiteboard on a desktop, web browser, or mobile device, the setup process is crucial to a smooth experience. In this section, we'll guide you through the initial steps, including signing in to your Microsoft account, accessing your whiteboards, configuring personal preferences, and organizing your whiteboard projects. By the end of this chapter, you'll have a fully functional workspace tailored to your needs.

1.2.1 Signing in and Accessing Whiteboards

The first step to accessing Microsoft Whiteboard is signing into your Microsoft account. Microsoft Whiteboard is integrated into the Microsoft 365 ecosystem, so it works seamlessly across devices and platforms if you are logged in. Let's go over the steps for signing in, accessing your previous whiteboards, and starting new ones.

Step 1: Signing in to Microsoft Whiteboard

To begin using Microsoft Whiteboard, you need to sign in using a Microsoft account. This could be a personal account, a work account, or a school account, depending on how you plan to use the tool.

1. Open Microsoft Whiteboard:

- On Desktop: If you're on a desktop or laptop computer, you can download Microsoft Whiteboard as a standalone app from the Microsoft Store for Windows 10 or 11. Alternatively, you can use the Whiteboard web version by navigating to the official Microsoft Whiteboard website (whiteboard.microsoft.com).

- On Mobile Devices: For iOS and Android users, the Whiteboard app is available on the App Store and Google Play, respectively. Download and install the app for easy access on the go.

- In Microsoft Teams or Other Microsoft 365 Apps: If you're already using Microsoft Teams or another Microsoft 365 app like Outlook or OneNote, you can open Whiteboard directly from there. Microsoft Whiteboard integrates seamlessly across the Microsoft 365 suite.

2. Click the 'Sign In' Button:

- After launching Microsoft Whiteboard, the first prompt you'll encounter is the sign-in screen. Here, click on the "Sign In" button to proceed.

- If you're using the Whiteboard app within another Microsoft 365 tool, it may automatically use your existing credentials to sign in.

3. Enter Your Microsoft Account Credentials:

- If you already have a Microsoft account, simply enter your email address and password. If your organization uses Microsoft 365, enter the work or school account details.

- If you don't have a Microsoft account yet, you can create one for free. You can do this directly from the sign-in screen by clicking the "Create Account" link. Follow the prompts to set up a new account.

4. Enable Two-Factor Authentication (Optional but Recommended):

- For enhanced security, Microsoft allows you to enable two-factor authentication (2FA). If you have this enabled, after entering your password, you'll be asked to confirm your identity via a text message, email, or authentication app.

- This added layer of security ensures that your whiteboards and data remain safe, particularly if you're using the tool for business or sensitive information.

Step 2: Accessing Existing Whiteboards

Once you're signed in, you'll gain access to any whiteboards you've previously created. Microsoft Whiteboard automatically saves your work to the cloud, ensuring that all your boards are accessible across different devices.

1. Viewing Recent Whiteboards:

- After signing in, you'll be taken to the dashboard or home screen, which displays a list of your recently used whiteboards. This section is particularly useful for quickly accessing whiteboards that you've been working on recently.

- If you're working on a collaborative whiteboard with others, those whiteboards will also appear in this section. Each whiteboard shows the most recent activity, making it easy to find ongoing projects.

2. Using the Search Bar:

- As your collection of whiteboards grows, it may become more challenging to find specific boards quickly. Thankfully, Microsoft Whiteboard has a built-in search function at the top of the dashboard.

- Simply type in keywords related to your whiteboard, such as its title, the date you created it, or collaborators' names. The search feature will pull up relevant results, allowing you to easily locate any whiteboard, no matter how old or recent it is.

3. Filtering Whiteboards by Category:

- Another helpful organizational tool is the ability to filter your whiteboards by category. You may have different categories of whiteboards such as Personal, Work, or School. Use the filter option on the dashboard to narrow down the list of whiteboards displayed based on these categories.

- If you work in a corporate or educational environment, you may also have access to shared whiteboards. These whiteboards are part of teams or group projects and will be listed under a different tab, making it easy to separate personal work from collaborative efforts.

4. Accessing Shared Whiteboards:

- If you've been invited to collaborate on a whiteboard, you can find these under the Shared with Me section. Whiteboards shared with you via email, link, or Microsoft Teams will automatically appear here.

- When accessing a shared whiteboard, Microsoft Whiteboard ensures that all changes are synced in real-time, so you can collaborate with your colleagues or classmates seamlessly.

Step 3: Creating a New Whiteboard

Now that you're signed in, it's time to create your first whiteboard. Starting a new whiteboard is a simple and straightforward process that takes just a few clicks.

1. Click on "Create New Whiteboard":

- On the dashboard or home screen, there's a button that says "Create New Whiteboard." Click on it to start a fresh, blank whiteboard.

- Depending on the device or platform you're using, the button may appear as a large, prominent feature on the main screen, or in a menu labeled "New Whiteboard" or "Create."

2. Naming Your Whiteboard:

- Once the new whiteboard opens, it's a good idea to name your whiteboard for easy reference later. At the top of the screen, there will be a "Title" or "Untitled Whiteboard" field. Click on it to rename your whiteboard.

- Choose a name that reflects the purpose of your whiteboard, whether it's a brainstorming session, project plan, or team collaboration. Keeping names descriptive will help you find them quickly in the future.

3. Exploring the Blank Canvas:

- You'll now see the whiteboard's blank canvas, ready for you to add your content. You can draw, add text, insert images, or use any of the tools available on the toolbar (which we'll explore in detail in later sections).

- Microsoft Whiteboard is an infinite canvas, meaning you can zoom in or out, scroll in any direction, and add as much content as you need without worrying about running out of space.

Whiteboard

Whiteboard 1

Board name

Whiteboard 1

Step 4: Syncing Across Devices

One of the most powerful features of Microsoft Whiteboard is its ability to sync your whiteboards across all devices. Since your work is saved automatically to the cloud, you can start working on your desktop and pick up right where you left off on your phone or tablet.

1. Enabling Sync on Different Devices:

- To ensure that your whiteboards are synced across devices, make sure you're signed in with the same Microsoft account on each device. Your whiteboards are tied to your account, so as long as you're logged in, all changes and updates are reflected across devices.

- If you're using Microsoft Whiteboard on a new device, simply download the app, sign in, and all your existing whiteboards will automatically appear.

2. Checking Sync Status:

- Sometimes, due to network connectivity issues, your whiteboard may not sync immediately. To check the sync status, look for the sync icon on the whiteboard dashboard or within the whiteboard itself. If there's a problem, Microsoft Whiteboard will notify you and allow you to retry syncing once you're reconnected to the internet.

- For collaborative whiteboards, it's essential to ensure that syncing is working correctly so all team members can see the latest updates in real time.

3. Working Offline:

- Microsoft Whiteboard also allows you to work offline. If you lose internet access, you can continue making changes to your whiteboards. Once you reconnect to the internet, your work will sync automatically.

By following these steps, you can confidently sign in, access, and set up your whiteboards for seamless collaboration and creativity. In the next sections, we'll dive deeper into how you can customize your whiteboard to match your unique preferences and workflow needs.

1.2.2 Setting Up Your Preferences

Setting up preferences in Microsoft Whiteboard allows you to customize the tool according to your needs and working style. By adjusting preferences, you can enhance your workflow, improve collaboration with team members, and create an environment that supports your creative process. In this section, we will explore various customization options and features that allow you to personalize your experience within Microsoft Whiteboard.

Customizing the Pen and Drawing Settings

The drawing tools in Microsoft Whiteboard are fundamental to its use, especially for sketching ideas, taking notes, or annotating documents. You can customize the pens and other writing tools to match your preferences.

1. Choosing Pen Styles: Microsoft Whiteboard offers several pen styles that you can use, including ballpoint pens, markers, highlighters, and pencils. You can select different pen thicknesses and colors to suit your task. For example, a fine pen might be useful for writing text, while a thicker marker could be better for diagrams.

2. Adjusting Pen Colors: Color plays a vital role in visual presentations, and the ability to choose from a wide variety of colors allows you to make your whiteboards more engaging. The default palette includes a range of basic colors, but you can also customize colors by clicking on the color picker, which lets you define specific hues using a color wheel.

3. Saving Pen Preferences: If you often use the same pen settings, you can save them for easy access. By doing so, your preferred pen color, thickness, and style will always be available when you start a new session.

4. Ink to Shape Conversion: One of the most powerful features of Microsoft Whiteboard is its ability to automatically convert hand-drawn shapes into perfect geometric forms. You can enable or disable this feature in the preferences, depending on whether you prefer to draw freehand or need precision for diagrams.

5. Ink to Text: Similarly, the ink-to-text feature converts handwritten words into typed text. This feature is particularly useful for presentations, as it can make your writing more readable. In the preferences, you can toggle this option on or off, depending on whether you want your handwriting converted automatically.

Language and Input Settings

Microsoft Whiteboard supports multiple languages and input methods. Setting the correct language and input options can greatly enhance the tool's usability, particularly for international teams or users who prefer to work in languages other than English.

1. Changing the Interface Language: By default, Microsoft Whiteboard will use the language of your operating system, but you can change this in the settings. To adjust the language, go to the settings menu, where you will find a list of supported languages. Select your preferred language, and Microsoft Whiteboard will update the interface accordingly. This is useful for teams that speak different languages or for users who are more comfortable working in their native language.

2. Input Method Preferences: Depending on your device, you may have various input methods at your disposal, including touch, stylus, and keyboard. In the preferences, you can prioritize your preferred method. For example, if you're using a tablet, you might want to enable touch input for quick navigation. If you're using a stylus, you can customize pressure sensitivity and the functions assigned to stylus buttons.

3. Text Input Settings: When working with text boxes or sticky notes, you can adjust the default font style, size, and color. Setting these preferences allows you to maintain a consistent look and feel throughout your whiteboards. For instance, if you often use a specific font for brainstorming sessions or presentations, you can set it as the default to save time.

3. Enabling or Disabling Collaboration Features

Microsoft Whiteboard is a powerful tool for collaboration, but depending on how you use it, you may want to enable or disable certain collaboration features. By setting up these preferences, you can control how your whiteboards are shared, who can edit them, and how changes are tracked.

1. Sharing Permissions: One of the most important preferences to consider is how you share your whiteboards with others. You can set your whiteboard to be view-only or allow others to edit it. In a collaborative environment, you may want to enable full editing permissions so that team members can contribute in real-time. Alternatively, for presentations or lectures, a view-only mode might be more appropriate to prevent unintended changes.

2. Real-Time Collaboration: By enabling real-time collaboration, you can work simultaneously with team members on the same whiteboard. You can choose whether to allow anonymous users to join the session or require them to sign in with their Microsoft account. Additionally, you can set preferences to receive notifications when someone joins or makes changes to the board.

3. Collaboration Tools: Microsoft Whiteboard includes several collaboration tools that you can customize. For instance, you can enable or disable comment features, control who can add sticky notes, and set preferences for tagging and assigning tasks. Adjusting these settings allows you to create a collaborative environment tailored to your team's needs.

4. Customizing Board Background and Layout

Visual presentation is key to creating effective whiteboards, especially when you're using them for brainstorming, project planning, or teaching. Microsoft Whiteboard offers several customization options for board backgrounds and layout to help you organize your ideas clearly.

1. Changing the Background Color: The default white background can be changed to other colors that better suit your task or preference. For example, darker backgrounds might be easier on the eyes during long sessions, while lighter backgrounds may be ideal for presentations. You can choose from a set of predefined colors or select custom colors.

2. Grid and Lined Backgrounds: In addition to solid colors, Microsoft Whiteboard offers grid and lined backgrounds, which are helpful for tasks like drawing diagrams, creating charts, or writing neatly. In the preferences, you can toggle between these backgrounds, and you can also adjust the size of the grid or line spacing to match your needs.

3. Custom Layouts and Templates: If you frequently use Microsoft Whiteboard for specific tasks like brainstorming, project management, or mind mapping, you can set up custom layouts or use templates. By saving your preferred layout, you can quickly load it whenever you start a new session. For example, you might create a template that includes pre-arranged sections for brainstorming or project tracking, complete with specific background colors, text formatting, and other elements.

4. Scaling and Zoom Preferences: Microsoft Whiteboard allows you to zoom in and out of your workspace, but you can set up default scaling preferences to match how you typically work. For instance, if you prefer to work on a zoomed-out view to see the entire whiteboard at once, you can set this as your default view. Alternatively, if you focus on detailed sections at a time, you might set the default to zoom in more closely.

5. Setting Up Auto-Save and Cloud Sync Preferences

Microsoft Whiteboard saves your work automatically, but there are several settings that allow you to control how and when your whiteboards are saved and synced across devices. By customizing these preferences, you can ensure that your work is always accessible, whether you're on a computer, tablet, or smartphone.

1. Enabling Auto-Save: By default, Microsoft Whiteboard saves your work in real-time to the cloud. However, you can adjust how frequently these auto-saves occur and whether they are saved to your local device as well. If you're working on sensitive material, you may want to disable automatic cloud saving and instead save manually at key points.

2. Syncing Across Devices: If you use Microsoft Whiteboard across multiple devices (such as a desktop, tablet, or smartphone), you can enable automatic syncing, ensuring that any changes made on one device are reflected on the others. In the preferences, you can control which devices are synced and how frequently this happens. For instance, you might set it to sync in real-time or choose to sync only when connected to Wi-Fi.

3. Offline Mode: Microsoft Whiteboard can also be used offline, but to enable this feature, you need to set up offline preferences. When working offline, your changes are saved locally and then synced to the cloud when an internet connection becomes available. You can adjust how often these offline saves occur and how they are managed when you go back online.

6. Accessibility and Ease of Use Preferences

Accessibility is an essential aspect of modern software design, and Microsoft Whiteboard includes several features to make the tool easier to use for individuals with disabilities or those who prefer certain usability enhancements.

1. High Contrast Mode: For users with visual impairments, high contrast mode can make it easier to differentiate between different elements on the screen. In the preferences, you can enable high contrast mode, which will adjust the colors of the interface to improve visibility.

2. Keyboard Shortcuts and Navigation: For users who prefer to navigate the interface using a keyboard rather than a mouse or stylus, Microsoft Whiteboard includes a wide range of keyboard shortcuts. You can customize these shortcuts to fit your working style, enabling quicker access to key tools and functions.

3. Speech-to-Text: If you prefer to dictate rather than type, Microsoft Whiteboard supports speech-to-text functionality. You can enable this feature in the preferences, allowing you

to add text to the whiteboard using your voice. This is particularly useful for users with limited mobility or those who simply prefer a hands-free approach to note-taking.

4. Zoom and Magnification: For users with low vision, zoom and magnification tools can be invaluable. You can set up preferences that allow for quick zooming in and out using keyboard shortcuts, mouse gestures, or touch inputs. Additionally, you can adjust the default zoom level to ensure that the whiteboard is always displayed at a size that is comfortable for you to view.

By setting up your preferences in Microsoft Whiteboard, you can create an environment that is tailored to your needs, improving both productivity and the overall user experience. Whether you are using the tool for individual tasks or collaborating with a team, these customization options ensure that you can work efficiently and effectively.

1.2.3 Organizing Your Whiteboards

Effective organization is key to making the most out of Microsoft Whiteboard. Whether you're working on multiple projects or collaborating with a team, keeping your whiteboards well-organized ensures easy access to your ideas, seamless collaboration, and a smoother workflow. In this section, we'll cover several strategies to help you organize your whiteboards efficiently, from naming conventions to grouping and archiving.

1. Naming Your Whiteboards for Easy Access

The first step to organizing your whiteboards is adopting a consistent naming convention. Without clear and descriptive names, it's easy for your workspace to become cluttered and confusing, especially when you have multiple whiteboards open. Here are some tips to help you name your whiteboards effectively:

- Be Descriptive: Instead of vague names like "Meeting" or "Notes," use descriptive titles that reflect the content or purpose of the whiteboard. For example, "Team Meeting - March 2024," or "Project A - Brainstorming Session."

- Use Dates: If you frequently create whiteboards for recurring meetings or sessions, consider adding dates to the titles to help differentiate between them. This allows you to quickly find the most up-to-date whiteboard while keeping older versions for reference.

- Project and Department Tags: If you're working in a larger organization, you may have whiteboards for different teams, departments, or clients. Adding tags such as "Marketing," "Design," or "Client X" to the title will make it easier to search for specific whiteboards later.

- Consistent Format: Develop a consistent naming structure, such as "[Project Name] - [Meeting Purpose] - [Date]." Having a uniform naming convention across your team ensures that everyone knows where to find the right whiteboard quickly.

2. Grouping Whiteboards by Category or Purpose

Microsoft Whiteboard allows you to manage your whiteboards more effectively by grouping them based on categories or projects. Grouping whiteboards can reduce clutter and provide a more organized workspace, especially when working on multiple projects simultaneously. Here are some methods to group your whiteboards:

- Create Folders or Categories: While Microsoft Whiteboard doesn't have a native folder feature yet, you can simulate this by applying consistent naming conventions. For instance, prefixing whiteboard names with specific projects, such as "Project X - [Whiteboard Name]," can help group all whiteboards related to that project.

- Organize by Purpose: Another approach is to group whiteboards based on their purpose, such as "Brainstorming," "Meetings," "Client Work," and "Internal Notes." This helps you quickly locate whiteboards based on what you need to work on at any given time.

- Organizing by Team Members or Department: If you collaborate with multiple teams, it might be useful to group whiteboards based on the team or department that's working on them. For example, you can have a group for "Marketing Team Whiteboards" and another for "Development Team Whiteboards."

By taking the time to group your whiteboards, you can streamline your workflow, reduce time spent searching for specific content, and ensure that every team member knows where to find the right whiteboards.

3. Archiving and Deleting Old Whiteboards

As your work progresses, you'll inevitably accumulate whiteboards that are no longer in active use. Instead of leaving them cluttering your dashboard, it's important to archive or delete old whiteboards that you don't need anymore.

- Archiving Completed Whiteboards: Instead of deleting a whiteboard, consider archiving it. While there's no official "archive" feature in Microsoft Whiteboard, you can achieve a similar effect by renaming old whiteboards and moving them to a separate section of your workspace. For instance, you can add "Archive" to the name and organize it with other archived boards, like "Project X - Brainstorming - Archive." This way, you can refer to old ideas without cluttering your active workspace.

- Deleting Unnecessary Whiteboards: If you no longer need a whiteboard and don't expect to reference it again, it's a good idea to delete it to declutter your workspace. To delete a whiteboard, simply locate it in your list, right-click, and choose the "Delete" option. Be cautious, though, as once a whiteboard is deleted, you won't be able to recover it unless you've saved a copy.

- Exporting Whiteboards for Long-Term Storage: If you want to keep a record of completed whiteboards without cluttering your workspace, consider exporting them as PDFs or images. This way, you can store them in cloud storage or file them in project folders for future reference, freeing up your Whiteboard interface for active work. To export a whiteboard, go to the options menu and choose "Export as Image" or "Export as PDF."

By implementing a regular archiving and deletion process, you can maintain a clean and organized workspace while still preserving important past work.

4. Tagging and Labeling Content for Quick Searches

To quickly locate specific whiteboards, it's useful to take advantage of tags or labels in your naming system. While Microsoft Whiteboard doesn't currently support metadata tagging, you can replicate this process by incorporating keywords and categories in your whiteboard titles or using sticky notes to add visible labels directly within whiteboards.

- Keyword Tags in Titles: Consider including relevant keywords in your whiteboard titles to make searching easier. For example, adding tags like "Research," "Marketing," or "Design" to your titles will help you quickly filter through whiteboards when you're looking for content related to a specific topic.

- Color-Coding Sticky Notes for Categorization: Within the whiteboard, you can use different colored sticky notes or text boxes to label sections of the board or differentiate ideas. For instance, use green sticky notes for "ideas," blue for "tasks," and yellow for "feedback." This visual organization helps break up content on large whiteboards and makes it easier to navigate.

- Sticky Notes as Labels for Important Sections: You can also use sticky notes as a form of labeling within the whiteboard. Add a note at the top of your whiteboard that serves as a label, such as “Marketing Campaign Ideas” or “Team Meeting Notes.” This label acts as an easy-to-spot identifier, especially on boards that contain a lot of information.

5. Regular Maintenance for Your Whiteboards

Organizing your whiteboards is not a one-time task but an ongoing process. To maintain an organized workspace, schedule regular clean-ups, whether weekly or monthly, to review your whiteboards and ensure that they remain relevant and well-organized. Here are some tips for maintaining order in your whiteboards:

- Set a Schedule for Reviewing Whiteboards: Regularly check through your whiteboards to identify which ones are still active and which can be archived or deleted. By scheduling a review, such as at the end of each month, you prevent your workspace from becoming too cluttered.

- Update and Refresh Whiteboards as Needed: Sometimes, whiteboards that were once organized can become cluttered as more information is added. Periodically review your active whiteboards to remove outdated information, rearrange content, or consolidate ideas into more cohesive layouts.

- Consistent Naming and Tagging: Make sure you follow consistent naming and tagging conventions across all your whiteboards. If you make changes to one naming convention or process, apply it to all relevant whiteboards to maintain a cohesive system.

By regularly reviewing and updating your whiteboards, you can maintain an efficient and streamlined workspace that enhances productivity and collaboration.

6. Collaborating on Whiteboard Organization

When working with a team, it's important to develop shared organizational standards so that everyone can easily navigate the whiteboards. Without consistent guidelines, it can become confusing for team members to find the content they need or contribute effectively.

- Develop Team-Wide Naming Conventions: Agree on a consistent naming structure for all team members to use. This ensures that everyone is on the same page when creating new whiteboards or searching for existing ones.

- Create a Shared Archive System: If you're working on long-term projects, create a shared archive system that all team members can access. This could be a dedicated section for archived whiteboards or a folder in cloud storage where exported whiteboards are saved.

- Assign Roles for Maintaining Whiteboards: Depending on the size of your team, you may want to assign specific individuals the responsibility of maintaining organization within the whiteboards. This ensures that there's someone consistently managing the structure of your whiteboards and keeping the system organized.

Collaboration on whiteboard organization will ensure smoother workflows and make it easier for team members to contribute effectively without getting lost in a sea of unorganized content.

7. Synchronizing with Other Apps for Enhanced Organization

Microsoft Whiteboard integrates with various Microsoft 365 apps like OneNote, Teams, and Outlook, allowing you to enhance your organizational system. By synchronizing your whiteboards with these apps, you can centralize your workflows and reduce duplication of tasks.

- Syncing Whiteboards with OneNote: Exporting or linking your whiteboards to OneNote allows you to store and organize whiteboards alongside other project materials, such as meeting notes, documents, and task lists.

- Collaborating via Microsoft Teams: Microsoft Whiteboard's integration with Teams allows you to manage and access your whiteboards directly from within your project channels or team meetings. This can streamline collaboration and ensure that whiteboards remain organized by project or team.

- Scheduling Whiteboard Reviews in Outlook: Use Outlook to schedule regular review meetings where team members can go through active whiteboards, discuss changes, and ensure everything is up to date and well-organized.

By integrating Microsoft Whiteboard with other apps in the Microsoft ecosystem, you can extend your organizational capabilities and maintain a more cohesive project management system.

By following the strategies outlined in this section, you can develop a highly organized and efficient workflow in Microsoft Whiteboard. Whether you're working alone or with a team, these organizational techniques will help you stay on top of your projects, easily access key information, and collaborate more effectively.

1.3 Basic Tools Overview

In Microsoft Whiteboard, understanding the basic tools is crucial for maximizing your productivity and creativity. The toolset is designed to be intuitive, allowing both beginners and experienced users to harness the power of visual collaboration. From drawing and annotating to organizing content, the basic tools form the foundation for effective use of Microsoft Whiteboard.

Microsoft Whiteboard offers a range of tools that help users create, collaborate, and share ideas in real-time. By mastering these basic tools, you'll be able to capture your ideas more effectively, whether you're brainstorming with a team, sketching out concepts, or organizing thoughts for a project. This section will provide an in-depth look at these essential tools, starting with the drawing tools.

1.3.1 Drawing Tools

The drawing tools in Microsoft Whiteboard are one of its most versatile features. Whether you're jotting down notes, sketching ideas, or creating visual diagrams, these tools give you the flexibility to express your ideas visually in a way that words alone often can't. Drawing on a digital whiteboard is not just about doodling; it's about organizing thoughts, communicating visually, and making ideas come to life.

a. Pen and Pencil Options

The pen and pencil tools in Microsoft Whiteboard are designed to offer a smooth and natural drawing experience, making them perfect for a variety of uses. Whether you're writing text, sketching diagrams, or creating artistic designs, the pen and pencil tools allow for precision and flexibility.

When you first open the drawing tools, you'll notice that there are several pen types available. The default pen option offers smooth, freehand lines that mimic the fluidity of writing on a traditional whiteboard. For more detailed or artistic work, the pencil tool offers a textured line, providing the feel of sketching with an actual pencil on paper.

You can customize the pen and pencil colors to suit your preferences. Microsoft Whiteboard offers a wide variety of preset colors, but you can also create custom shades to match your project's needs. Changing the pen thickness is also straightforward, allowing you to switch between fine lines for detailed work and thicker strokes for emphasis or structure.

Practical Uses:

- Note-taking: Use the pen tool for handwritten notes during meetings or brainstorming sessions.

- Sketching Diagrams: The pencil tool is great for creating rough sketches, wireframes, or diagrams before refining them.

- Highlighting: Use different colors to emphasize key points or differentiate between different sections of your whiteboard.

b. Adjusting Colors and Thickness

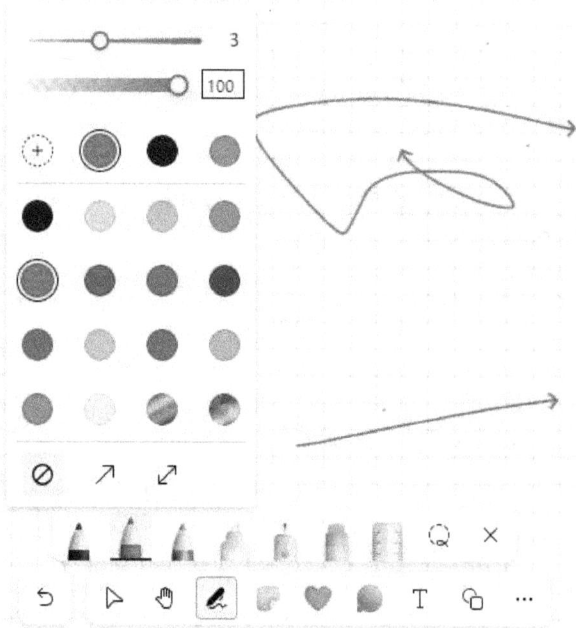

One of the standout features of Microsoft Whiteboard's drawing tools is the ability to adjust both the color and thickness of the pen and pencil. This allows for a high degree of customization, enabling users to differentiate between various elements on the board and create a more organized and visually appealing layout.

To change the color of your pen or pencil, simply click on the pen icon and choose from the available color palette. You can also select the color picker for even more options. Microsoft Whiteboard offers an extensive range of colors, from standard hues to unique shades, so you'll always have the right color for your needs.

Similarly, adjusting the thickness of your pen is simple. There are multiple preset thickness levels, ranging from thin lines that are ideal for detailed work to thick lines that can be used for bold statements or dividing sections. You can also use different thicknesses to simulate a multi-dimensional effect in your drawings.

Practical Uses:

- Color-Coding: Use different colors for different ideas or sections of your whiteboard. This helps in organizing thoughts and makes it easier to understand at a glance.

- Layering Information: Vary pen thicknesses to create visual hierarchy on your board, emphasizing key points or creating distinct sections.

- Visual Differentiation: By using contrasting colors and thicknesses, you can easily differentiate between annotations, drawings, and key ideas.

c. Using Highlighters

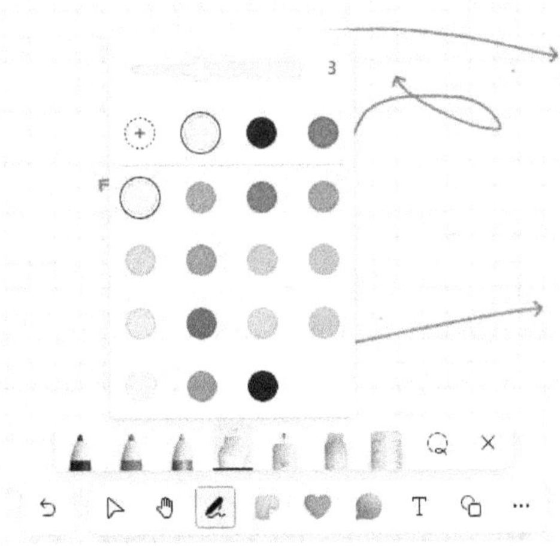

The highlighter tool is an essential feature for anyone looking to emphasize text or visual elements on their whiteboard. Like the pen tool, the highlighter can be customized in terms of color and thickness, making it versatile enough to suit a variety of tasks. Unlike the pen tool, however, the highlighter allows you to draw translucent lines over existing content without obscuring the underlying information.

The highlighter tool is particularly useful for collaborative work, where multiple participants may want to emphasize different points during a discussion. Whether you're reviewing a document, commenting on a diagram, or simply pointing out important details, the highlighter makes it easy to draw attention to key areas.

Practical Uses:

- Emphasizing Ideas: Use the highlighter to draw attention to important text or visuals without overwriting or obscuring the underlying content.

- Reviewing Work: During a collaborative session, you can use the highlighter to mark areas for further review or discussion.

- Color-Coding Annotations: Assign different colors to different types of highlights, such as red for urgent tasks and green for completed ones.

d. Eraser Tool

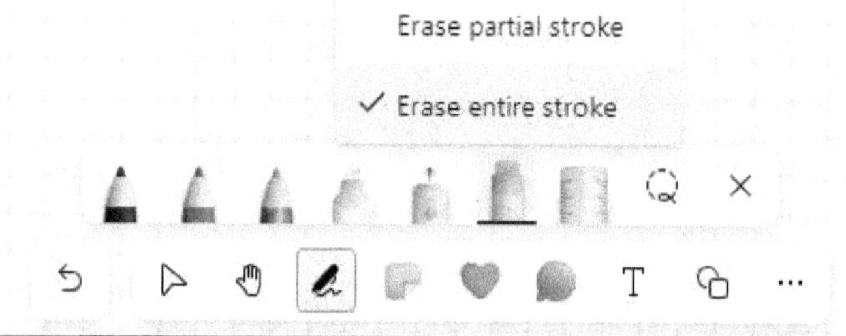

The eraser tool is a fundamental feature for correcting mistakes or removing content from your whiteboard. Unlike traditional whiteboards, where erasing often leaves behind streaks and smudges, the digital eraser in Microsoft Whiteboard ensures that your work remains clean and precise.

There are two main options for using the eraser tool: you can either erase individual strokes or use the "Erase All" feature to clear entire sections of the whiteboard. This flexibility allows for a high level of control over your workspace. For instance, if you've made a small mistake, you can simply tap the specific area to remove it. If a section no longer serves its purpose, you can quickly clear it and make space for new ideas.

The eraser tool also offers precision settings, allowing you to select specific parts of a stroke or drawing. This is especially useful when working with complex diagrams, where you may need to erase only certain sections without disturbing the surrounding content.

Practical Uses:

- Correcting Mistakes: Use the eraser tool to make quick corrections without disrupting the overall flow of your work.

- Clearing Space: When your board becomes cluttered, the eraser helps clear unused or outdated sections to make room for new ideas.

- Selective Erasing: The precision settings enable you to remove only specific parts of a drawing or annotation.

e. Undo and Redo Options

The Undo and Redo features in Microsoft Whiteboard provide an added layer of control, allowing you to reverse mistakes or restore previously deleted content. This is especially helpful during brainstorming sessions or collaborative work, where ideas and content may evolve rapidly.

With the Undo option, you can easily step back through your actions to reverse any mistakes or changes. For example, if you've accidentally erased an important section or drawn a line in the wrong place, the Undo feature lets you restore the previous state with a single click.

The Redo feature works in tandem with Undo, allowing you to reapply any actions that you've previously undone. This can be useful if you change your mind about a revision or deletion and want to restore it quickly without having to recreate the content manually.

Practical Uses:

- Reversing Mistakes: Quickly undo any accidental changes or mistakes to maintain the integrity of your work.

- Experimenting with Ideas: Use Undo and Redo while brainstorming to test out different concepts and easily switch between variations.

- Restoring Deleted Content: Accidentally erased something important? The Redo function can quickly bring it back, saving you time and effort.

f. Using the Ruler for Precision

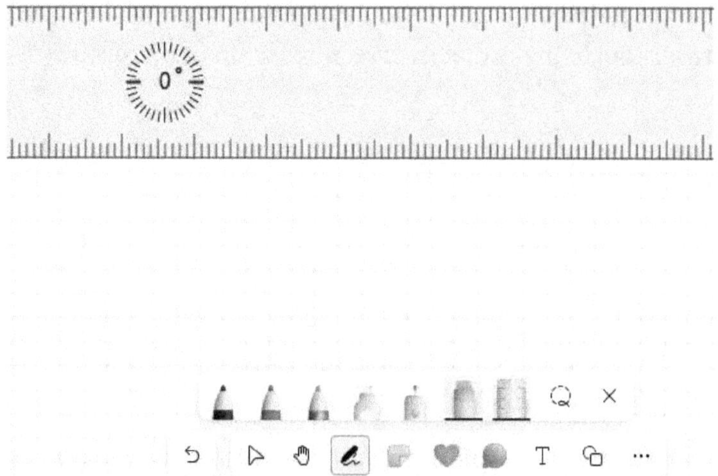

The Ruler tool is an invaluable asset when you need to create straight lines or align objects on the whiteboard. It works just like a physical ruler, allowing you to measure distances and angles with precision. This tool is particularly useful for diagramming, creating charts, or any task that requires accurate alignment.

The Ruler is easy to manipulate on the digital canvas. Simply rotate it to your desired angle, then draw along its edge to create perfectly straight lines. You can adjust the ruler by dragging it around the canvas, and you can also set it to specific angles for more complex drawings.

For more detailed work, the Ruler also offers an angle indicator that shows the exact degree at which the ruler is set. This ensures that your lines and drawings are perfectly aligned, even when working with intricate diagrams or multi-step processes.

Practical Uses:

- Diagramming: Use the Ruler to draw precise shapes, lines, and diagrams for presentations or collaborative work.

- Aligning Content: The Ruler ensures that all elements on the whiteboard are perfectly aligned, making your whiteboard visually organized and professional.

- Measuring Angles: For more advanced projects that require precision, the Ruler's angle feature allows for accurate drawing at specific degrees.

By mastering these drawing tools, you'll be able to create a more organized, visually appealing whiteboard that effectively communicates your ideas. Whether you're sketching, writing, or annotating, these tools will give you the freedom and flexibility to express your thoughts clearly and efficiently.

1.3.2 Eraser and Undo/Redo

In any creative or collaborative process, mistakes or revisions are an inevitable part of the journey. Microsoft Whiteboard recognizes this and provides powerful tools like the Eraser, Undo, and Redo to allow users to quickly correct errors or revert to previous states without the hassle of starting over. These tools play a significant role in enhancing your workflow by making the process of editing, correcting, and refining much smoother.

Understanding the Eraser Tool

The Eraser is a fundamental tool in any digital whiteboard or drawing application, allowing users to remove any ink or content they've drawn directly on the board. Microsoft Whiteboard's eraser is specifically designed to be user-friendly and effective, offering various options for clearing content from the board, whether it's small markings or large sections of a design.

How to Access the Eraser Tool

To access the Eraser tool in Microsoft Whiteboard:

1. Locate the Toolbar at the bottom of the screen.

2. Click or tap on the Eraser icon, which typically resembles a small rubber eraser.

3. Once selected, the Eraser tool is ready for use. Simply drag the cursor or your finger/stylus across the area you want to erase.

On touchscreen devices or when using a stylus, the eraser can be even more intuitive. Many digital pens, such as those used with Surface devices, come with an eraser on the opposite end. Flipping the pen around and using it as you would with a traditional pencil eraser will instantly activate the eraser feature in Microsoft Whiteboard.

Types of Erasers

Microsoft Whiteboard offers more than just a simple "one-size-fits-all" eraser. The tool can be customized for more efficient use depending on your needs:

- Stroke Eraser: The default mode for the eraser is the stroke eraser, which removes entire strokes or drawn lines with a single gesture. This is useful when you need to quickly clean up sketches or diagrams without worrying about precision erasing.

- Object Eraser: For more precise erasing, particularly when dealing with text or individual objects on the board, the object eraser allows you to target and remove specific items. This is handy for structured content such as text boxes or shapes.

Eraser Tips for Efficient Use

To use the Eraser tool effectively and avoid unnecessary frustration, here are some tips to keep in mind:

1. Use the Stroke Eraser for Speed: When you're rapidly brainstorming or sketching out ideas, you may need to erase large sections of content. The stroke eraser is perfect for this, as it quickly wipes away full lines or drawings with a single swipe. This keeps the workflow fast and fluid, without bogging you down in detail.

2. Zoom In for Precision Erasing: If you're working on intricate designs or small details, zooming in can give you greater control over the erasing process. This is especially helpful when you're working on complex diagrams or when erasing small portions of text or drawings.

3. Undo Instead of Erasing: Sometimes, erasing might not be the best option if you've made a recent mistake. Instead of using the eraser, consider using the Undo button, which can revert the whiteboard to a previous state without disrupting your workflow.

Eraser Shortcuts and Tips

For those who want to work efficiently with Microsoft Whiteboard, learning a few eraser-related shortcuts can greatly improve your workflow:

- Stylus Eraser: If you're using a Surface Pen or similar device, flipping the pen around and using the eraser end allows for quick switching between drawing and erasing, making the workflow smoother.

- Eraser Size Adjustments: Some versions of Microsoft Whiteboard may allow you to adjust the size of the eraser, giving you even more control over the erasing process. This is particularly useful when dealing with both large sketches and fine details.

Undo and Redo: A Safety Net for Creativity

One of the standout features of digital whiteboarding tools is the ability to Undo or Redo actions. Whether you're experimenting with ideas, sketching out concepts, or collaborating with a team, the ability to quickly backtrack or restore previous states is invaluable.

The Undo Function

The Undo button allows you to reverse your last action on the board, whether it's a drawing stroke, an object placement, or a text input. This feature is particularly useful in situations where you've accidentally erased something important, made a mistake in your drawing, or simply want to change direction with your brainstorming or project planning.

To use the Undo function:

1. Locate the Undo button in the top toolbar, which typically looks like a backward-facing arrow.

2. Click or tap the button to undo the most recent action.

Alternatively, if you're using a keyboard, the standard Ctrl+Z shortcut will perform the same action. For those on touchscreen devices or using a stylus, a quick two-finger tap on the screen also serves as an intuitive Undo command.

How Many Actions Can Be Undone?

Microsoft Whiteboard allows you to undo a significant number of previous actions. While the exact number may vary depending on the version of Whiteboard you're using, it's generally quite generous, allowing you to undo several dozen steps in your workflow. This gives you ample flexibility when experimenting with ideas or working through different iterations of a project.

The Redo Function

Just as valuable as the Undo function is the Redo feature. If you've undone an action but later decide that it was correct after all, you can quickly restore it using the Redo button. This function ensures that you don't lose progress if you accidentally go back too far in your edits.

To use the Redo function:

1. Locate the Redo button, typically next to the Undo button in the toolbar, represented by a forward-facing arrow.

2. Click or tap the Redo button to reinstate the most recently undone action.

As with Undo, there are shortcuts for Redo as well:

- Ctrl+Y or Ctrl+Shift+Z on a keyboard will perform the Redo action.

- A three-finger tap on touchscreen devices will also redo an action.

When to Use Undo and Redo

The Undo and Redo tools are particularly useful in the following scenarios:

1. Brainstorming Sessions: When you're quickly jotting down ideas, the ability to revert a few steps back without disrupting your flow can keep the momentum going. It allows you to experiment without fear of permanently losing earlier thoughts.

2. Collaborative Work: When multiple team members are contributing to a whiteboard, mistakes can happen. If someone accidentally erases or overwrites an important section, the Undo button can immediately restore the lost content, preventing miscommunication or the need to recreate work.

3. Detailed Design or Diagramming: When you're working on detailed designs or diagrams, mistakes can often go unnoticed until a few steps later. The Undo function lets you correct these mistakes quickly, while the Redo function allows you to experiment without worry, as you can easily restore previous versions.

Best Practices for Undo/Redo Use

To make the most out of the Undo and Redo tools, consider the following best practices:

- Undo Before Using the Eraser: If you've just made a mistake, it's often faster to use Undo rather than switching to the Eraser tool. This can save you time and effort, particularly when working with intricate or multi-step designs.

- Use Redo to Experiment: The ability to quickly undo and redo actions makes it easy to experiment with different ideas. If you're unsure whether a certain change improves your work, Undo it to see how the board looked before, and Redo to compare it with the new version.

- Undo in Collaborative Settings: During real-time collaboration, it's possible that changes made by others might conflict with your work. In these cases, use the Undo feature to revert changes without disrupting the flow of the session.

Undo/Redo in Collaborative Whiteboards

When working in a collaborative setting, Microsoft Whiteboard's Undo and Redo features extend to every participant in the session. This means that any user can undo or redo changes made by themselves or others, making it easy to reverse unintentional edits or restore lost content. However, this also introduces the possibility of accidental undos affecting someone else's work, so it's important to communicate with your team during collaborative sessions.

To avoid potential issues in collaborative settings:

- Assign Roles: In more structured sessions, assigning specific roles or areas of responsibility on the whiteboard can help avoid confusion when multiple people are making changes at once.

- Use Comments and Notes: Instead of undoing someone else's work directly, consider adding a note or comment suggesting revisions. This helps maintain a smooth flow and keeps everyone on the same page.

Summary

The Eraser, Undo, and Redo tools in Microsoft Whiteboard are indispensable for any user, whether you're an artist sketching out ideas, a business professional diagramming a project plan, or a teacher guiding students through collaborative exercises. These tools give you the flexibility to correct mistakes, refine your work, and collaborate effectively, all while maintaining a smooth and intuitive workflow.

By mastering the Eraser, Undo, and Redo features, you'll be able to maintain creative freedom, make quick corrections, and streamline your collaborative efforts, ensuring that your whiteboard sessions are productive and frustration-free.

1.3.3 Using the Ruler for Precision

One of the fundamental tools available in Microsoft Whiteboard is the ruler, which helps users draw straight lines and maintain accuracy in their designs and annotations. This feature is particularly beneficial when working on diagrams, charts, or any other visual content requiring precision. Whether you are an educator, designer, or team leader, mastering the ruler tool in Microsoft Whiteboard can significantly improve the clarity and professionalism of your whiteboard creations.

In this section, we'll explore the ruler tool's functionalities, discuss various ways it can be utilized for precision, and provide some practical tips on how to leverage it effectively.

1. What is the Ruler Tool?

The ruler in Microsoft Whiteboard is a versatile tool designed to help you draw straight lines at specific angles. It mimics a physical ruler, allowing you to rotate it to a desired angle and draw lines with precision. The ruler is especially useful when creating diagrams, geometric shapes, flowcharts, or any type of content that requires a clean, straight edge.

The tool operates much like a real ruler in that it offers a clear visual guide. This feature is often paired with Microsoft Whiteboard's other drawing tools, such as the pen, pencil, or highlighter, to enhance your ability to create professional-quality designs. Whether you're drawing a simple line, setting up the framework for a diagram, or marking important sections on your whiteboard, the ruler ensures that all your lines are straight and neat.

2. Accessing the Ruler Tool

Accessing the ruler tool in Microsoft Whiteboard is straightforward and easy to incorporate into your workspace:

1. Open the Whiteboard: Navigate to your desired whiteboard and ensure it's open and active.

2. Locate the Ruler Icon: At the bottom toolbar of Microsoft Whiteboard, you will find the ruler icon, represented by a straight ruler graphic. Simply click on this icon to activate the ruler.

3. Ruler Placement: Once selected, the ruler will appear directly on your whiteboard as an adjustable overlay.

The ruler can be moved, resized, and rotated to fit your exact needs. It will remain active until you decide to deactivate it by clicking on the ruler icon again. This flexibility ensures that it can be integrated seamlessly into your workflow, whether you need it for just a single line or for creating a detailed diagram.

3. Rotating and Adjusting the Ruler

One of the key features that makes the ruler tool in Microsoft Whiteboard so useful is its rotation capability. Unlike a traditional physical ruler, the digital version can be rotated to any angle with precision. This allows for the creation of straight lines not only vertically and horizontally but also at any desired angle, providing flexibility for geometric designs, architecture sketches, or any project requiring angled lines.

To rotate the ruler:

1. Two-Finger Gesture (Touchscreen): If you're using a touchscreen device, simply use two fingers to rotate the ruler. Place your fingers on the ruler and twist them in the direction you want the ruler to rotate.

2. Scroll Wheel (Mouse): If you're using a mouse, hover over the ruler and use your mouse's scroll wheel to rotate the ruler. Each scroll will rotate the ruler in small increments, allowing for fine-tuned adjustments.

3. Angle Display: As you rotate the ruler, you'll notice that the angle of rotation is displayed. This is particularly helpful when you need to set the ruler at a specific angle (e.g., 45 degrees or 90 degrees). By knowing the exact angle, you can create perfectly aligned lines and shapes without any guesswork.

4. Drawing with the Ruler

Once the ruler is positioned at your desired angle, you can use the drawing tools (pen, pencil, or highlighter) to create straight lines along its edge. Here's how to draw with the ruler:

1. Select a Drawing Tool: Choose one of the drawing tools from the toolbar, such as the pen or highlighter.

2. Align the Pen with the Ruler: Move the pen or cursor along the edge of the ruler, ensuring that it follows the ruler's guide. The drawing tool will naturally snap to the ruler, making it easy to create a straight line.

3. Draw the Line: Press down and draw along the ruler's edge. As you move, the line will form in perfect alignment with the ruler, ensuring precision.

You can repeat this process to draw multiple lines at various angles, depending on your needs. This method works well for creating structured designs, grid layouts, and even simple diagrams that require clean, straight lines.

5. Practical Uses of the Ruler Tool

The ruler tool is a versatile feature that can be applied to numerous practical scenarios within Microsoft Whiteboard. Below are some common uses:

1. Creating Charts and Graphs:

The ruler is incredibly useful for drawing the axes of graphs or dividing the whiteboard into sections. Whether you're creating a bar chart, line graph, or scatter plot, the ruler can ensure that all lines are perfectly straight and well-aligned.

2. Designing Geometric Shapes:

If you're working on geometry or design-related projects, the ruler can help you create accurate shapes such as triangles, rectangles, and polygons. You can adjust the ruler to specific angles, ensuring that all sides of the shape are perfectly straight and proportional.

3. Aligning Text and Sticky Notes:

In collaboration settings, you may want to arrange sticky notes or text boxes in an orderly fashion. The ruler can be used as a visual guide to align these elements, ensuring they are evenly spaced and positioned on the whiteboard.

4. Flowcharts and Process Diagrams:

When creating process diagrams or flowcharts, the ruler ensures that all connectors and lines between elements are straight. This enhances the clarity of the diagram, making it easier for others to understand.

5. Architectural and Engineering Sketches:

If you're using Microsoft Whiteboard for architectural or engineering projects, the ruler helps maintain accuracy in your designs. You can use it to draw straight lines for floor plans, technical diagrams, and other structural elements.

6. Advanced Techniques with the Ruler

While the ruler is simple to use, there are a few advanced techniques that can elevate your whiteboard creations:

1. Combining the Ruler with Freehand Drawing:

Although the ruler helps create perfectly straight lines, you can combine it with freehand drawing to add detail and creativity to your whiteboard. For example, use the ruler to create a framework and then switch to freehand drawing to add more organic shapes or annotations.

2. Using Multiple Rulers for Complex Designs:

In some projects, you may need multiple guidelines at different angles. Microsoft Whiteboard allows you to move and rotate the ruler repeatedly without resetting the lines you've already drawn. This means you can use the ruler at one angle, draw your lines, then rotate it to a different angle for additional lines, creating complex and intricate designs.

3. Creating Perfect Shapes with Ruler and Shape Recognition:

Microsoft Whiteboard has a built-in shape recognition feature that automatically converts rough hand-drawn shapes into perfect geometric shapes. By combining the ruler with this feature, you can create exceptionally neat diagrams. For instance, use the ruler to draw straight lines for a triangle's sides, and the shape recognition tool will ensure the angles and sides are perfectly proportional.

4. Precision Scaling:

When drawing to scale (especially for technical or architectural drawings), the ruler tool becomes indispensable. You can manually calculate and adjust the length of each line using the ruler as a guide, ensuring the drawing follows the required dimensions.

7. Troubleshooting Common Issues

While the ruler tool is intuitive, there are a few common issues that users may encounter. Let's take a look at how to troubleshoot them:

1. Ruler Won't Rotate Properly:

If you're unable to rotate the ruler using touch gestures or the scroll wheel, try the following:

- Ensure your touchscreen or mouse is functioning correctly.

- If using a touch device, make sure your fingers are placed directly on the ruler and that your screen isn't locked in a specific orientation.

- For mouse users, ensure the scroll wheel is clean and working properly.

2. Lines Don't Align with the Ruler:

If your drawn lines don't align correctly with the ruler, it may be due to inaccurate positioning. Make sure the pen tool is closely following the edge of the ruler and that you are drawing straight along the guide.

3. Difficulty Drawing Diagonal Lines:

If diagonal lines aren't coming out as expected, check the angle of the ruler. Rotate the ruler precisely to the angle you want, using the angle display as a guide to ensure accuracy.

8. Tips for Effective Use of the Ruler

To maximize your productivity when using the ruler tool, keep the following tips in mind:

1. Use Shortcuts: Learn keyboard shortcuts and gestures to quickly access and rotate the ruler. This will save time and make your workflow more efficient.

2. Combine with Zoom: If you're working on a large whiteboard, use the zoom feature to get a closer look at fine details. This is especially helpful when drawing smaller, more intricate lines with the ruler.

3. Experiment with Angles: Don't limit yourself to vertical and horizontal lines. Experiment with different angles to create dynamic and interesting designs. Whether you're working on flowcharts or creative diagrams, angled lines can add a unique touch to your work.

4. Practice Makes Perfect: Like any tool, the more you use the ruler, the more comfortable and precise you'll become. Spend time practicing with different line types, shapes, and angles to master the tool fully.

In conclusion, the ruler tool in Microsoft Whiteboard is an invaluable feature that provides precision, accuracy, and flexibility to your whiteboard designs. By mastering its use, you can ensure that all your lines, diagrams, and shapes are neat, aligned, and professional.

Whether you're creating technical drawings or organizing a brainstorming session, the ruler will help you present your ideas with clarity and confidence.

1.4 Saving and Exporting Whiteboards

1.4.1 Saving Automatically in the Cloud

One of the most powerful features of Microsoft Whiteboard is its seamless integration with Microsoft 365, allowing users to automatically save their work to the cloud. This feature ensures that your whiteboards are always up to date, accessible from anywhere, and protected from data loss. Understanding how this feature works and how to maximize its benefits is crucial for both individual users and teams who rely on real-time collaboration.

1. The Importance of Cloud Saving

Cloud saving is a fundamental aspect of modern digital tools, and Microsoft Whiteboard fully leverages this technology. When your work is saved in the cloud, it offers several significant advantages:

- Continuous Access: Whether you're working on your desktop, laptop, tablet, or mobile device, you can seamlessly switch between them and pick up where you left off. This accessibility means that your ideas and projects are never confined to one device, making it easy to work remotely or share your whiteboard during meetings or collaboration sessions.

- Real-Time Synchronization: With cloud saving, any changes you make to a whiteboard are updated in real-time across all your devices. This is particularly important in collaborative settings, where multiple users may be working on the same board simultaneously. Cloud syncing ensures that everyone sees the most recent version of the whiteboard without the need for manual updates or file exchanges.

- Backup and Security: Saving to the cloud provides an additional layer of security by ensuring your work is backed up on Microsoft's servers. This eliminates the risk of losing important whiteboards due to device failure, accidental deletions, or software crashes. Microsoft's cloud infrastructure is highly secure, with multiple layers of encryption and protection to safeguard your data from unauthorized access or breaches.

In addition to these benefits, cloud storage with Microsoft Whiteboard also makes it easy to share your work with others, either through direct collaboration within a shared whiteboard or by exporting your whiteboard to share with a wider audience. Whether you're brainstorming ideas with a team or developing a personal project, cloud saving ensures your work is always safe, accessible, and up-to-date.

2. How Cloud Saving Works in Microsoft Whiteboard

Microsoft Whiteboard is designed to save your work automatically in the cloud. As soon as you start working on a whiteboard, the changes are constantly being saved to your account. This automatic saving process eliminates the need for manual saving, allowing you to focus entirely on your creative work without worrying about losing progress.

- Microsoft Account Integration: To take advantage of cloud saving, users must be signed in with their Microsoft account. This account is linked to other Microsoft services such as OneDrive, Teams, and Outlook, making it part of the larger Microsoft 365 ecosystem. If you don't have a Microsoft account, you can create one for free, which will give you access to cloud saving and other services.

- Auto-Save Functionality: Once signed in, the auto-save feature begins working as soon as you create or edit a whiteboard. Every change you make—whether it's drawing, adding text, or moving objects around—will be automatically saved to your cloud account. This feature is designed to work continuously in the background, ensuring that your whiteboard is always saved without requiring any manual intervention.

- Syncing Across Devices: One of the key advantages of cloud saving is the ability to sync your whiteboards across multiple devices. If you're using Microsoft Whiteboard on a laptop at work and later switch to a tablet at home, your work will be synchronized instantly. The cloud ensures that you can access the latest version of your whiteboard from any device where you're signed in.

3. Ensuring a Reliable Cloud Connection

While cloud saving is designed to be automatic, it relies on a stable internet connection. If you're working offline, your changes won't be saved until you reconnect to the internet. In such cases, Microsoft Whiteboard will store your changes locally on the device, and once your device reconnects, it will sync your updates with the cloud. To ensure a smooth experience, it's important to be aware of your connection status, especially if you're working in an environment with intermittent or unreliable internet access.

Here are some tips to ensure that your whiteboards are always saved and synced properly:

- Check Your Connection: Before starting a session on Microsoft Whiteboard, make sure that your device has a stable internet connection. This will ensure that any changes you make are uploaded to the cloud in real-time, reducing the risk of unsaved work.

- Offline Mode: Microsoft Whiteboard does allow for offline work. However, it's important to note that when working offline, your changes will only be saved locally. Once you reconnect to the internet, the whiteboard will automatically sync and update the cloud version of your work. Always make sure to allow some time for syncing if you've been working offline for an extended period.

- Monitor Sync Status: You can usually tell if your whiteboard is synced by checking the sync icon, which is often displayed in the toolbar or status bar. If the sync symbol indicates any errors, you can troubleshoot the connection or check Microsoft's service status to ensure their cloud servers are operating correctly.

4. Troubleshooting Cloud Saving Issues

In rare cases, users may encounter issues with cloud saving or syncing. This can happen due to network problems, account conflicts, or temporary outages with Microsoft's cloud services. Here are some common issues and how to resolve them:

- Network Connectivity Problems: If your internet connection is unstable, Microsoft Whiteboard may not be able to sync your changes to the cloud. Ensure that you're connected to a reliable Wi-Fi or Ethernet network, and if necessary, restart your router or device to resolve connection issues.

- Account Conflicts: Occasionally, users may experience problems if they are signed in with multiple Microsoft accounts on the same device. To avoid account conflicts, ensure that you are signed in to the correct account linked to your whiteboards. You can verify this by checking your account settings in the app.

- Service Outages: If Microsoft's cloud services are experiencing temporary outages or disruptions, your whiteboards may not sync until the service is restored. You can check Microsoft's service status page or consult your organization's IT support if this happens. Once the outage is resolved, your changes will automatically sync.

- Local Device Storage: If you're working offline, be aware that your changes are being saved locally on your device. In some cases, if your device runs out of storage or faces other issues, it could interfere with the local saving process. Regularly check your device's storage capacity and clear out unnecessary files to prevent this from happening.

5. Maximizing Cloud Saving for Team Collaboration

The cloud-saving feature in Microsoft Whiteboard is not just useful for individual users—it also plays a vital role in team collaboration. When working on a shared whiteboard, all team members can contribute simultaneously, with changes being saved in real-time across all devices. This ensures a seamless collaboration experience, as everyone always sees the most updated version of the whiteboard.

- Collaborative Cloud Saving: When multiple users are working on the same whiteboard, all changes are automatically saved to the cloud. This means that there's no need to manually update or sync files—everything is done automatically, ensuring that the entire team is always on the same page.

- Version Control: While Microsoft Whiteboard does not have a formal version control system, the continuous saving feature ensures that all changes are captured. If a mistake is made, users can easily undo changes or use the undo/redo buttons to revert the whiteboard to an earlier state.

- Cross-Platform Collaboration: Cloud saving also supports collaboration across different devices and platforms. Whether team members are using Windows, iOS, or web versions of Microsoft Whiteboard, cloud saving ensures that the same whiteboard can be accessed and edited from anywhere.

6. Customizing Your Cloud Saving Settings

Although cloud saving in Microsoft Whiteboard is automatic by default, there are a few ways users can customize their experience. In particular, users can manage how their whiteboards are saved, where they are stored, and how they are shared with others.

- Managing Storage Locations: By default, Microsoft Whiteboard saves your files to your personal or organizational cloud storage. If you're using an organization's Microsoft 365 account, your whiteboards will likely be saved within the organization's designated cloud environment, such as OneDrive for Business or SharePoint. Individual users can also save whiteboards to their personal OneDrive accounts.

- Sharing Options: Cloud saving makes it easy to share whiteboards with others. Through the sharing options, you can decide who has access to your whiteboards and what level of permissions they have. You can choose to give others full editing access, view-only access, or even restrict access entirely if needed.

- Data Management: For those concerned with data management and storage limits, Microsoft Whiteboard's integration with Microsoft 365 allows users to track their storage usage. Microsoft typically provides ample storage for cloud users, but it's good practice to occasionally review your saved whiteboards and delete any that are no longer needed.

1.4.2 Exporting as Image or PDF

Exporting your whiteboard content as an image or PDF allows you to share your work with others who might not have access to Microsoft Whiteboard or simply prefer a static version of your visual content. Microsoft Whiteboard provides straightforward export options to ensure that your digital whiteboard can be shared across various platforms or used in different formats. Here, we'll walk through the steps to export your whiteboard and discuss best practices for managing your exported content.

1. The Importance of Exporting

Exporting a whiteboard is an essential feature, especially in scenarios where you need to share your ideas with a broader audience, such as during meetings or project reviews. It is particularly useful for the following purposes:

- Sharing with external team members: While Microsoft Whiteboard facilitates real-time collaboration for users within your organization, exporting as an image or PDF ensures that you can share your whiteboard with colleagues or clients outside of your organization, who may not have access to Whiteboard or prefer a non-interactive document format.

- Creating archives of your work: Sometimes you need to document your work in static formats for future reference. Exporting your whiteboard ensures that you have a snapshot of your brainstorming session or project plan, which can be reviewed at any time, even if the original whiteboard is modified later.

- Presenting in meetings: Exporting your whiteboard as a PDF or image can be handy when presenting in meetings, especially if you want to include the content in slide decks, reports, or email summaries. It offers a professional way to present visual ideas in a polished format.

2. Exporting a Whiteboard as an Image

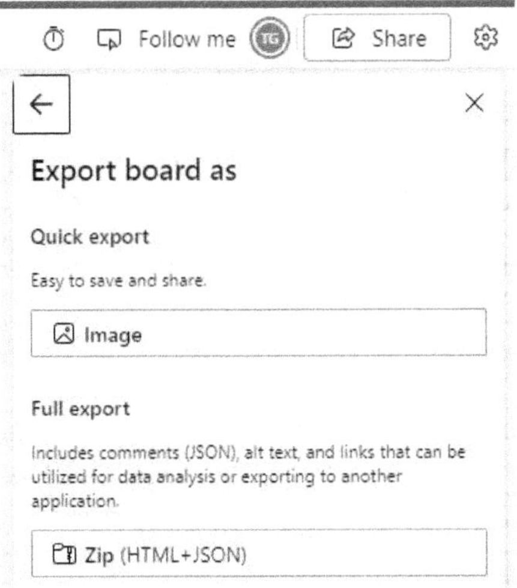

Exporting your whiteboard as an image file is a convenient option when you want to share or embed your content in a visual format that's easy to distribute. Microsoft Whiteboard supports exporting as high-quality images, typically in PNG format, which is widely used and compatible with most devices and platforms.

Here's how you can export your whiteboard as an image:

1. Open the Whiteboard you want to export. Navigate to the specific whiteboard that you wish to export from your collection or open a new one if needed.

2. Access the Export Options. In the upper-right corner of the Whiteboard window, you'll see a menu icon (three dots). Click on this menu to open the additional options for the whiteboard.

3. Select 'Export Image.' From the drop-down menu, choose the option that says 'Export as Image.' A dialogue box will appear asking where you want to save the image and what resolution you prefer.

4. Choose the Export Settings. Depending on your needs, you can select different image resolutions. For example, if you are embedding the image in a document or sharing it via

email, a lower resolution might suffice. However, for presentations or printing purposes, it's a good idea to select a higher resolution for clarity.

5. Save the Image. Once you've selected the desired resolution, click on 'Save' and choose the destination folder on your device. You can also rename the image file if necessary before saving.

Best Practices for Exporting as an Image:

- Organize before exporting: Make sure that your whiteboard is well-organized before exporting. Rearrange items, adjust the spacing, and ensure that no important content is cropped or hidden. This will result in a more professional and polished image.

- Consider image resolution: If you plan to print your whiteboard or display it on large screens, choose a higher image resolution. Lower resolutions are best for quick sharing or embedding into documents, but they may lose detail when enlarged.

- Export multiple whiteboards: If your content is spread across multiple whiteboards, consider exporting them separately and compiling them in a shared folder or ZIP file. This makes it easier to share large projects or brainstorming sessions with team members.

3. Exporting a Whiteboard as a PDF

PDF is one of the most widely used formats for sharing documents, and it's a great option for exporting whiteboard content in a format that's compatible across devices and operating systems. Unlike image files, PDFs can contain multiple pages, making them ideal for complex or multi-layered whiteboards.

Here's how to export your whiteboard as a PDF:

1. Open the Whiteboard you want to export. Navigate to your desired whiteboard that you wish to convert to a PDF.

2. Access the Export Menu. Similar to exporting an image, click the menu icon (three dots) in the upper-right corner of the whiteboard interface.

3. Select 'Export as PDF.' From the options, click on 'Export as PDF.' A dialogue box will pop up, prompting you to select your export preferences.

4. Configure PDF Settings. Microsoft Whiteboard allows you to configure the layout and formatting of your exported PDF. You can choose between exporting the entire whiteboard

as a single page or breaking it into multiple pages. Additionally, you can adjust the orientation (portrait or landscape) and scale.

5. Save the PDF. After configuring the settings, click 'Save' and choose the folder where the PDF will be stored. If necessary, rename the file before saving it.

Best Practices for Exporting as PDF:

- Optimize layout: If your whiteboard contains a lot of content, consider breaking it into multiple pages to make it more readable. You can also arrange different sections of your whiteboard into distinct PDF pages.

- Choose the right orientation: Select either portrait or landscape orientation based on the layout of your whiteboard. Landscape is typically better for visual-heavy content, while portrait is better for whiteboards with more text.

- Use multi-page PDFs for detailed whiteboards: If your whiteboard contains complex information spread across multiple layers or frames, exporting it as a multi-page PDF helps to preserve the content in an organized manner.

4. Managing Exported Files

Once you have exported your whiteboard, managing your exported files effectively is key to maintaining an organized workflow, especially when working on larger projects that may involve multiple whiteboards and frequent updates. Here are a few tips for managing your exported image and PDF files:

1. Create a Folder System: Set up a folder structure on your device or cloud storage system to keep all exported files organized. For example, you can create a folder for each project and within each project folder, store images and PDFs in separate subfolders.

2. Version Control: If you regularly update and export the same whiteboard, consider using a version control system in your file names, such as "Project_Whiteboard_V1" or "Brainstorming_Session_Aug2024_V2." This allows you to track changes and easily refer back to previous versions of your whiteboard.

3. Backup Exported Files: Always back up your exported whiteboards to a secure cloud storage solution, such as OneDrive or Google Drive. This ensures that you don't lose important whiteboard content if your local storage is compromised.

4. Sharing with Colleagues: When sharing whiteboard content with colleagues, compress the files into a ZIP folder if you're sharing multiple images or PDFs. You can also use a file-sharing service to distribute the content more efficiently, especially when dealing with large file sizes.

5. Exporting for Different Scenarios

There are various scenarios in which exporting a whiteboard can be highly useful. Here are a few examples:

- Exporting for Presentations: If you're preparing for a presentation and need to include whiteboard content in a PowerPoint, export the whiteboard as an image. Once exported, you can easily insert the image into your presentation slides.

- Sharing with Clients or Stakeholders: When sharing ideas or brainstorming sessions with clients, exporting as a PDF provides a professional format. The PDF can be reviewed by the client at any time, ensuring that they have a clear visual representation of your work.

- Archiving Completed Projects: For completed projects, it's important to archive all relevant materials, including whiteboards. Export your final whiteboards as high-resolution images or PDFs and store them alongside other project files for future reference.

6. Common Issues When Exporting

While exporting whiteboards is generally a smooth process, you may occasionally run into a few issues. Here are some common problems and how to resolve them:

- Export Error: If you encounter an error while trying to export, ensure that you are connected to the internet and that Microsoft Whiteboard is properly synced. Restarting the application may also resolve temporary issues.

- Low-Resolution Exports: If your exported image appears pixelated or low-quality, ensure that you have selected a high-resolution setting during the export process. Additionally, check the size and complexity of your whiteboard, as very large whiteboards may require adjustment in export settings for optimal resolution.

- Missing Content in Export: If some parts of your whiteboard are missing in the exported file, it may be because certain elements are off-screen or hidden. Zoom out to ensure that all content is visible within the whiteboard canvas before exporting.

Conclusion

Exporting your whiteboard as an image or PDF allows you to share your visual ideas with a wider audience, preserve important information, and present your work in a variety of formats. By following the steps and best practices outlined above, you can ensure that your exported whiteboards are clear, professional, and easy to distribute. Whether you're sharing with colleagues, presenting to clients, or archiving your work, exporting in the right format ensures that your whiteboard content remains useful long after the brainstorming session has ended.

CHAPTER II Mastering the Whiteboard Tools

2.1 Drawing and Inking Tools

Drawing and inking tools form the core of visual collaboration in Microsoft Whiteboard. Whether you're brainstorming ideas, mapping out processes, or creating diagrams, the intuitive pen and pencil options allow for fluid and creative expression. In this section, we will explore the different pen and pencil tools, customization options for colors and thickness, and how to make the most of inking features to enhance your workflow.

2.1.1 Pen and Pencil Options

Microsoft Whiteboard's inking capabilities are among its standout features, providing users with a set of digital pens and pencils designed for intuitive drawing, writing, and annotating. These tools are crucial for brainstorming sessions, sketching out ideas, and communicating visually in meetings or educational environments.

Introduction to the Pen and Pencil Tools

Upon opening Microsoft Whiteboard, you'll find the pen and pencil tools prominently located on the toolbar at the bottom of the screen. These tools are easy to access and work seamlessly with both touch input and stylus devices like the Microsoft Surface Pen. Even without a stylus, you can use a mouse to draw or write, although the experience might feel more fluid with a stylus.

Pen and Pencil Differences:

- The pen tool is ideal for writing or drawing with smooth, sharp lines, mimicking the effect of using a traditional ink pen.

- The pencil tool offers a softer, textured effect, similar to sketching with a graphite pencil, making it better suited for freehand drawings or shading.

Both tools serve distinct purposes but work well together, allowing users to create everything from precise annotations to more artistic, hand-drawn visuals.

Choosing the Right Tool for the Task

When to use the pen and pencil often depends on the context of your work:

- Pen Tool: Ideal for precise tasks like writing text, underlining key points, or drawing diagrams. Its sharper lines make it great for making annotations, adding clarity to presentations, or highlighting specific details.

- Pencil Tool: Perfect for creative tasks like sketching, shading, or creating softer, freehand visuals. It's also useful when you want to create rough drafts or explore ideas without committing to defined, sharp lines.

You can switch between these tools at any time based on the level of precision or texture required.

Using the Pen Tool

The pen tool is designed to replicate the smooth, clean strokes of a traditional pen, making it particularly useful for:

- Handwriting: Whether you are jotting down notes during a meeting or labeling sections of a diagram, the pen tool is sharp enough to ensure your text remains clear and readable. With the pen tool, you can simulate the feeling of writing on paper, but with the added benefits of digital flexibility.

- Precise Markups: When presenting information to others, whether in a classroom or during a virtual meeting, you may need to mark up a document or whiteboard quickly. The pen tool allows you to underline or circle specific parts of a diagram, making it a helpful tool for explaining ideas clearly.

Pen Customization Options

The power of Microsoft Whiteboard's pen tool lies in its versatility. You can customize the pen to suit your needs in various ways:

1. Pen Colors:

Choosing the right color is crucial for ensuring your work is both visually appealing and easy to follow. Microsoft Whiteboard offers a variety of preset colors for the pen tool, ranging from standard black and blue to more vibrant hues like red, green, and purple. Here's how to change the color of your pen:

- *Steps to Change Pen Color:*

1. Click on the pen icon located on the toolbar.
2. A color palette will appear, displaying a range of colors.
3. Select the desired color, and the pen will now draw in that color.

For more flexibility, Microsoft Whiteboard also offers a custom color picker, allowing you to choose any color by entering a hex code or adjusting sliders to get the perfect shade.

Best Practices for Color Selection:

- Black and Blue Pens are best suited for general writing and annotations.

- Red Pens are great for highlighting errors or areas that require attention.

- Green and Other Colors can be used to add visual diversity to your notes, helping to categorize information.

2. Pen Thickness:

The thickness of your pen strokes can be adjusted based on your needs. Thin lines are great for writing or adding detailed annotations, while thicker lines are better for highlighting or drawing attention to larger areas.

- *Steps to Adjust Pen Thickness:*

1. Select the pen tool.
2. Click on the thickness icon next to the pen color options.
3. Choose from the available thickness levels, ranging from very thin to extra thick.

The pen's thickness slider offers several options, allowing you to create everything from thin, detailed lines to bold, impactful strokes. This flexibility is particularly useful when you need to switch between tasks such as writing notes and drawing attention to key points.

Using the Pencil Tool

The pencil tool is designed to mimic the textured, freehand feel of a traditional pencil, making it ideal for:

- Sketching and Shading: The pencil tool is perfect for creating rough drafts, sketches, or diagrams. Its textured effect makes it particularly useful for artists or those who prefer freehand drawing over structured lines.

- Brainstorming: During brainstorming sessions, the pencil tool can be used to quickly jot down ideas or sketch out rough concepts. The softer lines make it easy to experiment without the need for precision.

- Creative Projects: For users who enjoy adding a creative touch to their presentations, the pencil tool can be used to add artistic flair to your whiteboard.

Pencil Customization Options

Similar to the pen tool, the pencil can also be customized in terms of color and thickness. However, the pencil offers a more textured appearance, which can add depth to your drawings or annotations.

1. Pencil Colors:

The pencil tool comes with a selection of colors similar to the pen tool. You can access these colors via the same palette:

- *Steps to Change Pencil Color:*

1. Click on the pencil icon in the toolbar.
2. A color selection menu will appear.
3. Choose the color you wish to use for the pencil tool.

Just like with the pen tool, you can choose from preset colors or use the custom color picker for more personalized options. When sketching or shading, choosing a softer color (such as gray or light blue) can add a natural, pencil-like appearance to your work.

2. Pencil Thickness:

Adjusting the thickness of the pencil strokes is essential for achieving the right balance between light shading and bold sketches. The pencil's thickness slider functions similarly to the pen's but allows for a slightly softer edge to your lines.

- *Steps to Adjust Pencil Thickness:*

1. Select the pencil tool from the toolbar.
2. Click on the thickness icon beside the color options.
3. Select the appropriate thickness for your task.

When sketching out ideas, you might start with a thinner line for basic shapes and switch to a thicker line to add shading or emphasis to certain areas.

Using Pen and Pencil Together

One of the strengths of Microsoft Whiteboard is the ability to use the pen and pencil tools together, allowing for a richer and more dynamic visual experience. Here are some ways to use both tools effectively:

- Annotating and Sketching: You might use the pen tool to annotate a document or diagram with precise text, while using the pencil tool to sketch out ideas or add shading around those annotations.

- Layering Information: The pen tool's sharp lines can be layered over the softer pencil strokes to create depth. For example, you could sketch a rough diagram using the pencil tool, then go over it with the pen to highlight key areas.

Optimizing the Inking Experience

1. Using a Stylus vs. Mouse:

While both a stylus and mouse can be used with the pen and pencil tools, the experience is much smoother with a stylus, particularly for tasks that require precision or fluid motion. A stylus allows for pressure sensitivity, meaning that pressing harder results in thicker lines, just like using a real pen or pencil.

2. Taking Advantage of Pressure Sensitivity:

For those using a pressure-sensitive stylus, the pen and pencil tools can respond to the amount of pressure applied. Pressing harder on the screen will result in thicker, bolder lines, while light strokes will produce thinner lines. This is especially useful for sketching and shading, as it allows for more control and creativity.

Conclusion

The pen and pencil options in Microsoft Whiteboard are powerful tools for expressing ideas visually. With customizable colors, thicknesses, and the ability to switch between precision and freehand sketching, these tools cater to a wide variety of tasks, from basic annotations to complex brainstorming sessions. Whether you're using a mouse, touch input, or a stylus, mastering the pen and pencil features will greatly enhance your ability to collaborate and communicate effectively using Microsoft Whiteboard.

2.1.2 Adjusting Colors and Thickness

One of the key features that make Microsoft Whiteboard such a versatile tool for collaboration and creativity is the ability to adjust the colors and thickness of your drawing and inking tools. These adjustments provide flexibility, allowing you to create visual variety, emphasize certain ideas, and add a personal touch to your digital whiteboard. Whether you're brainstorming with colleagues, planning projects, or teaching a concept, color and line thickness are critical components of how information is presented and interpreted. This section will explore how to efficiently use and customize these options, helping you to take full advantage of Microsoft Whiteboard's capabilities.

1. Understanding the Importance of Colors and Thickness

The right use of colors and line thickness can make a big difference in how content is perceived. Using different colors, for example, allows you to categorize, prioritize, and organize information visually. This can make your whiteboard content more accessible and easier to follow for collaborators. Similarly, adjusting the thickness of lines enables you to distinguish between major points and finer details, creating a visual hierarchy that enhances communication.

In educational or business settings, the strategic use of color and line thickness can drive engagement and comprehension. Instructors might use bold lines and bright colors to highlight important concepts, while project managers might use color-coded categories to keep track of various tasks and team members.

The primary benefits of adjusting colors and thickness include:

- Visual Organization: Differentiating between different topics, sections, or layers of information.

- Enhanced Readability: Using thicker lines for emphasis, or thinner lines for less critical information.

- Better Engagement: Colorful and well-organized content can keep your audience's attention focused on the task at hand.

- Aesthetic Appeal: A whiteboard filled with varied colors and line thicknesses is visually pleasing and more professional-looking.

Now, let's walk through how to adjust colors and thickness in Microsoft Whiteboard.

2. Navigating the Color and Thickness Options

The Pen and Pencil tools in Microsoft Whiteboard come with customizable options for both color and thickness. These options are accessible from the toolbar at the bottom of the Whiteboard screen. Whether you're using a mouse, touchpad, or stylus, making adjustments is intuitive and user-friendly.

Step 1: Selecting the Drawing Tool

Before adjusting any properties, you must first choose either the Pen or Pencil tool from the toolbar:

- Pen Tool: Best for smooth, clean lines. Useful for underlining or writing text on the whiteboard.

- Pencil Tool: Offers a more freehand, casual line that mimics the natural strokes of handwriting.

Once you've selected your drawing tool, you'll be able to modify its color and thickness.

Step 2: Adjusting the Color

Next, look for the color palette icon, which will appear once you click on either the Pen or Pencil tool. Microsoft Whiteboard provides a set of pre-selected colors, and adjusting your drawing color is as easy as clicking the color that best fits your needs.

1. Preset Colors: These include common colors like red, blue, black, and green. The preset colors offer quick access to commonly used hues and are perfect for fast, on-the-fly drawings.

2. Custom Color Palette: In some versions or with future updates, Microsoft Whiteboard may allow you to access an extended color palette or even input specific hex color codes. This can be helpful if you are working within strict branding guidelines or if you want to maintain a specific color scheme.

How to Use Colors Effectively:

- Categorization: Assigning colors to different categories or tasks can help make information more structured. For example, you can use red for urgent tasks, green for completed items, and blue for ongoing projects.

- Highlighting: To draw attention to important information, use bright or contrasting colors.

- Aesthetic Appeal: Well-chosen colors make your whiteboard more engaging and easier to navigate. For instance, soft pastel shades are good for background or less important notes, while darker or vibrant shades can be reserved for key points.

Step 3: Adjusting the Thickness

In addition to color, you can also adjust the thickness of your lines. This feature is accessible from the same toolbar menu, next to the color palette. The thickness adjustment is represented by different-sized lines or circles, which represent the width of your stroke.

The thickness settings are often displayed as:

- Thin: Best used for detailed work, fine outlines, or small annotations.

- Medium: A versatile option that is good for regular writing and general drawing.

- Thick: Ideal for bold lines, highlights, or when you want to make something stand out.

By default, the Pen and Pencil tools will likely be set to a medium thickness, but you can change this based on the task you're performing.

Tips for Using Thickness:

- Emphasis: Use thicker lines to emphasize important sections or to outline key areas. For example, if you're drawing a chart, the axes can be in a thick, bold color while the lines representing data points remain thin for better clarity.

- Contrast: Adjusting thickness in combination with color can help create contrast. For instance, a thick, dark line can frame a section of your whiteboard, drawing attention to the information within it.

- Layering Information: Using varying thicknesses helps you create a layered approach to presenting information, making your whiteboard content more digestible. Important ideas can be drawn in bold, while supporting details are rendered with thinner lines.

3. Practical Examples of Using Colors and Thickness

Now that you understand the basics of adjusting colors and thickness, let's explore some practical examples of how you might use these features in real-world scenarios.

Example 1: Project Planning and Task Management

Imagine you are using Microsoft Whiteboard to manage a team project. You might want to use different colors and line thicknesses to organize tasks:

- Colors: Use red to indicate tasks that are high priority, green for completed tasks, and blue for tasks that are still in progress.

- Thickness: Use a thick line for the overall project timeline or key milestones, and thin lines for the individual tasks that fall under each milestone.

This method not only makes the whiteboard easier to read but also helps team members quickly understand the status of the project at a glance.

Example 2: Teaching a Concept in a Classroom

A teacher using Microsoft Whiteboard to explain a complex concept, such as a math equation or a diagram, can utilize colors and thicknesses to make the lesson clearer:

- Colors: Assign a different color to each step of a math problem to guide students through the process. For example, blue for the equation, green for simplification steps, and red for the final answer.

- Thickness: Use a bold line to underline the critical points or outcomes of the problem and thinner lines for less important annotations.

This visual differentiation not only keeps students engaged but also makes it easier for them to follow the logical flow of the lesson.

Example 3: Brainstorming Session

In a collaborative brainstorming session, color and thickness can be used to categorize and prioritize ideas. For example:

- Colors: Use one color for ideas related to marketing, another color for product development, and a third for customer feedback.

- Thickness: Important ideas or main themes can be written in bold, while supporting details or additional thoughts can be rendered with thinner lines.

This approach helps participants quickly navigate the whiteboard and contributes to a more organized and productive session.

4. Accessibility and Inclusivity

It's also important to consider the role that colors and thickness play in accessibility. Not everyone interprets colors in the same way, especially people with color vision deficiencies (color blindness). When choosing colors and line thicknesses for your whiteboard, keep in mind the following best practices:

- High Contrast: Ensure there is a significant difference between the colors used for foreground (text and drawings) and background. This helps ensure that all users can easily see the content.

- Avoiding Red-Green Confusion: Many individuals with color blindness have difficulty distinguishing between red and green. Consider using additional visual cues, such as different line thicknesses or annotations, to convey important information.

- Clear Visual Hierarchy: Use thickness in combination with color to create a clear visual hierarchy, ensuring that your content is organized in a way that's easy to follow, regardless of color vision ability.

5. Saving Custom Color and Thickness Combinations

To streamline your workflow, Microsoft Whiteboard may allow you to save custom combinations of color and thickness. This feature is especially useful if you frequently use the same settings in your whiteboards, such as for brand colors or standardized project templates.

- Saving Settings: Some versions of Microsoft Whiteboard automatically save your last-used color and thickness settings. However, in more advanced versions, you may be able to save custom color palettes and thickness settings for easy access in future whiteboards.

- Restoring Defaults: If you need to reset your whiteboard tools to the original settings, you can easily do so by navigating to the toolbar and selecting the default options for color and thickness.

Conclusion:

Adjusting colors and thickness in Microsoft Whiteboard is a simple yet powerful way to elevate your visual communication. By thoughtfully applying these options, you can create whiteboards that are not only functional but also visually engaging. Whether you're using the platform for team collaboration, education, or personal projects, mastering these customization options will greatly enhance your whiteboard experience.

In the next section, we will dive into Adding and Manipulating Shapes, where you'll learn how to further organize and enhance your whiteboards with precision and clarity.

2.1.3 Using Highlighters

The highlighter is one of the most versatile and useful tools in Microsoft Whiteboard, perfect for drawing attention to specific elements on your canvas. Unlike the pen or pencil, which are more focused on drawing and writing, the highlighter serves to emphasize or underline existing content without overpowering it. In this section, we'll explore how to effectively use the highlighter to enhance your whiteboard sessions and boost visual communication.

Understanding the Role of the Highlighter

The highlighter tool is designed to mimic the functionality of a real-world highlighter marker. In any collaborative space or presentation, certain key points, areas, or details often need to stand out. Highlighting is the ideal way to achieve this because it lets you mark these areas while keeping the underlying content legible and clear.

Microsoft Whiteboard's highlighter tool works in much the same way. It's intended for situations where you need to draw your collaborators' attention to specific details without altering the overall content. This could include underlining key ideas, spotlighting portions of text or images, or creating emphasis on particular sections of diagrams or charts.

Accessing the Highlighter Tool

The highlighter is part of the Inking Tools in Microsoft Whiteboard. Here's how to access it:

1. Open the Whiteboard Toolbar: When you open Microsoft Whiteboard, you'll see the toolbar at the bottom of the screen. This contains all your basic drawing and inking tools.

2. Select the Inking Tools: Click on the pen icon to open the inking tools. This will display the various writing and drawing tools available, including pens, pencils, and the highlighter.

3. Choose the Highlighter: Among the inking tools, you'll notice an icon resembling a highlighter marker. Click on it to select it as your current tool.

4. Adjust Color and Thickness: Just like with the pen tool, you can adjust the color and thickness of the highlighter by clicking on the color options next to the highlighter icon. Microsoft Whiteboard allows you to choose from a variety of colors, ensuring that your highlights can match the theme or purpose of your whiteboard session.

Practical Uses of the Highlighter

Let's explore some practical situations where the highlighter tool shines in a Microsoft Whiteboard session.

1. Highlighting Key Points in Text

When using text boxes or sticky notes, there may be certain keywords, phrases, or sentences that require additional emphasis. Using the highlighter tool, you can draw over or underline these key points without obscuring the content. This can be particularly useful during brainstorming sessions, project planning, or instructional lessons.

For example, if you're outlining a project plan with different phases and tasks, you can use the highlighter to mark the most urgent tasks or the ones that need special attention. The ability to use different colors also allows you to color-code your highlights based on priority or categories.

2. Emphasizing Visual Elements

Besides text, you can use the highlighter to bring attention to certain parts of diagrams, charts, or drawings. For instance, if you have drawn a flowchart or a mind map on the whiteboard, you can highlight the most important connections, decision points, or outcomes to make them stand out.

In educational settings, the highlighter is often used to mark critical areas in images, such as labeling parts of a diagram or emphasizing a portion of a chart in a lesson. By using the highlighter, you ensure that important visual information is not lost amidst other details.

3. Creating a Visual Hierarchy

The highlighter tool is not just about marking specific words or areas—it can also help you create a visual hierarchy on your whiteboard. For example, if you have a list of items, you can highlight the most important items to visually separate them from the rest. This makes it easier for collaborators to immediately focus on what's most crucial.

Similarly, in a meeting where you're jotting down multiple ideas, you can highlight the ones that have been selected for further action, leaving the rest in a neutral tone. This kind of visual organization helps streamline collaborative sessions, especially when multiple people are working on the same whiteboard.

4. Organizing Thoughts and Ideas

When brainstorming or ideating, you often generate a large number of ideas in a short period. Using the highlighter tool to group or emphasize related ideas can help organize them visually. For example, after a brainstorming session, you might want to highlight the ideas that are related to marketing strategies in yellow and product development ideas in blue. This kind of categorization allows for easier navigation through complex or crowded whiteboards.

Best Practices for Using the Highlighter

While the highlighter is a simple tool, using it effectively requires some forethought. Here are a few best practices for ensuring that your highlights have the intended impact without overwhelming your whiteboard:

1. Use Color Purposefully

The ability to change the color of the highlighter means you can establish a color-coding system that adds clarity to your work. However, avoid using too many colors without a clear purpose. A general rule of thumb is to stick to three or four colors at most—each with a specific meaning. For example:

- Yellow could indicate urgency.

- Blue could be for general emphasis.

- Green could highlight tasks completed or ideas approved.

By assigning meaning to your highlighter colors, you ensure that your whiteboard remains organized and visually coherent.

2. Maintain Legibility

It's important to use the highlighter in a way that doesn't obscure the content beneath it. While it's tempting to use a thick highlighter stroke to make something stand out, this can make the underlying text or image difficult to read. Always ensure that your highlights complement the content rather than overpower it. If necessary, adjust the thickness of the highlighter tool to keep your markings subtle and non-intrusive.

3. Avoid Over-Highlighting

Highlighting can lose its impact if overused. If everything is highlighted, then nothing stands out. Be selective about what you choose to emphasize. Use the highlighter sparingly to mark only the most important information. Over-highlighting can create visual clutter, making it harder for your team to focus on what truly matters.

4. Layering Highlights for Complex Information

Sometimes, you may need to emphasize several different aspects of the same section of the whiteboard. In this case, you can use layered highlighting to create depth. For instance, you can first highlight key text in yellow and then add a secondary highlight in blue to show a second layer of information. Just be mindful not to overdo this technique, as it can make the content hard to interpret.

Collaborating with the Highlighter in Real-Time

One of the advantages of Microsoft Whiteboard is its collaborative nature. When working with a team in real-time, the highlighter tool becomes a valuable asset for group discussions, feedback, and decision-making. Here's how the highlighter can be used collaboratively:

1. Real-Time Feedback

In a live brainstorming session or team meeting, participants can use different highlighter colors to provide real-time feedback or mark key points. This allows for quick visual cues during discussions, helping everyone stay on the same page without interrupting the flow of conversation.

For example, one team member can highlight areas that need further discussion, while another can use a different color to mark agreed-upon action points. This dynamic use of the highlighter enables smoother, more organized meetings.

2. Tracking Changes and Decisions

The highlighter is also effective in tracking changes or decisions made during a whiteboard session. As your team works through a problem or project plan, you can highlight the agreed-upon solutions or decisions directly on the whiteboard. This makes it easy to look back at the whiteboard and see the progression of the discussion, as well as the final outcomes.

3. Assigning Tasks and Priorities

If you're using the whiteboard for project management, the highlighter can be used to visually assign tasks or set priorities. For instance, after listing out tasks on the whiteboard, you can highlight the ones that are high priority in red or yellow. This provides a clear visual indication of what needs immediate attention, and helps team members stay aligned on project goals.

Conclusion

The highlighter tool in Microsoft Whiteboard may seem simple, but when used effectively, it can significantly enhance your ability to organize information, collaborate with others, and emphasize key points. Whether you're using it for real-time feedback, visual hierarchy, or categorizing ideas, the highlighter serves as a valuable tool for both individual work and team collaboration. By understanding how to properly adjust and apply this tool, you can ensure that your whiteboard sessions are productive, clear, and visually engaging.

2.2 Adding and Manipulating Shapes

2.2.1 Drawing Perfect Shapes

One of the most powerful features of Microsoft Whiteboard is its ability to help you easily draw and manipulate shapes. Whether you're working on a brainstorming session, creating a mind map, or designing a visual flowchart, shapes are essential tools for structuring information and communicating ideas effectively. This section will guide you through the process of drawing perfect shapes on Microsoft Whiteboard, as well as explain how to make the most of this feature for various purposes.

Why Use Shapes in Microsoft Whiteboard?

Shapes serve multiple purposes when it comes to collaboration and visual communication. They help organize thoughts, segment different parts of a project, and visually clarify concepts that might be difficult to explain with text alone. Shapes are also useful for highlighting key points in your ideas or diagrams, making them easier to follow and understand. They form the building blocks of everything from simple to complex diagrams.

Whether you're teaching a class, working on a business proposal, or organizing a creative project, shapes provide a foundation for building more sophisticated visuals. Microsoft Whiteboard allows users to create and manipulate shapes with precision, ensuring that your boards look professional and organized.

Drawing Shapes Manually

In Microsoft Whiteboard, you can draw shapes freehand or use the shape recognition feature to automatically convert your sketches into precise geometric shapes. Here's how you can use both methods:

1. Drawing Freehand Shapes:

- You can simply use the pen tool to draw shapes such as circles, squares, triangles, and rectangles freehand.

- This method allows for complete freedom in drawing, making it ideal when you need a rough sketch or when precision isn't required.

- However, keep in mind that manually drawn shapes might not always look perfect, especially if you are using a mouse or trackpad instead of a stylus.

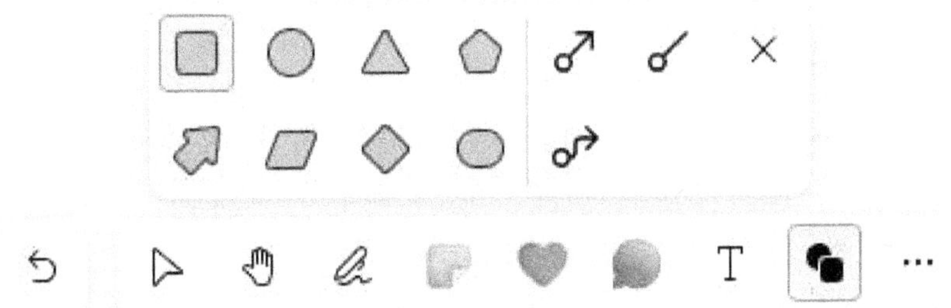

2. Using Shape Recognition:

- Microsoft Whiteboard includes a feature that automatically recognizes your hand-drawn shapes and converts them into neat, geometrically accurate versions. This is particularly useful if you want your diagrams to have a professional and clean look.

- To use this feature, simply draw the desired shape (such as a rectangle or circle) on the Whiteboard, and the software will automatically refine the edges and corners to make it a perfect version of that shape.

Shapes Available in Microsoft Whiteboard

Microsoft Whiteboard offers a variety of shapes that are commonly used in diagrams, flowcharts, and other visual presentations. Some of the key shapes include:

- Circles: Often used to represent cycles, focus points, or nodes in a diagram.

- Squares and Rectangles: Ideal for categorizing ideas, creating lists, or grouping information.

- Triangles: Useful for flowcharts, hierarchical diagrams, or indicating movement/direction.

- Lines and Arrows: Essential for connecting ideas, showing relationships, and indicating flow or sequence.

These shapes can be drawn quickly, and Microsoft Whiteboard's shape recognition ensures that they will always appear neatly and professionally.

Step-by-Step Guide to Drawing Perfect Shapes

Now, let's walk through the process of drawing perfect shapes on Microsoft Whiteboard using the shape recognition feature. Follow these steps to create accurate shapes in your whiteboard sessions:

1. Activate the Pen Tool:

 - On the toolbar, select the pen tool to begin drawing. You can choose from various pen styles and colors to suit your preferences.

2. Draw the Desired Shape:

 - Freehand draw the shape you want to appear on the board. For example, if you want a perfect circle, draw a rough circle using your stylus, mouse, or trackpad.

3. Watch the Shape Recognition:

 - As soon as you finish drawing, Microsoft Whiteboard's shape recognition will automatically adjust your freehand drawing into a clean, accurate version of the shape. It will smooth the edges and make the shape appear geometrically perfect.

4. Refining the Shape:

 - After the shape has been automatically adjusted, you can refine its size or position by clicking on it and using the handles around the shape. Drag the corners or sides to resize the shape to your liking.

5. Multiple Shape Drawing:

 - If you're creating a complex diagram that includes multiple shapes, you can repeat the above process to continue adding shapes one after the other. Each shape will automatically snap into place with clean lines and proportions.

Customizing Shapes

Once you've drawn a shape, Microsoft Whiteboard offers several ways to customize it to fit the needs of your project. Here are some common customizations you can apply:

1. Resizing Shapes:

- After selecting a shape, you'll notice small handles around its edges. By clicking and dragging these handles, you can increase or decrease the size of the shape.

- Microsoft Whiteboard ensures that the aspect ratio of geometric shapes is maintained, meaning that a circle won't turn into an ellipse unless you manually change its proportions.

2. Changing Colors and Outline:

- You can change the fill color and outline of a shape to match your design needs. Simply select the shape and choose from a wide range of colors in the toolbar. This feature is particularly helpful when you're using shapes for color-coded diagrams.

3. Adding Text to Shapes:

- One of the most useful features in Microsoft Whiteboard is the ability to add text inside shapes. To do this, simply click inside the shape and start typing. This allows you to label shapes, create titles, or add notes to specific parts of a diagram.

- The text automatically fits inside the shape, adjusting its size if necessary to accommodate longer words or sentences.

4. Aligning and Grouping Shapes:

- If you have multiple shapes on the Whiteboard, you may want to align them neatly for a professional look. Microsoft Whiteboard offers alignment guides that help you position shapes perfectly relative to one another.

- Additionally, you can group several shapes together by selecting them and using the "Group" option. Grouped shapes move as a unit, making it easy to rearrange complex diagrams without losing their structure.

Practical Applications of Shapes

Shapes are versatile tools that can be used in a wide variety of contexts, including business, education, and personal projects. Here are a few ways you can make the most of shapes in Microsoft Whiteboard:

1. Mind Mapping:

- When brainstorming ideas, shapes such as circles and squares can help you visually structure your thoughts. You can use arrows and lines to connect related concepts and create a clear visual representation of your mind map.

2. Flowcharts:

- Flowcharts are a staple in business and project management. Using rectangles for processes, diamonds for decisions, and arrows to indicate the flow, Microsoft Whiteboard makes it easy to create detailed and professional flowcharts for your team.

3. Classroom Diagrams:

- Teachers can use Microsoft Whiteboard's shapes to create engaging visuals for their students. Diagrams can help explain complex subjects such as geometry, biology (using labeled shapes), or historical timelines (using shapes to denote key events).

4. Organizational Charts:

- If you're working on organizational planning, shapes can help you create clear and informative org charts. Use rectangles or circles to represent individuals or departments and connect them with lines to show reporting structures.

Tips for Drawing Perfect Shapes Efficiently

Here are a few expert tips for drawing and manipulating shapes more efficiently on Microsoft Whiteboard:

- Use a Stylus for Greater Precision: While you can draw shapes using a mouse or trackpad, a stylus provides far greater accuracy, especially when drawing detailed shapes or fine adjustments.

- Leverage the Ruler for Straight Lines: If you need to draw perfectly straight lines, use the built-in ruler tool. This ensures that your lines are perfectly aligned and consistent.

- Snap-to-Grid Feature: Enable the snap-to-grid option to align shapes perfectly with one another. This is particularly useful when working on structured diagrams or flowcharts where alignment matters.

Conclusion

Drawing and manipulating shapes in Microsoft Whiteboard is an essential skill for creating professional and organized visuals. Whether you're using it for brainstorming, presentations, or teaching, understanding how to draw perfect shapes and utilize the customization options will elevate the quality of your work. By mastering the various tools available, from shape recognition to grouping and alignment, you'll be able to create visually appealing and effective diagrams, enhancing both personal and collaborative projects.

2.2.2 Grouping and Aligning Shapes

Grouping and aligning shapes is one of the most crucial aspects of creating organized and visually appealing whiteboards. When you work with multiple shapes, text boxes, or other elements, the ability to group them together and align them properly can significantly improve the clarity and professional appearance of your whiteboard. In this section, we'll explore in depth how to group and align shapes, including the tools available in Microsoft Whiteboard, best practices, and some advanced tips to optimize your workflow.

Understanding the Importance of Grouping and Aligning

Grouping and aligning shapes go beyond mere aesthetics; they are essential to maintaining clarity in your whiteboard sessions, especially when dealing with complex information. Whether you are mapping out a process flow, brainstorming ideas, or presenting a plan to your team, well-organized content can make the difference between confusion and understanding. Here are a few reasons why grouping and aligning shapes matter:

- Clarity: When elements are grouped and aligned, it becomes easier for others to follow your ideas.

- Efficiency: Grouping multiple shapes allows you to move, resize, or adjust them together, saving time.

- Consistency: Alignment ensures that your board looks neat and professional, which is particularly useful in business or educational settings.

- Focus: Well-organized whiteboards help focus attention on the most important points, reducing distraction from scattered elements.

Grouping Shapes

Grouping shapes in Microsoft Whiteboard allows you to combine several elements into one unified group. Once grouped, you can move, resize, or manipulate the entire group as a single entity. This feature is especially useful when you have multiple components—such as shapes, sticky notes, or text—that form part of a larger idea or visual representation.

How to Group Shapes

1. Select the Shapes:

First, select the shapes you want to group. You can do this by clicking and dragging your cursor over the shapes, or by clicking on each shape while holding down the Ctrl key (or Cmd on Mac).

2. Group the Shapes:

Once the shapes are selected, right-click on any one of them to bring up the context menu. In the options menu, click on Group. Alternatively, you can use a shortcut (such as Ctrl+G or Cmd+G) to quickly group the selected items.

3. Manipulating the Group:

After the shapes are grouped, you can now treat them as one object. This means you can move the group around the whiteboard by clicking and dragging it, resize the group by clicking on the corner and dragging to adjust the dimensions, or rotate the group using the rotation tool.

Ungrouping Shapes

If at any point you need to work with individual shapes within a group again, you can easily ungroup them. Simply select the group, right-click, and choose Ungroup from the context menu. You can also use a shortcut like Ctrl+Shift+G (or Cmd+Shift+G on Mac) to quickly ungroup the shapes.

When to Use Grouping

Grouping is particularly useful in the following scenarios:

- Flowcharts and Diagrams:

Grouping multiple shapes together in a process flow or diagram can help you maintain structure and move the entire process as one unit.

- Mind Maps:

When you're brainstorming ideas and organizing them into a mind map, grouping related items (such as an idea and its sub-ideas) keeps them together, making it easier to reorganize thoughts later.

- Presentations:

If you're using Microsoft Whiteboard for a presentation, grouping elements that need to be moved or resized together can help keep everything aligned when transitioning between different sections of your board.

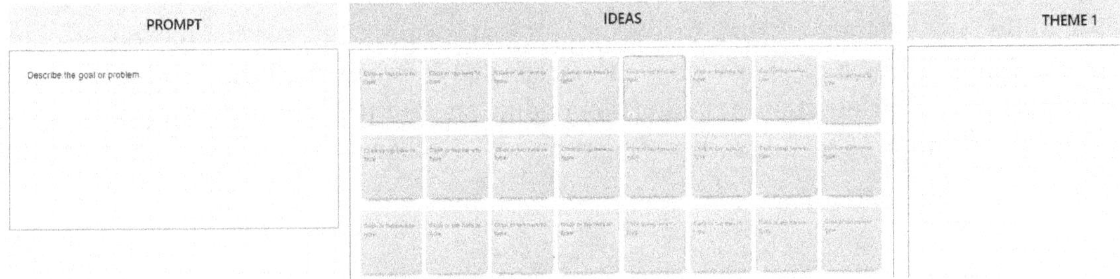

Aligning Shapes

Alignment is another key component of creating a clean and visually appealing whiteboard. Microsoft Whiteboard offers multiple ways to ensure that your shapes and other elements are properly aligned. By aligning shapes, you create a sense of order and consistency, making your whiteboard easier to understand and more professional-looking.

How to Align Shapes

1. Manual Alignment:

One of the simplest ways to align shapes is by using the grid lines that appear when you move shapes around the canvas. These lines help you visually align shapes relative to each other. As you drag a shape, grid lines will automatically appear when it is aligned with another shape either horizontally or vertically. This gives you a quick and easy way to ensure that shapes are in line with one another.

2. Snap-to-Grid:

Microsoft Whiteboard has a Snap-to-Grid feature that helps you align shapes more precisely. When this feature is enabled, shapes will automatically "snap" into place along an invisible grid on the canvas, making alignment easier and faster. This feature is especially helpful when working with several shapes that need to be evenly spaced.

3. Align Using the Ruler Tool:

The Ruler Tool is a highly effective feature for precise alignment. You can activate the ruler by clicking on the Ruler Icon in the toolbar. Once activated, the ruler will appear on your whiteboard, and you can rotate it to different angles by using the Arrow Keys or by manually dragging the edges. Once the ruler is in place, you can draw perfectly straight lines that help align other shapes or text boxes.

4. Aligning Text within Shapes:

In addition to aligning shapes themselves, it's also important to ensure that any text within those shapes is properly aligned. Microsoft Whiteboard allows you to align text inside shapes to the left, right, or center, depending on your preference. This is particularly useful when you are creating labels, diagrams, or flowcharts that require clear, readable text.

Best Practices for Aligning Shapes

To ensure the best results when aligning shapes on your whiteboard, consider these best practices:

- Use Alignment Guides:

The visual alignment guides (the grid lines that appear when moving shapes) are your best friends. They will help you make sure that elements are in line without too much manual effort.

- Keep Consistent Margins:

When working on complex whiteboards, ensure that there is an equal amount of space between shapes. This not only improves the overall appearance but also makes it easier for others to follow your ideas.

- Center Important Elements:

For whiteboards that are used in presentations or where certain elements are more important than others, ensure that the most crucial parts are centered or prominently aligned to draw attention.

Advanced Alignment Techniques

Microsoft Whiteboard also allows for more advanced alignment techniques that you can use to further refine your whiteboard layout.

- Distribute Shapes Evenly:

If you're working with multiple shapes that need to be spaced evenly apart, you can select all the shapes, right-click, and choose the Distribute Evenly option. This will automatically space the shapes equally either horizontally or vertically.

- Align to Center or Edge:

For more precise control, you can align multiple shapes to either the center or edge of the board. Select the shapes you want to align, right-click, and choose either Align Center, Align Left, or Align Right based on your preference.

- Combine Grouping and Aligning:

Grouping and aligning are powerful when used together. For example, you can group related shapes, align the group to the center or edge of the whiteboard, and then fine-tune the individual elements within the group.

Best Practices for Grouping and Aligning Shapes

While it's easy to use these tools in Microsoft Whiteboard, the key to success lies in adopting best practices that ensure your whiteboards are functional, clear, and visually appealing. Here are some best practices to consider:

1. Plan Before You Group or Align:

Before grouping or aligning shapes, it's a good idea to have a rough layout in mind. Decide where major elements will go and how they will interact. This will save time and effort when you start manipulating the elements.

2. Avoid Over-Grouping:

While grouping shapes can be incredibly useful, over-grouping can make it harder to edit individual elements later. Be selective about what you group together. Group only those elements that are logically connected or need to move together as a single unit.

3. Regularly Check Alignment:

As you add more shapes to your whiteboard, it's important to regularly check your alignment. Make sure that elements remain consistent in spacing and positioning, especially when you add new content to an existing layout.

4. Use Alignment to Highlight Key Information:

If certain shapes or elements are more important than others, you can use alignment as a way to highlight them. For example, centering key information or aligning important shapes in a prominent position can draw the viewer's eye.

5. Maintain a Clean Layout:

A cluttered whiteboard can be distracting. Make sure there is enough spacing between shapes and text, and avoid overlapping elements unless absolutely necessary.

6. Use the Ruler Tool for Precision:

For whiteboards that require precision, such as flowcharts or technical diagrams, the ruler tool is indispensable. It will help you ensure that all lines and shapes are perfectly straight and aligned.

By mastering the art of grouping and aligning shapes, you'll be able to create professional, organized, and visually appealing whiteboards that effectively communicate your ideas. Whether you're working solo, collaborating with a team, or presenting to a large audience, these skills will ensure that your whiteboard sessions are both productive and engaging.

2.2.3 Resizing and Moving Shapes

Shapes are a core element of any visual collaboration tool, and in Microsoft Whiteboard, they offer a powerful way to visually represent ideas, organize content, and create more structured diagrams. After you've added shapes to your whiteboard, the ability to resize and move them flexibly is key to keeping your workspace organized and adapting your visual elements as needed. This section will explore the different ways you can resize and move shapes to optimize your whiteboard for both individual and collaborative use.

Resizing Shapes: Adjusting Dimensions for Clarity and Emphasis

One of the most useful features of Microsoft Whiteboard is the ability to resize shapes dynamically. Whether you're trying to emphasize a particular concept, fit more content into your whiteboard, or align shapes with other elements, resizing can help you tailor your workspace to meet your needs.

1. Resizing Shapes Using the Handles

When you select any shape in Microsoft Whiteboard, you'll notice small circular handles appear around the edges of the shape. These are your resizing handles, and they make it easy to adjust the size of the shape. Here's how you can resize your shapes:

- Step 1: Click on the shape you want to resize. Handles will appear around its edges.

- Step 2: Hover your cursor over one of the handles. When the cursor changes to a double-sided arrow, you can drag the handle to resize the shape.

- Step 3: Click and drag the handle inward or outward to decrease or increase the size of the shape, respectively. You can resize both horizontally and vertically, depending on the handle you choose.

By using the corner handles, you can maintain the shape's proportions, whereas using the handles on the sides or top allows you to stretch or compress the shape in one direction, giving you greater control over the appearance of your shapes.

2. Resizing Multiple Shapes Simultaneously

In cases where you have multiple shapes on your whiteboard and you want to resize them together, Microsoft Whiteboard allows for multi-shape selection and resizing. This is particularly useful when you need to resize groups of shapes uniformly.

- Step 1: Use the lasso tool or hold down the "Ctrl" (or "Cmd" on Mac) key and click on each shape you want to select.

- Step 2: Once all the shapes are selected, resizing handles will appear around the group.

- Step 3: Use the corner or side handles to resize all the shapes at once. This ensures that the relative proportions between the shapes remain intact.

This feature helps in maintaining consistency across a series of related shapes, making your whiteboard content look clean and professional.

3. Aspect Ratio and Shape Integrity

Maintaining the aspect ratio of shapes can be crucial in ensuring that the original proportions are retained. For instance, circles can turn into ovals and squares into rectangles if resized without maintaining their aspect ratios. Microsoft Whiteboard provides a simple solution to this:

- Hold Shift: While dragging a corner handle, hold the "Shift" key to lock the shape's aspect ratio. This is particularly helpful for shapes like circles or triangles where proportionality is important for visual clarity.

By keeping the aspect ratio consistent, you ensure that your diagrams remain visually balanced, and your audience can easily recognize shapes without distortion.

4. Resizing for Precision

In some instances, you might need to resize shapes with greater precision, especially when working with detailed diagrams. In such cases, rather than relying solely on the mouse for resizing, you can use the Whiteboard's ruler tool or gridlines:

- Step 1: Enable the ruler tool to align your shapes accurately. This will help in maintaining straight lines and equal proportions.

- Step 2: Use grid snapping to automatically align shapes to a grid, ensuring uniformity when resizing or positioning shapes.

These additional tools allow for finer control over the size and alignment of your shapes, making Microsoft Whiteboard a robust tool for detailed work.

Moving Shapes: Organizing and Reorganizing Your Content

Once your shapes are in place, you'll often find the need to move them around the whiteboard as your ideas evolve or as you collaborate with others. Moving shapes is essential for organizing your content and creating logical, readable diagrams.

1. Moving Shapes Individually

Moving shapes in Microsoft Whiteboard is straightforward and intuitive. Here's how you can do it:

- Step 1: Click on the shape you want to move. A border will appear around the shape, indicating it is selected.

- Step 2: Click and hold the shape, then drag it to the desired location on the whiteboard.

- Step 3: Release the mouse button to place the shape.

This method works well for moving shapes individually. The whiteboard offers a fluid experience, allowing you to quickly reposition shapes without disrupting the overall structure of your board.

2. Moving Multiple Shapes Together

If you've created a group of shapes and need to move them together, Microsoft Whiteboard provides an easy way to move multiple shapes as a unit:

- Step 1: Use the lasso tool to draw around the shapes you want to move, or hold down the "Ctrl" (or "Cmd" on Mac) key and click on each shape to select them.

- Step 2: Once selected, click and drag any of the shapes within the selection to move the entire group.

- Step 3: Release the mouse button when you're happy with the new location.

Moving multiple shapes at once is particularly helpful when working on larger projects with complex diagrams that need restructuring or when collaborating in a team where different parts of the whiteboard need to be shifted.

3. Aligning Shapes While Moving

As you move shapes, keeping them aligned with other elements is crucial for maintaining a neat and professional-looking whiteboard. Microsoft Whiteboard offers alignment aids that automatically help you snap shapes into place:

- Guidelines: As you move shapes, the whiteboard may display temporary guidelines to help you align shapes with other elements on the board.

- Grid snapping: If you have gridlines enabled, shapes will automatically snap to the nearest grid intersection, making it easier to align multiple shapes in a structured layout.

These alignment aids ensure that your shapes are positioned in a way that enhances the visual flow of your content, helping both you and your collaborators quickly understand the relationships between different elements.

4. Layering and Stacking Shapes

In more complex whiteboard designs, you may have shapes that overlap. Understanding how to control the layering of shapes can make your designs more functional and visually appealing.

- Sending to Back/Bringing to Front: When you have overlapping shapes, right-click on a shape to access the context menu, and then choose "Send to Back" or "Bring to Front" to adjust the stacking order of shapes. This is useful when you want certain elements to be more prominent or when some shapes are obscuring others.

- Layering for Visual Impact: By strategically layering shapes, you can create visual hierarchies that guide the viewer's eye and emphasize the most important elements of your diagram.

These tools make Microsoft Whiteboard highly versatile, allowing you to create complex, multi-layered diagrams that remain clear and effective.

5. Moving Shapes with Precision

If you're dealing with a detailed layout or diagram, moving shapes precisely is crucial to maintain consistency and balance on your whiteboard. Microsoft Whiteboard allows for fine-tuned movement:

- Arrow Keys for Precision: Once a shape is selected, you can use the arrow keys on your keyboard to nudge the shape in small increments. This is ideal for making small adjustments that are difficult to achieve with a mouse.

- Using Ruler and Gridlines: For even greater precision, enabling the ruler and gridlines helps ensure that your shapes are perfectly aligned. The ruler can be rotated to any angle, providing an exact guide for positioning your shapes.

This precision can be especially useful in professional settings where clean, accurate diagrams are essential for communicating complex ideas effectively.

Organizing Shapes: Best Practices for a Clear and Effective Whiteboard

Now that you know how to move and resize shapes, it's important to consider how these actions contribute to the overall clarity and organization of your whiteboard. Here are some best practices to ensure your whiteboard remains clear, functional, and easy to navigate:

1. Group Related Shapes Together: By clustering related shapes, you can create visual groupings that make it easier for your audience to follow your ideas. For example, use color coding or proximity to group shapes by topic or function.

2. Use Consistent Sizes and Spacing: Consistency in shape size and spacing makes your whiteboard look more professional and easier to read. Try to use the same size for similar shapes and maintain even spacing between them to avoid clutter.

3. Avoid Overcrowding: Resist the temptation to pack too much information into a small space. Overcrowded whiteboards can be difficult to follow, especially in collaborative settings. Instead, spread shapes out and use blank space to give each element room to breathe.

4. Label Shapes Clearly: Use text boxes or sticky notes to label shapes so that their meaning is clear. This is especially important in collaborative environments where multiple people may be working on the same whiteboard.

By following these best practices, you'll create whiteboards that are not only visually appealing but also functional and easy to understand.

With these tips, you're well-equipped to make the most of Microsoft Whiteboard's shape resizing and moving features. Whether you're designing a flowchart, creating a mind map, or organizing a team brainstorm, mastering these tools will allow you to adapt your whiteboard to any situation.

2.3 Using Sticky Notes and Text Boxes

Microsoft Whiteboard is a powerful tool for visualizing ideas, brainstorming, and organizing information in a collaborative setting. One of the essential features for efficient idea capture is the use of sticky notes and text boxes. These features allow users to add text quickly, structure information logically, and communicate ideas effectively in a virtual space. In this chapter, we will explore how to create and format text using sticky notes and text boxes, enabling you to leverage these tools for productive and engaging whiteboard sessions.

2.3.1 Creating and Formatting Text

Text is fundamental in any whiteboard or brainstorming session. Whether you're jotting down ideas, labeling a diagram, or organizing information, Microsoft Whiteboard offers a versatile text toolset through sticky notes and text boxes. Both options allow you to create, customize, and arrange text in ways that suit your workflow.

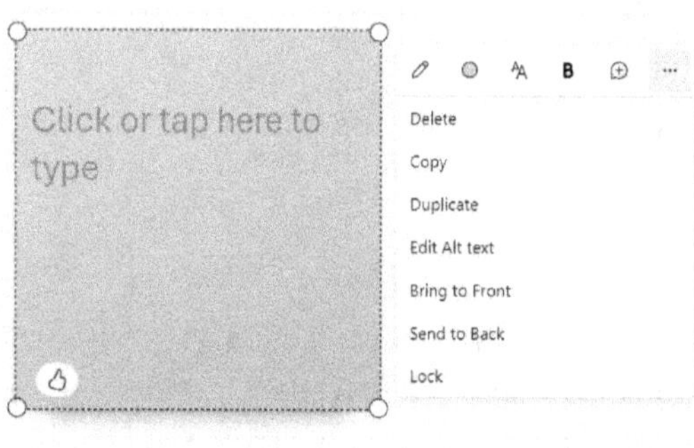

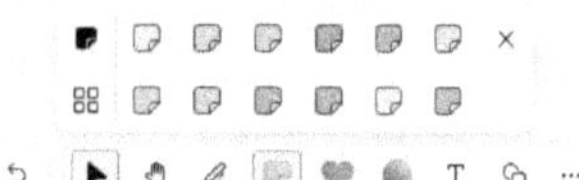

1. Creating a Sticky Note

Sticky notes are one of the most frequently used features in Microsoft Whiteboard, offering a fast and intuitive way to capture thoughts, ideas, or tasks in a visually distinct manner. Here's how you can create and use sticky notes effectively:

- *Step 1: Adding a Sticky Note*

To add a sticky note, click on the "Sticky Note" icon in the toolbar, typically represented by a small note or square symbol. This will open a blank sticky note in the whiteboard area, ready for text input.

- *Step 2: Typing into the Sticky Note*

Once the sticky note appears, simply click on it and begin typing. Sticky notes are ideal for capturing short, concise points. Whether you're brainstorming ideas or organizing tasks, the sticky note format helps keep your content clear and visually separated from other elements on the whiteboard.

- *Step 3: Customizing the Sticky Note Color*

Microsoft Whiteboard allows you to choose from several color options for sticky notes, making it easy to categorize information visually. For example, you might use yellow sticky notes for important points, green for tasks, and blue for questions. To change the color of a sticky note, click on the note to highlight it, then select the color palette icon from the toolbar. Choose your preferred color from the available options.

- *Step 4: Moving and Resizing Sticky Notes*

Sticky notes can be easily repositioned by clicking and dragging them to a new location on the board. This allows for flexibility in organizing information as you add more notes or change the structure of your whiteboard content. Additionally, you can resize the sticky note by clicking on the note and dragging the corner handles, ensuring your text fits perfectly within the note's boundaries.

2. Formatting Text within Sticky Notes

While sticky notes are a great way to capture information quickly, formatting options within the note itself are somewhat limited compared to text boxes. However, you can still make some basic adjustments to ensure your sticky notes are easy to read and visually appealing:

- *Text Alignment:* By default, text in a sticky note is left-aligned. Unfortunately, Microsoft Whiteboard doesn't provide extensive formatting options within sticky notes (such as bold or italic text), but the simplicity keeps the focus on capturing thoughts swiftly without distraction.

- *Clear and Concise Wording*: Given the size limitations of sticky notes, it's best to keep your text concise. Use bullet points or short phrases to convey ideas. If a thought requires more elaboration, consider linking the sticky note to a more detailed text box or another section of the whiteboard.

3. Creating a Text Box

In addition to sticky notes, text boxes offer a more robust way to display larger amounts of text. Text boxes are ideal when you need to add longer explanations, detailed notes, or titles to sections of your whiteboard.

- *Step 1: Adding a Text Box*

To insert a text box, click on the "Text" icon in the toolbar. This will insert a blank text box on the whiteboard. You can immediately begin typing, or reposition the text box to the desired location before adding text.

- *Step 2: Adjusting Text Box Size and Position*

After typing your text, you can click and drag the text box to move it around the whiteboard. You can also resize the text box by clicking and dragging the corners. This flexibility allows you to structure your whiteboard more effectively, especially when working with larger groups or during complex brainstorming sessions.

- *Step 3: Changing Font Size and Style*

Unlike sticky notes, text boxes offer more extensive formatting options. You can adjust the font size to make certain text stand out or appear more subtle depending on the content's importance. To change the font size, select the text, and you will see options to increase or decrease the size from the toolbar. This makes text boxes ideal for adding titles, headings, or important annotations to your whiteboard.

4. Formatting Options for Text Boxes

Text boxes in Microsoft Whiteboard come with a broader range of formatting options, allowing you to tailor the appearance of the text to suit your needs. These formatting options can enhance clarity, improve the visual flow of the whiteboard, and ensure that key points are emphasized.

- *Bold, Italic, and Underline Text*

You can emphasize certain words or phrases by using bold, italic, or underline formatting. To do this, simply highlight the text you want to format, then select the appropriate option from the formatting toolbar that appears when you click into the text box. Bold can be used to highlight important concepts, while italics might be used for quotations or subtle emphasis.

- *Adjusting Text Alignment*

Text alignment can play a key role in structuring your whiteboard's layout. You can left-align, center-align, or right-align text depending on your preference. Center-aligned text is often useful for titles or headings, while left-aligned text works best for longer bodies of information. This flexibility ensures that your content remains organized and easy to read.

- *Changing Text Color*

Microsoft Whiteboard allows you to change the color of your text within a text box. To do this, highlight the text and select the color palette from the formatting toolbar. Text color changes can be used to group related ideas visually, distinguish between different contributors, or highlight important points.

- *Using Bullet Points and Numbered Lists*

When working with more extensive content, especially in brainstorming sessions, bullet points or numbered lists can help organize thoughts and ideas effectively. To add bullet points or a numbered list, click the list icon in the formatting toolbar. Lists are particularly useful for creating to-do lists, outlining tasks, or summarizing key points.

- *Resizing Text Boxes for Better Readability*

One of the great advantages of using text boxes over sticky notes is that they can be resized both vertically and horizontally. This feature allows you to fit larger amounts of text without compromising the readability of your whiteboard. You can also adjust the overall font size for better readability, particularly in group presentations or when sharing the whiteboard remotely.

5. Best Practices for Using Text in Whiteboards

Now that you know how to create and format text in sticky notes and text boxes, it's essential to consider best practices for using text effectively on your whiteboards. Here are a few tips to keep in mind:

- *Keep it Concise:* Whiteboards are typically used for brainstorming and collaboration, so avoid long blocks of text whenever possible. Summarize key points, and keep explanations short to maintain clarity.

- *Use Color Wisely:* Text colors can help differentiate between topics, categories, or contributors. However, avoid using too many different colors, as it can lead to visual clutter. Stick to a consistent color scheme that enhances rather than distracts from the content.

- *Maintain Readability:* Ensure that your font size is appropriate for the audience. If you are sharing the whiteboard with a group, larger fonts will help participants read the content more easily, especially in remote meetings where screen size may vary.

- *Structure Your Content:* Organize your whiteboard content by using text boxes for titles and headings, and sticky notes for quick thoughts and ideas. This structure will help participants navigate the whiteboard more efficiently and ensure that important information stands out.

- *Collaborate with Clarity:* If you're working in a team setting, clearly label each section or contribution with names or roles. This helps everyone stay organized and ensures that ideas or tasks don't get lost during collaboration.

2.3.2 Organizing Ideas with Sticky Notes

In any collaborative brainstorming session or solo ideation process, one of the most effective ways to visualize and structure your thoughts is through sticky notes. Microsoft Whiteboard brings this familiar physical tool into the digital realm, allowing you to organize ideas in a way that fosters creativity, enhances clarity, and promotes collaboration. This section will guide you through the benefits of using sticky notes, how to organize them effectively, and tips to get the most out of this powerful feature.

Why Use Sticky Notes for Idea Organization?

Before diving into the specifics of organizing sticky notes in Microsoft Whiteboard, it's important to understand why sticky notes are so useful for brainstorming and idea generation. Sticky notes allow for flexibility, spontaneity, and a hands-on approach to visualizing abstract concepts. Whether you're conducting a brainstorming session, creating a to-do list, or planning a project, sticky notes help break down ideas into manageable, bite-sized chunks. In a collaborative environment, sticky notes also make it easy for team members to add, move, and adjust thoughts on the fly.

Sticky notes promote a non-linear way of thinking, which encourages creativity and allows participants to explore multiple ideas simultaneously. With Microsoft Whiteboard, the process is made even more seamless, as users can create as many sticky notes as needed without worrying about running out of physical space or materials. The digital nature of Whiteboard means you can always expand, rearrange, or categorize ideas in real time.

Creating Sticky Notes in Microsoft Whiteboard

In Microsoft Whiteboard, adding sticky notes is straightforward. The sticky note tool is located in the toolbar, allowing you to quickly add notes with just a click. You can select the color, format the text, and position them anywhere within the Whiteboard canvas. Here's how to create and customize your sticky notes:

1. Click the Sticky Note Icon: Find the sticky note icon in the toolbar at the bottom of your screen. Clicking it will open a blank sticky note on the board.

2. Type Your Idea: Once the sticky note appears, you can type directly into the note. Microsoft Whiteboard supports different font sizes and colors, making it easy to create visual distinctions between various ideas or categories.

3. Choose the Color: Microsoft Whiteboard offers several color options for sticky notes. Using different colors can help differentiate between different types of ideas, tasks, or phases of a project.

4. Resize and Move Sticky Notes: You can easily drag your sticky notes across the canvas and resize them to make them more prominent or reduce clutter.

These sticky notes can then be grouped, aligned, and categorized to help organize your ideas efficiently.

Strategies for Organizing Sticky Notes

Once you've added a few sticky notes, the real challenge begins: how do you organize them effectively? Organization is key to transforming a brainstorm from a chaotic explosion of ideas into a structured, actionable plan. Here are several strategies to help you organize your sticky notes within Microsoft Whiteboard:

1. Grouping by Category or Theme

One of the simplest and most effective ways to organize sticky notes is by grouping them into categories or themes. This method allows you to identify patterns and relationships between ideas. For example, during a product development meeting, you could categorize sticky notes into sections such as "Features," "User Experience," "Technical Challenges," and "Marketing." Within Microsoft Whiteboard, you can group sticky notes together simply by dragging them into clusters.

To further enhance organization, try color-coding your sticky notes based on these themes. Using different colors for each category creates a visual system that allows team members to quickly identify related ideas. For example, you could use yellow sticky notes for features, blue for user experience ideas, and green for marketing strategies.

2. Using Connectors for Relationships

In complex brainstorming sessions, your ideas might not exist in isolation. Some concepts will be connected or dependent on others. To highlight these relationships, Microsoft Whiteboard offers the ability to add connectors between sticky notes. This can help you create mind maps or flowcharts where ideas are connected by lines, showing cause-and-effect relationships or dependencies.

For instance, if you're developing a new app, you could create sticky notes for different features, then use connectors to show how one feature impacts another or how the development of one feature depends on the completion of another.

3. Prioritization Using Size and Position

Once you've grouped your sticky notes, it's helpful to start prioritizing ideas. Not all ideas are equally important, so you may want to make certain sticky notes stand out more. One way to do this is by adjusting the size of your sticky notes. In Microsoft Whiteboard, you can easily resize your sticky notes to make the most important ones larger and more prominent.

Another technique is to arrange your sticky notes by priority. Sticky notes that represent urgent tasks or high-priority ideas can be placed at the top of your board, while less critical items can be placed further down. This visual prioritization helps you and your team focus on the most important tasks first.

4. Creating a Kanban Board

If you're managing a project or a workflow, using sticky notes to create a digital Kanban board can be highly effective. A Kanban board visually represents tasks as they move through different stages of completion, such as "To Do," "In Progress," and "Done."

In Microsoft Whiteboard, you can easily set up a Kanban board by creating columns or sections on your canvas and populating them with sticky notes. Each sticky note represents a task, and you can move them between columns as they progress through the workflow. This method is particularly useful for team collaboration, as it allows everyone to see the status of tasks at a glance.

5. Organizing Sticky Notes by Time

For project planning or brainstorming sessions that involve timelines, organizing your sticky notes chronologically can help create a clear picture of what needs to be done and when. Arrange your sticky notes in a timeline format, where tasks or ideas are placed based on their order of execution.

For instance, if you're planning a marketing campaign, you could organize sticky notes into phases like "Initial Research," "Content Creation," "Launch," and "Post-Launch Review." This visual timeline helps ensure that tasks are completed in the right order and that no steps are missed.

6. Clustering Ideas for Brainstorming Sessions

When running a brainstorming session with multiple participants, it can be helpful to cluster sticky notes based on the flow of ideas. For example, during an open brainstorming session, different team members may add sticky notes rapidly, covering a range of topics. Once the brainstorming phase is complete, go back and cluster similar ideas together to identify trends or recurring themes.

In Microsoft Whiteboard, you can easily drag and drop sticky notes to cluster them together, creating a sense of order from the chaos of free-form idea generation. This step is critical in taking a brainstorming session from raw creativity to actionable insights.

7. Using Layers and Depth for Hierarchical Ideas

In some cases, ideas have a hierarchical relationship. You may want to organize ideas so that broader categories are at the top and subcategories or specific actions are layered underneath. Microsoft Whiteboard allows you to create multiple layers by placing sticky notes on top of one another or organizing them in a nested structure.

For example, in a product design session, you could have a top-level sticky note labeled "User Interface Design" and beneath it, several sub-notes detailing specific design elements like "Buttons," "Navigation," and "Color Scheme." This hierarchical organization helps to break down complex ideas into manageable pieces, making it easier to tackle large projects.

Collaboration Tips for Organizing Sticky Notes

Sticky notes become even more powerful when used in a collaborative setting. Microsoft Whiteboard's real-time collaboration features allow team members to simultaneously add, edit, and organize sticky notes from different locations. Here are a few collaboration tips to make the most of this functionality:

1. *Assigning Sticky Notes to Team Members*: You can assign ownership of sticky notes by labeling them with team members' initials or using a specific color for each person. This helps keep track of who is responsible for which tasks or ideas during a collaborative session.

2. *Real-Time Feedback and Adjustments:* Encourage team members to provide real-time feedback on sticky notes by adding comments or creating new sticky notes that suggest improvements or changes. This ongoing dialogue keeps the brainstorming or project planning process dynamic and inclusive.

3. *Avoid Overcrowding:* It's important to avoid overcrowding your whiteboard with too many sticky notes. If the board starts to look cluttered, consider creating separate boards for different themes or categories. Microsoft Whiteboard makes it easy to switch between different boards, so you can keep each one organized and focused on specific topics.

Maximizing the Value of Sticky Notes

To truly get the most out of sticky notes in Microsoft Whiteboard, it's essential to follow best practices for ideation and organization. Here are a few additional tips for ensuring that your sticky note sessions are productive:

- *Limit the number of words per note:* Sticky notes work best when they contain concise ideas. Limit each note to a short phrase or sentence to keep the board visually clean and easy to scan.

- *Encourage color-coding:* Use color strategically to differentiate between categories, priorities, or team members. Color-coding provides a visual shorthand that makes it easy to understand the organization of ideas at a glance.

- *Regularly review and reorganize:* As projects evolve, make it a habit to review and reorganize your sticky notes. Ideas that were initially brainstormed might need to be revisited, reprioritized, or even discarded. Regularly updating your whiteboard keeps it aligned with the current state of the project.

Conclusion

Sticky notes are a simple yet powerful

tool for organizing ideas in Microsoft Whiteboard. Whether you're working solo or with a team, they offer endless possibilities for brainstorming, project planning, and problem-solving. By mastering the art of organizing sticky notes, you can transform scattered thoughts into a clear and actionable plan, enhancing both creativity and productivity. Keep experimenting with different organizational strategies, and soon you'll find the approach that works best for you and your team.

2.3.3 Grouping Text and Sticky Notes

In Microsoft Whiteboard, organizing and grouping different elements like text boxes and sticky notes is a key feature for enhancing clarity and structuring your ideas. Grouping allows users to combine multiple pieces of content into meaningful clusters, making it easier to organize brainstorming sessions, mind maps, or any other collaborative work. In this section, we'll explore how to effectively group text and sticky notes, why grouping is useful, and different ways to take advantage of this powerful feature.

Why Grouping Matters

Whether you're leading a team meeting, planning a project, or simply brainstorming on your own, grouping elements like sticky notes and text helps streamline your process in several ways:

1. *Visual Organization:* Grouping allows you to keep related ideas together in a clean, organized way. For example, during brainstorming sessions, sticky notes can quickly pile up on your whiteboard, making it hard to follow. Grouping them by theme, priority, or category helps keep everything clear.

2. *Efficient Collaboration:* When collaborating with others, grouped elements help convey the structure of your thought process to the entire team. Everyone can see how individual ideas or notes relate to larger goals or concepts. This leads to more focused discussions and smoother collaboration.

3. *Easier Management of Large Projects:* When working on complex projects with many moving parts, it's crucial to track different components, tasks, or responsibilities. Grouping

sticky notes and text boxes into clusters (like "To-Do," "In Progress," and "Completed") simplifies progress tracking and helps ensure nothing gets overlooked.

How to Group Text and Sticky Notes in Microsoft Whiteboard

Microsoft Whiteboard offers simple yet powerful grouping options. Let's walk through the process step-by-step to show how to group text boxes and sticky notes:

1. Selecting Multiple Elements

The first step in grouping elements is to select multiple sticky notes or text boxes. You can do this by:

- Lasso Tool: Use the Lasso tool from the toolbar to circle around the elements you want to group. The lasso feature allows you to capture multiple elements at once, making it ideal for grouping.

- Click and Drag: Alternatively, click and drag across the whiteboard to select the text boxes and sticky notes that you wish to group.

- Hold Shift: You can also select multiple items manually by clicking on each one while holding down the Shift key.

2. Aligning the Elements

Once selected, you'll notice that you can move all elements together. It's important to align them in a way that's visually meaningful. For instance:

- Grid Alignment: If you're dealing with categories or phases of a project, aligning sticky notes and text boxes in a grid format makes it easier to visualize progress.

- Freeform Grouping: If the session is more creative and free-flowing, you might want to group sticky notes in non-linear arrangements. In this case, consider using shapes or lines (discussed in section 2.2) to emphasize relationships between elements.

3. Creating a Group

To officially group the items, follow these steps:

- Right-click or Long-press: After selecting the items, right-click (or long-press on touch devices) to bring up a contextual menu.

- Select 'Group': From the menu, choose the option to "Group" the items. This will lock them together as a single entity, allowing you to move or manipulate them as a whole. You can still edit individual sticky notes or text boxes within the group.

- Ungrouping: If you need to make changes or rearrange items, you can easily ungroup the elements by selecting the group and choosing "Ungroup" from the same contextual menu.

4. Using Labels and Colors for Better Organization

One of the most useful techniques in grouping text and sticky notes is leveraging labels and color coding to add another layer of organization. Here's how:

- Color Coding: Assign different colors to sticky notes based on categories, priorities, or departments. For instance, use yellow sticky notes for "Marketing Ideas," blue for "Engineering Tasks," and green for "Finance."

- Adding Labels: Text boxes can serve as headers or labels for different groups of sticky notes. For example, you might have a text box labeled "Brainstorming Ideas" with a collection of sticky notes beneath it representing various suggestions.

5. Resizing and Moving Groups

Once grouped, the entire cluster behaves like a single object. You can resize and move groups of sticky notes and text boxes with ease:

- Resizing: Click on the group to bring up the corner handles. Drag the corners to adjust the size of the entire group, ensuring that the text and sticky notes remain proportional.

- Moving: Once resized, you can click and drag anywhere on the group to move it around the canvas. This is especially helpful when rearranging ideas during a collaborative brainstorming session.

Practical Applications of Grouping

1. Brainstorming Sessions

In brainstorming sessions, sticky notes are frequently used to capture individual ideas. However, without some form of organization, the sheer volume of notes can become overwhelming. By grouping related sticky notes (e.g., grouping ideas into themes such as "Marketing," "Product Features," and "Customer Feedback"), you can better manage the flow of information and enhance the session's productivity.

2. Project Planning

When planning a project, it's common to split tasks into different phases or categories. For instance, a project might have phases such as "Research," "Development," and "Launch." You can create sticky notes for each task within these phases and group them together accordingly. This not only helps keep your project plan organized but also visually indicates the progress of each phase.

3. Task Management

Grouping is an excellent way to manage tasks, especially in a collaborative environment. You can create sticky notes for each task, color-code them based on priority (e.g., red for urgent tasks, yellow for medium-priority tasks, and green for low-priority tasks), and group them into categories such as "To Do," "In Progress," and "Completed." This approach is perfect for Agile teams, Kanban boards, or anyone who wants a visual task management system.

4. Mind Mapping

Mind mapping is a popular technique used for brainstorming, problem-solving, and idea generation. Grouping sticky notes and text boxes allows you to create meaningful connections between ideas. For example, the central concept can be represented by a text box, while related ideas can be captured as sticky notes surrounding it. Grouping these related sticky notes keeps the mind map organized and easy to follow.

5. Event Planning

When planning an event, there are often multiple components to consider—logistics, catering, guest lists, marketing, etc. You can create sticky notes for each task or responsibility and group them under categories like "Pre-Event," "During Event," and "Post-Event." Grouping ensures that each aspect of the event is accounted for, helping you manage your planning process more efficiently.

Best Practices for Grouping Sticky Notes and Text Boxes

While grouping is a simple feature, there are several best practices you can follow to make the most of it:

- *Use Colors Wisely:* Overloading your whiteboard with too many different colors can be overwhelming. Stick to a limited palette (3-4 colors) and use them consistently to represent specific themes or categories.

- *Keep Groups Manageable:* Don't overcrowd groups with too many items. If a group becomes too large, consider breaking it into sub-groups. For example, a "Marketing Ideas" group could be split into "Online Marketing," "Print Marketing," and "Event Marketing."

- *Regularly Review and Update Groups:* Groups are not static; they should evolve with your project or brainstorming session. Regularly review and reorganize groups as necessary to keep the whiteboard relevant and focused.

By mastering the grouping feature in Microsoft Whiteboard, you can significantly improve how you organize, visualize, and communicate ideas. Whether you're leading a brainstorming session, managing a project, or collaborating with a team, grouping sticky notes and text boxes provides a flexible and powerful way to structure your thoughts.

In the next section, we'll explore how to incorporate images and files into your whiteboard to further enrich your collaborative experience.

2.4 Incorporating Images and Files

One of the most powerful features of Microsoft Whiteboard is its ability to incorporate images and external files. Whether you're brainstorming ideas, visualizing concepts, or collaborating with team members, the ability to add images and files enhances communication and creativity. By using images and files, you can bring in visual elements that help clarify ideas, organize thoughts, and make your whiteboard sessions more interactive and engaging.

In this section, we'll walk through the different methods of adding images and files to your whiteboard, how to manipulate these elements, and the various ways they can be used to enhance your productivity.

2.4.1 Importing Images

Adding images to Microsoft Whiteboard is a simple process that allows you to visually enhance your workspace. Images can be used in a variety of ways, such as creating visual aids for presentations, illustrating ideas during brainstorming sessions, or providing context to abstract concepts. Here's how you can effectively import images into your whiteboard and make the most of this feature.

Finding and Preparing Your Images

Before you begin importing images, it's important to consider what type of image is most suitable for your whiteboard session. Depending on your objective, you might want to use diagrams, photos, illustrations, or icons. For example, if you're using the whiteboard for a project meeting, diagrams and flowcharts might be more appropriate, while photos might be helpful when collaborating on a design or creative task.

To prepare your images for import, make sure they are in a compatible format. Microsoft Whiteboard supports popular image formats such as JPG, PNG, and GIF. If you're working with more complex visual elements, such as a layered design file, consider exporting it as an image to ensure compatibility with the whiteboard environment.

Importing an Image from Your Device

The simplest way to add an image to your whiteboard is by importing it directly from your device. Whether you're using a desktop, laptop, or tablet, Microsoft Whiteboard makes this process seamless.

1. *Open Your Whiteboard:* Start by opening the whiteboard where you want to add the image. Ensure that your whiteboard is saved, and you're working in the correct space.

2. *Access the Insert Menu:* On the toolbar, look for the Insert icon, which typically appears as a small image or a "+" symbol. Click on this icon to reveal a menu of import options.

3. *Select 'Import Image':* From the menu, choose the Image option. This will prompt you to browse your device for the image file you wish to import.

4. *Choose the Image:* Browse through your device's files and select the image you want to import. Once selected, click Open or Insert to upload the image onto your whiteboard.

5. *Position the Image:* After the image is imported, you can click and drag it to reposition it within the whiteboard space. You can also resize the image by clicking and dragging the corners, allowing you to fit it perfectly into your layout.

Importing an Image from the Web

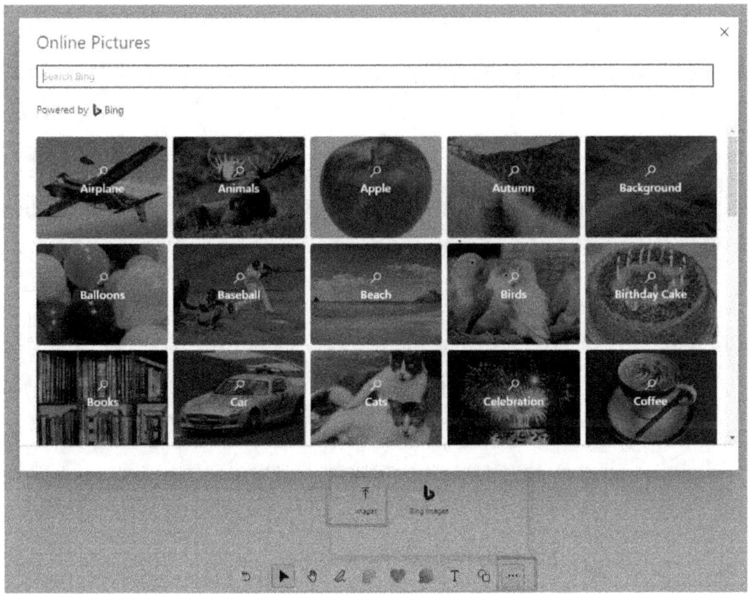

If the image you want to add isn't saved on your device but is available online, you can still bring it into your whiteboard without leaving the app. Microsoft Whiteboard provides a built-in option for adding web images, making it easy to search and incorporate visuals without switching between applications.

1. *Use the Built-in Web Search:* Open the Insert menu as you would when importing from your device. Instead of selecting the file option, click on Bing Image Search or a similar web search option, depending on your app version.

2. *Search for Your Image:* Type a relevant keyword to search for the image you need. For example, if you're working on a presentation about marketing strategies, you could search for terms like "marketing diagram" or "business flowchart."

3. *Select and Insert the Image:* Once you've found the image you need, click on it, and then press Insert to add it to your whiteboard. The image will appear, and you can manipulate it just like any other image imported from your device.

Best Practices for Using Images

While adding images can significantly enhance your whiteboard sessions, it's essential to ensure that you're using them effectively. Here are a few tips to make the most out of imported images:

- *Clarity is Key:* Ensure that the images you import are clear and high-quality. Blurry or pixelated images can detract from the clarity of your ideas and make collaboration more difficult. If you're using diagrams or charts, make sure the text is legible even when resized.

- *Avoid Clutter:* It's easy to overload a whiteboard with too many images, which can make it harder to focus on key concepts. Use images sparingly and only when they add value to the discussion.

- *Group Related Images:* If you're working with multiple images, consider grouping them together to create a visual cluster. This helps in keeping your workspace organized and makes it easier for collaborators to follow along.

- *Use Annotations:* Don't just drop images onto the whiteboard without context. Use text boxes, sticky notes, or drawing tools to annotate the images and explain how they fit into the larger discussion.

Enhancing Collaboration with Images

Images play a critical role in collaboration, especially in remote work environments. They allow team members to quickly grasp complex ideas, provide feedback on designs, and contribute to visual brainstorming sessions.

1. *Using Images for Brainstorming:* During brainstorming sessions, you can use images to inspire creativity or illustrate ideas that are difficult to explain with words alone. For example, if you're brainstorming a new product design, you could add images of similar products or inspiration boards directly onto the whiteboard.

2. *Creating Visual Summaries:* After a meeting or discussion, use images to create a visual summary of the key points. Import charts, graphs, or infographics that represent the data discussed and place them in a central location on the whiteboard for easy reference.

3. *Collaborative Design and Feedback:* If your team is working on a design or visual project, images can be used to present drafts and collect feedback. Each team member can contribute by adding annotations or comments directly on the image, allowing for real-time collaboration and faster iteration.

Accessibility and Copyright Considerations

When using images in your whiteboard sessions, it's important to consider both accessibility and copyright. Here are a few guidelines to keep in mind:

- *Alt Text for Accessibility:* If you're sharing the whiteboard with a broader team, including individuals with visual impairments, consider providing alt text descriptions for important images. This ensures that everyone can understand the content, regardless of their ability to see the image.

- *Use Copyright-Free Images:* When importing images from the web, make sure they are either free to use or properly attributed. Sites like Unsplash, Pexels, and Pixabay offer a wide range of royalty-free images that you can safely incorporate into your work without worrying about copyright violations.

By following these steps, you can effectively incorporate images into your Microsoft Whiteboard, enhancing collaboration, creativity, and communication within your team. Images help bridge the gap between ideas and execution, making complex concepts more tangible and accessible to everyone involved.

2.4.2 Attaching PDFs and Documents

Incorporating various types of files, such as PDFs and documents, is a powerful feature of Microsoft Whiteboard. This capability transforms Whiteboard from a simple brainstorming tool into a comprehensive platform for presentations, collaboration, and real-time document annotation. By learning how to attach and work with PDFs and other documents, you can streamline group projects, presentations, or even training sessions, all within a digital whiteboard environment.

The Importance of Attaching Files to Your Whiteboard

When collaborating with a team, it's often necessary to refer to or annotate various types of documents, such as reports, forms, or guidelines. With Microsoft Whiteboard, you can easily attach PDFs, Word documents, Excel spreadsheets, and other file types to your whiteboard, giving your team access to all the resources they need in one convenient place.

Attaching files directly into your workspace helps ensure that everyone is on the same page — quite literally. Instead of switching between different applications to refer to external documents, everything is seamlessly integrated into the Whiteboard. This integration helps improve workflow and reduces time lost in switching between applications, searching for files, or keeping multiple windows open.

How to Attach PDFs and Documents in Microsoft Whiteboard

Microsoft Whiteboard provides an intuitive interface to incorporate files. Here's how you can attach PDFs, Word documents, Excel sheets, and other formats to your whiteboard:

1. Open Microsoft Whiteboard

Start by launching the Microsoft Whiteboard app or opening it in your browser if you're using the web version. Open an existing whiteboard or create a new one where you plan to add the documents.

2. Access the File Insertion Option

On the Whiteboard interface, look for the Insert menu on the toolbar. This button allows you to add various types of content to your whiteboard, including text, sticky notes, images, and files.

3. Select "Documents"

Within the Insert menu, select the Documents option to begin attaching PDFs or other types of documents. This option allows you to browse your local device, OneDrive, or any integrated cloud storage where your document is saved.

4. Choose the File to Attach

After selecting the Documents option, a file browser window will pop up. From here, navigate to the folder where your desired file is stored. You can attach multiple file types, but PDFs are often the most common as they are widely used for reports, presentations, and publications.

5. Insert and Position the File

Once you've selected the file, click Insert. The document will appear on your whiteboard as a small thumbnail image that represents the file. From there, you can drag and position the file wherever you want on the whiteboard workspace.

6. Preview or Expand the Document

Clicking on the thumbnail will give you a preview of the attached file. You can expand the document to view its full contents within the Whiteboard interface. This is especially useful when working with longer PDFs or complex documents that require frequent reference.

7. Resize and Move the Document

You can also resize the thumbnail to make the file preview larger or smaller depending on how much space you want it to take up on your whiteboard. To resize, simply click on one of the corners of the file and drag it to your desired size.

Benefits of Attaching PDFs and Documents in Microsoft Whiteboard

Attaching files directly to your Microsoft Whiteboard offers several distinct benefits:

1. Easy Reference and Access

By having the document directly on the whiteboard, everyone in the team can quickly access the same file. Whether it's a report that needs reviewing or a guide that must be followed, you no longer have to search for the file in your email or cloud storage. This ease of access improves team efficiency.

2. Seamless Collaboration and Annotation

After attaching a file to the whiteboard, team members can collaborate by annotating the document. For instance, you can use the inking tools to highlight sections of a PDF, add sticky notes for comments, or draw attention to specific points in a report. These annotations can be saved and shared with the team, making collaboration more interactive and hands-on.

3. Visualize Ideas Alongside Documents

One of the standout features of Microsoft Whiteboard is its ability to visually organize thoughts, concepts, and files in one place. You can add sticky notes, text, and drawings around the attached document to better brainstorm or plan projects. It's particularly helpful when working on projects that require combining data from multiple sources.

4. No Need for Multiple Applications

Attaching documents directly onto your whiteboard eliminates the need to switch between apps. For example, in a brainstorming session, you might need to refer to a detailed PDF while simultaneously jotting down ideas or creating diagrams. Microsoft Whiteboard allows you to do this without breaking your workflow.

5. Version Control and Organization

Files on Microsoft Whiteboard are automatically saved along with the whiteboard itself, meaning you don't have to worry about losing any documents or annotations. If the file changes, you can always update it and continue working on the same board, ensuring that everyone is viewing the latest version.

Annotation on Attached Files

One of the most powerful features of attaching PDFs and documents in Microsoft Whiteboard is the ability to annotate them directly. For example, you might want to highlight certain sections of a report, cross out irrelevant text, or even add comments and feedback. Here's how to effectively annotate attached files:

1. Using the Inking Tools

After attaching a file, you can immediately start annotating it using the drawing or inking tools available in Microsoft Whiteboard. Select the pen or highlighter tool from the toolbar, choose a color and thickness, and start marking up the document. Annotations are dynamic and can be adjusted or erased as needed.

2. Highlighting Important Sections

If you're working with long documents, using the highlighter tool to emphasize key sections is particularly useful. For example, in a project meeting, team members can highlight different parts of a contract or specification document to discuss during a presentation.

3. Adding Sticky Notes for Feedback

Sticky notes are a great way to add feedback without altering the original document. By placing sticky notes next to specific points in a report or PDF, you can leave comments for others or note down important talking points for future reference.

4. Collaborating in Real-Time

When working with others, Microsoft Whiteboard allows for real-time collaboration. This means multiple users can annotate and comment on the same document at the same time. For instance, while one person highlights a section, another could be leaving notes or drawing arrows to signify key points.

Best Practices for Attaching and Annotating Documents

To ensure you're getting the most out of attaching and annotating documents in Microsoft Whiteboard, consider these best practices:

1. Attach Only What's Necessary

While attaching files is useful, avoid cluttering your whiteboard with unnecessary documents. Focus on attaching only those files that are critical to your discussion or project. This keeps your whiteboard organized and easy to navigate.

2. Use Annotations to Enhance, Not Overwhelm

Annotations are a powerful tool for collaboration, but over-annotating can make documents difficult to read. Keep your highlights, drawings, and sticky notes concise and focused on the most important sections of the document.

3. Organize Files Neatly on the Whiteboard

When attaching multiple documents, keep them organized on the whiteboard so they are easy to locate. You can group related documents together or use whiteboard sections to divide the workspace into different categories (e.g., "Reference Documents," "Feedback," etc.).

4. Update Files as Needed

If you're working on a long-term project, make sure to update the attached files as the project progresses. This ensures that everyone is working with the latest information and that older versions of the document don't cause confusion.

5. Leverage Microsoft 365 Integration

If you're working within the Microsoft 365 ecosystem, consider leveraging integrations between Whiteboard and other apps like OneDrive and Teams. For example, you can save files to OneDrive directly from Whiteboard or share annotated documents via Teams for quick feedback from colleagues.

Conclusion

Attaching PDFs and documents to your Microsoft Whiteboard can dramatically improve how you collaborate and work on projects. This feature not only provides easy access to vital resources but also allows for real-time collaboration and annotation, turning your whiteboard into a dynamic space for brainstorming and project development. Whether you're working in a team environment or managing a personal project, learning how to effectively attach and annotate documents in Microsoft Whiteboard can save time, enhance creativity, and streamline your workflow.

2.4.3 Annotating on Imported Files

One of the standout features of Microsoft Whiteboard is the ability to annotate directly on imported files. This functionality provides an interactive and dynamic way of collaborating on documents, images, and presentations. Whether you're working on a PDF report, a presentation deck, or simply marking up a graphic or photo, annotating on files within Whiteboard opens up a world of possibilities for team collaboration, education, and personal productivity.

Why Annotate on Imported Files?

Annotating on files allows you to make notes, highlight important sections, or even brainstorm ideas in real-time on a shared document. Whether you are working with colleagues, students, or even clients, the ability to annotate creates a seamless, interactive experience. It enables clearer communication and a more hands-on approach to working through content, giving everyone involved the chance to contribute effectively.

When you import a file into Microsoft Whiteboard, you can:

- Highlight Key Sections: Draw attention to important details or areas of focus.

- Provide Feedback: Add comments and suggestions directly onto the document.

- Brainstorm Ideas: Jot down ideas or make notes alongside specific parts of the document.

- Collaborate in Real-Time: Multiple users can annotate on the same file simultaneously, making it an excellent tool for remote collaboration.

Importing Files for Annotation

Before diving into annotation, it's essential to understand how to import files. Microsoft Whiteboard allows you to import various file types, including images (JPG, PNG), PDFs, and Office documents like Word or PowerPoint files. Here's a quick refresher on importing files into Whiteboard:

1. Open a Whiteboard: Navigate to your desired whiteboard and open it.

2. Select the Insert Button: Tap on the "Insert" button from the toolbar, which provides options for adding content.

3. Choose File Type: Select the file type you want to import (e.g., image, PDF, document).

4. Position the File: Once the file is imported, you can position it anywhere within the workspace, resizing and moving it as needed.

Step-by-Step Guide to Annotating on Files

Once the file is imported into the Whiteboard, you can begin annotating it. The process is simple and highly customizable, allowing you to use all the drawing and inking tools available in Microsoft Whiteboard.

1. Selecting the Inking Tool

After importing a file, the first step to annotating is selecting the inking tool. The toolbar in Microsoft Whiteboard offers various inking options, including pens, pencils, and highlighters.

- Pen Tool: This tool allows you to write or draw with precision. You can select different pen colors and thicknesses, ensuring your annotations stand out or blend in as needed.

- Pencil Tool: The pencil tool is ideal for freehand sketching and rough notes. It offers a more natural feel, especially for sketching ideas or adding creative elements to your annotations.

- Highlighter Tool: If you're working with a document or report, the highlighter tool is an excellent choice for marking key points or passages.

To choose a tool, click on the appropriate icon from the toolbar. If you're using a touchscreen device, simply select the tool and start drawing or writing on the document.

2. Customizing Annotation Tools

The ability to customize annotation tools is one of the features that makes Microsoft Whiteboard versatile. By adjusting the pen's thickness or choosing a different color, you can tailor your annotations to the specific needs of your project.

To customize your annotation tools:

1. Select the Pen Icon: After selecting the pen or highlighter, tap on the pen icon again to access customization options.

2. Choose Color: A color palette will appear, allowing you to pick from various shades. Select a color that contrasts well with the document's background for clear visibility.

3. Adjust Thickness: Depending on the detail level required, you can adjust the pen's thickness. Use a thicker pen for bolder annotations and a thinner one for precision work.

These options provide flexibility and allow you to highlight information more effectively, making your annotations more visually appealing and functional.

3. Making Notes and Annotations

Once your tools are customized, you can begin making annotations on the file. Some of the most common types of annotations include:

- Circling Key Sections: Use the pen tool to circle or underline critical points in the document. This method is often used for drawing attention to specific details, figures, or headlines.

- Writing Comments: Write brief notes or comments in the margins of the document. This is especially useful when reviewing text-heavy documents or giving feedback on presentations.

- Highlighting: Use the highlighter tool to emphasize text, making it stand out for easy reference. This is particularly useful in educational settings or document reviews, where highlighting critical points can facilitate quick access to important information.

As you annotate, remember that Microsoft Whiteboard is a collaborative tool, meaning others can view and interact with your annotations in real-time. You can create shared notes, provide feedback, and even add new annotations as discussions progress.

4. Collaborative Annotation in Real-Time

One of the strengths of Microsoft Whiteboard is its real-time collaboration capabilities. Multiple users can annotate on an imported file simultaneously, creating a highly interactive and dynamic workspace. This feature is particularly useful for team-based projects, remote work environments, and collaborative learning.

- Collaborate with Others: Invite others to your whiteboard and give them permission to edit. They can use the same inking tools to annotate on the document, adding their insights or comments directly onto the file.

- Review Annotations Together: Collaborators can review the document together, discussing each other's annotations in real-time. This helps streamline decision-making and ensures everyone is on the same page.

- Keep Track of Changes: Microsoft Whiteboard keeps track of all annotations, so you can see who made specific edits or contributions. This feature is handy when working in large teams, allowing you to attribute feedback and changes to individual members.

For remote teams, the ability to collaborate on files and annotate in real-time replicates the in-person brainstorming or review process, making it easier to maintain productivity even when team members are in different locations.

Annotating on PDFs

Annotating on PDFs is one of the most popular use cases for Microsoft Whiteboard. PDFs are often used for formal documents, reports, and presentations, making them ideal for review sessions, project feedback, or brainstorming sessions.

- Importing the PDF: Start by importing the PDF into Microsoft Whiteboard as described earlier. Once imported, the PDF will appear as a static image on the canvas.

- Annotating the PDF: You can use the same inking tools (pens, highlighters, etc.) to annotate the PDF. Circling important data, highlighting sections of text, or adding handwritten notes are all possible with ease.

- Zooming and Navigating: Microsoft Whiteboard allows you to zoom in and out of the PDF document. If the PDF is more than one page, you can scroll through the different pages while annotating on each as needed.

- Feedback and Review: PDF annotation is perfect for reviewing proposals, legal documents, and even study materials. Teams can collectively analyze the content, mark areas that need attention, and share feedback directly on the document.

Annotating on Images and Graphics

Annotating on images and graphics can be incredibly useful for visual projects, brainstorming sessions, or even educational purposes. Whether you're marking up a design, adding notes to a chart, or giving feedback on a graphic, Microsoft Whiteboard makes it simple.

- Importing the Image: Similar to importing PDFs, images can be added to the whiteboard canvas and moved, resized, or rotated as needed.

- Annotating the Image: Use the pen, pencil, or highlighter tools to draw directly on the image. For example, you could circle a section of a graphic, write feedback, or even sketch ideas directly on the photo.

- Creative Collaboration: In group settings, this feature is ideal for brainstorming or creative sessions. Multiple users can add their thoughts, suggest improvements, or propose design changes by annotating directly on the image.

Enhancing Your Annotations with Visual Tools

Microsoft Whiteboard offers additional visual tools that can be used to enhance your annotations on imported files.

- Shapes and Icons: Adding shapes such as arrows, boxes, or circles can help highlight specific parts of a document or image. You can also use icons like checkmarks, question marks, or symbols to clarify your annotations.

- Text Boxes: While the inking tools are great for freehand notes, sometimes adding a structured text box is more appropriate. You can type detailed feedback or create labels that provide further context for your annotations.

- Sticky Notes: Sticky notes can be used to add short comments or reminders on top of the imported file. This is particularly useful when you want to add feedback without directly writing on the file itself.

Saving and Sharing Annotated Files

Once you've finished annotating, you may want to save or share the annotated file. Microsoft Whiteboard provides several options:

1. Export as Image or PDF: You can export the entire whiteboard, including your annotations, as an image or PDF file. This option is ideal if you need to send the annotated document to someone who doesn't have access to the Whiteboard app.

2. Share the Whiteboard Link: If you want to continue collaborating or allow others to review your annotations, you can share the whiteboard link directly. This option allows others to interact with the file and continue making annotations.

3. Save to OneDrive: For seamless integration with other Microsoft 365 apps, you can save the annotated file directly to OneDrive. This ensures that the document is securely stored and accessible from any device.

Conclusion:

Annotating on imported files within Microsoft Whiteboard is a powerful tool for collaboration, communication, and idea generation. By using the inking tools, customizing your annotations, and collaborating in real-time, you can transform static documents into interactive spaces where ideas flourish. Whether you're working on a business proposal, a design concept, or an educational project, mastering the art of annotation in Microsoft Whiteboard will help you and your team work more efficiently and effectively.

CHAPTER III
Collaborating in Real-Time

In a world that relies heavily on remote work and virtual collaboration, the ability to work on a single platform with your team in real-time is invaluable. Microsoft Whiteboard provides a seamless environment for teamwork by allowing users to collaborate on a shared canvas. This chapter will explore how to invite others to your whiteboard and enable collaborative features, including inviting participants, setting permissions, and working together in real time.

3.1 Inviting Others to Your Whiteboard

Inviting others to your whiteboard is the first step in collaborative work. Microsoft Whiteboard makes it easy to bring team members into your workspace, whether they are across the room or across the globe. By allowing participants to join your whiteboard, you can create a dynamic and interactive environment where ideas flow freely, and everyone can contribute in real-time. Whether it's for a brainstorming session, project planning, or team meeting, understanding how to invite collaborators and set permissions is crucial for ensuring smooth and productive teamwork.

Before diving into the technical aspects of sharing your whiteboard, let's explore why inviting others to your whiteboard is such a powerful tool.

Why Collaboration is Key in Microsoft Whiteboard

Collaboration in Microsoft Whiteboard offers several benefits:

- Enhanced Brainstorming: Multiple perspectives can lead to more innovative solutions and creative ideas.

- Increased Engagement: When everyone can contribute simultaneously, team members feel more engaged and invested in the process.

- Real-Time Feedback: You can receive and give feedback instantly, speeding up decision-making and project development.

- Efficiency in Remote Work: Whiteboard bridges the gap in remote environments by providing a shared virtual space where everyone can contribute, no matter where they are.

Now, let's explore the specific steps to invite others to collaborate on your whiteboard

3.1.1 Sharing via Link or Email

Microsoft Whiteboard offers two primary methods for inviting collaborators: sharing via a link or sending an invitation through email. Both options are simple, and each has its own advantages depending on the scenario. This section will guide you through both processes in detail, helping you understand when and how to use them effectively.

Sharing via Link

Sharing a whiteboard via a link is one of the quickest and most convenient ways to invite collaborators. By generating a unique link, you can provide access to anyone with the link, allowing them to join the whiteboard instantly. This method is particularly useful for spontaneous collaborations or when you need to quickly invite a large group of people.

Steps to Share a Whiteboard via Link

Here's a step-by-step guide to sharing your whiteboard via a link:

1. Open the Whiteboard: Begin by opening the whiteboard you want to share. Make sure you are signed into your Microsoft account and have access to the whiteboard you wish to share.

2. Click the 'Invite' Button: In the top right corner of your whiteboard, you'll find an 'Invite' button, often represented by an icon of a person with a plus sign. Click this button to open the sharing menu.

3. Generate a Shareable Link: After clicking 'Invite,' a window will appear with the option to generate a link. Simply click the 'Create sharing link' button, and a unique URL will be generated for your whiteboard.

4. Copy the Link: Once the link is generated, click the 'Copy link' button. The URL is now saved to your clipboard, ready to be shared.

5. Distribute the Link: You can now paste this link into an email, chat, or any other communication platform to invite others. Anyone with the link can access the whiteboard, depending on the permissions you set.

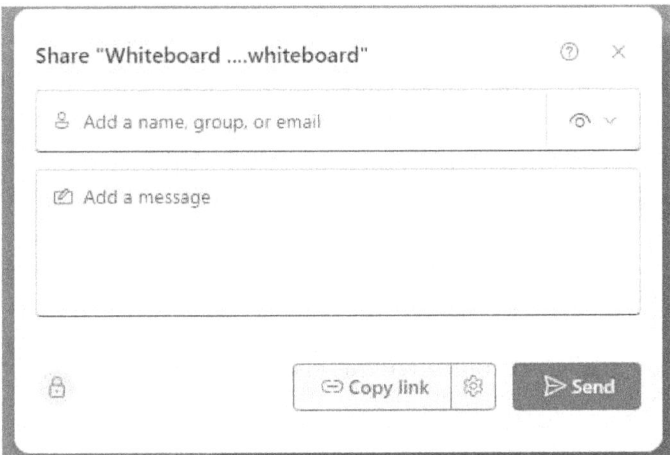

Best Practices for Sharing via Link

While sharing via link is easy, it's important to consider how you distribute the link and what permissions you give to the recipients. Here are some best practices to ensure a smooth experience:

- Consider Permissions Carefully: By default, anyone with the link will have the ability to view or edit the whiteboard, depending on the settings you choose. Make sure you understand the implications of these permissions, especially when sharing the link with a large group or externally.

- Limit Access When Needed: For sensitive whiteboards, consider limiting access by sharing the link only with specific individuals rather than a large group or publicly. If necessary, you can restrict editing permissions and limit the link to view-only access.

- Use Expiration Links: If you are sharing a whiteboard for a temporary project, it might be useful to create a link that expires after a certain period. While this option is not natively supported within Microsoft Whiteboard, third-party tools or platforms you use for communication may offer this feature.

- Track Participation: While the link-sharing method is quick and convenient, it can be difficult to track who has joined the whiteboard. If you need to know exactly who is collaborating, consider using the email invitation method instead.

Sharing via Email

For more controlled collaboration or when you need to track exactly who is accessing the whiteboard, inviting participants via email is an excellent option. This method allows you to send a personalized invitation directly to the people you want to collaborate with and set specific permissions for each participant.

Steps to Share a Whiteboard via Email

1. Open the Whiteboard: As with sharing via link, start by opening the whiteboard you wish to share. Ensure you are signed in and have access to the whiteboard.

2. Click the 'Invite' Button: Again, click the 'Invite' button in the top right corner to open the sharing menu.

3. Enter Email Addresses: In the sharing window, there is a field labeled 'Invite People by Email.' Enter the email addresses of the people you want to invite. You can invite multiple people at once by separating their email addresses with commas.

4. Set Permissions: Before sending the invitations, you'll need to decide whether each participant can 'Edit' or 'View' the whiteboard. These permissions can be adjusted individually, allowing some people to contribute actively while others may only observe.

5. Send the Invitation: Once you've added the email addresses and set the appropriate permissions, click the 'Send' button. The recipients will receive an email invitation containing a link to the whiteboard. From there, they can join the whiteboard and begin collaborating.

Advantages of Sharing via Email

While sharing via a link is quick and flexible, there are distinct advantages to using the email invitation method:

- Controlled Access: By sending invitations directly to specific email addresses, you maintain greater control over who can access your whiteboard. This method ensures that only those invited can join, reducing the risk of unauthorized access.

- Tracking Participants: Unlike link sharing, which may allow anonymous participation, email invitations allow you to see exactly who is accessing the whiteboard. This is particularly useful in business or educational settings where accountability is important.

- Personalized Permissions: Sharing via email gives you the ability to set customized permissions for each participant. You can give certain individuals full editing access while restricting others to view-only access, ensuring that the collaboration process remains organized.

Best Practices for Sharing via Email

When inviting others via email, it's important to follow some best practices to ensure a smooth and secure collaboration process:

- Double-Check Email Addresses: Always double-check the email addresses before sending invitations. A small typo can result in the wrong person gaining access or an important team member missing out.

- Assign Appropriate Permissions: Carefully consider the permissions for each individual you invite. For example, project managers may need full editing access, while other team members or clients may only need to view the whiteboard.

- Communicate Expectations Clearly: When sending email invitations, it's a good idea to follow up with a message or meeting that outlines the purpose of the whiteboard and the role each participant will play. This helps avoid confusion and ensures that everyone is on the same page.

- Manage Permissions Over Time: As the project progresses, you may need to adjust the permissions for different participants. For example, you might grant a team member editing access during the brainstorming phase, then change it to view-only once the whiteboard is finalized.

Conclusion

Sharing your Microsoft Whiteboard via link or email is the gateway to unlocking powerful real-time collaboration. By understanding the differences between the two sharing methods, you can choose the one that best suits your needs and manage your whiteboard effectively. Whether you opt for the speed of link-sharing or the control of email invitations, both options allow you to create an engaging and collaborative workspace where everyone can contribute their ideas and expertise. In the next section, we will dive deeper into Setting Permissions to ensure that your collaborative process remains efficient and secure.

3.1.2 Setting Permissions

When inviting others to collaborate on a Microsoft Whiteboard, controlling who can do what on the board is essential for ensuring smooth collaboration. Setting the right permissions helps in managing the flow of the collaboration process, safeguarding sensitive content, and preventing accidental changes. In this section, we will dive deep into how to set permissions effectively when sharing your Whiteboard, and why understanding these settings can greatly enhance your collaborative experience.

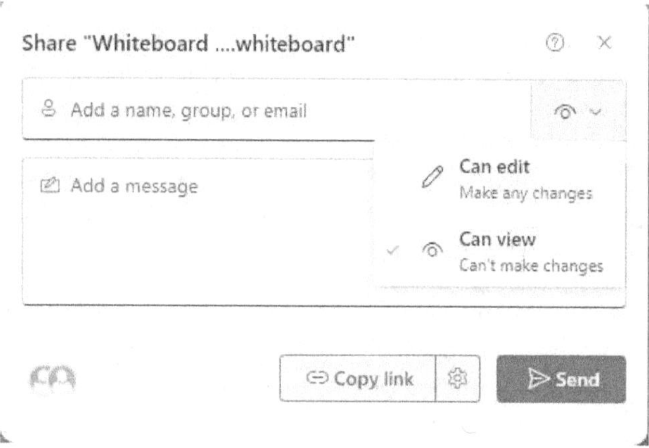

Understanding Permission Levels

Microsoft Whiteboard offers different permission levels that dictate what other participants can do on your board. These permissions are important to ensure the right level of control over your content. Primarily, there are two key roles:

1. Can Edit: This permission allows the collaborator to interact with the Whiteboard fully. They can add, modify, delete, and move content on the Whiteboard. This is useful when you're working with colleagues or team members who need to contribute ideas, notes, or visuals in real-time.

2. Can View: This is a more restricted permission, where collaborators can only see what's on the Whiteboard but cannot make any changes. This is ideal when you want to present information to an audience without the risk of someone accidentally moving or deleting

content. This setting is commonly used during presentations or educational sessions where one person controls the content, and others are passive participants.

Setting the appropriate permission level for each user or group is crucial for maintaining order, especially in large collaborative sessions. For example, in a brainstorming session, it may be appropriate to allow everyone to edit the Whiteboard, while in a review or presentation, you might limit most participants to view-only mode.

How to Set Permissions

Setting permissions in Microsoft Whiteboard is an intuitive process, but it requires a few key steps to ensure the right people have the right access.

1. Share Your Whiteboard: First, to access the permission settings, you need to share your Whiteboard. To do this, click on the "Share" button, usually located in the upper-right corner of the Whiteboard interface. This will open a sharing dialog where you can invite others via email or generate a shareable link.

2. Invite by Email or Link: After clicking the "Share" button, you'll see two main options to invite collaborators. You can either enter specific email addresses to send an invite, or generate a shareable link that can be sent out through other communication channels.

- Invite by Email: This method is more secure because it limits access to specific people, ensuring that only those invited can join the Whiteboard.

- Shareable Link: This is a more flexible method, but it's important to manage how this link is distributed, as anyone with the link can access the Whiteboard depending on the permissions you set.

3. Choose Permission Levels: Once you've chosen how you want to share the Whiteboard, you'll be prompted to set permissions. Here you can choose between Can Edit and Can View options.

- If inviting by email: You can assign permissions to each person individually. For example, you might want to give a co-worker editing privileges while allowing a supervisor to view the content only.

- If sharing via link: You can set a global permission for everyone who has the link. If you choose "Can Edit," everyone with the link will be able to modify the Whiteboard. If you choose "Can View," they will only be able to observe the content.

4. Adjust Permissions After Sharing: Sometimes, the requirements of the collaboration change. Fortunately, Microsoft Whiteboard allows you to modify permissions after sharing the board. You can go back to the sharing settings, find the list of participants, and adjust their individual permissions. For example, you can change someone from "Can Edit" to "Can View" if their role in the project shifts.

5. Revoking Access: In some cases, you may want to remove someone's access to the Whiteboard entirely. This can be done through the sharing panel by removing their email address or disabling the shareable link.

Best Practices for Managing Permissions

While Microsoft Whiteboard's permissions are easy to set up, there are some best practices to consider for optimal collaboration. Managing permissions effectively can prevent issues like version control problems, accidental deletions, or miscommunication among team members. Here are some strategies to ensure smooth collaboration:

1. Limit the Number of Editors: While it may seem beneficial to allow everyone to edit the Whiteboard, this can quickly lead to chaos, especially in large teams. By limiting the number of editors, you can maintain better control over the content and avoid the risk of accidental changes. Reserve editing privileges for key team members who are responsible for adding or organizing content.

2. Assign Roles Early: Before sharing the Whiteboard, it's a good idea to assign specific roles to each participant. Determine who will be in charge of adding content, who will organize the information, and who will review or give feedback. By setting these roles early, you can avoid confusion and ensure that the Whiteboard is used efficiently.

3. Use the "Can View" Permission for Large Audiences: If you're sharing your Whiteboard with a large group for review or presentation purposes, it's generally best to use the "Can View" permission. This way, you can present your ideas clearly without interruptions or accidental modifications by viewers. For example, during a company-wide presentation, you could have a small group of contributors actively working on the Whiteboard, while the rest of the participants are limited to viewing mode.

4. Regularly Review Permissions: If you're using Microsoft Whiteboard for ongoing projects, it's a good idea to review permissions periodically. As the project evolves, you may need to adjust permissions based on changing roles or responsibilities. For example, you might need to grant editing privileges to someone who was previously only a viewer, or vice versa.

5. Be Cautious with Shareable Links: While shareable links provide flexibility, they also come with risks. Anyone with the link can access the Whiteboard based on the permission level you've set. If security is a concern, especially in a business setting, it's better to invite specific people by email rather than relying on shareable links. Additionally, if you do use a shareable link, consider setting a time limit on the link or disabling it once the collaboration is over.

6. Monitor Activity on Your Whiteboard: With multiple editors working on a Whiteboard, it's important to keep track of what's happening. Regularly review the changes made by others to ensure that the Whiteboard stays organized and on track. If your team is using Microsoft Whiteboard as part of a larger project, it might be helpful to schedule regular reviews of the board to make sure everything is progressing smoothly.

Use Cases for Permission Settings

To better understand how to manage permissions effectively, let's look at some common scenarios where different permission settings are useful.

1. Brainstorming Sessions: In a brainstorming session, you'll likely want all participants to have editing privileges. This allows everyone to contribute ideas freely, whether through text, sticky notes, or drawings. Once the session is over, you may want to review the content and limit future changes by switching participants to "Can View" mode, preserving the integrity of the brainstorming output.

2. Project Planning: When using Microsoft Whiteboard for project planning, it's common to have a core team responsible for adding and organizing the content. In this case, it makes sense to grant editing privileges to this core group while giving other stakeholders view-only access. This ensures that the project plan is only modified by those directly involved in its development, while other team members can review the plan and offer feedback without altering the content.

3. Classroom or Training Sessions: In educational settings, Microsoft Whiteboard is often used to present information to students or trainees. In these cases, the instructor typically controls the Whiteboard, while students are given view-only access. This setup ensures that the lesson content remains clear and organized, while still allowing students to interact with the material in a structured way.

4. Review and Approval Process: During a review or approval process, you might want a small group of people to be able to comment on or mark up a Whiteboard, while a larger group is limited to viewing the content. For example, in a product development review, the

design team might have editing privileges to refine the design, while other stakeholders can view the Whiteboard and provide feedback without making changes themselves.

Security Considerations

While Microsoft Whiteboard is designed with collaboration in mind, it's important to consider the security implications of sharing your Whiteboard with others, especially if you're working with sensitive information. Here are some security best practices to keep in mind when setting permissions:

1. Use Two-Factor Authentication: If your organization uses Microsoft 365, make sure two-factor authentication (2FA) is enabled for all accounts. This adds an extra layer of security, ensuring that only authorized users can access the Whiteboard, even if someone else gains access to their credentials.

2. Set Permissions Based on Sensitivity: For highly sensitive projects, consider limiting editing access to a very small group and using "Can View" permissions for everyone else. This reduces the risk of accidental or malicious changes to critical information.

3. Disable Links When Not in Use: If you've shared a Whiteboard via a link, make sure to disable the link once the collaboration is finished. This prevents anyone with the link from accessing the Whiteboard in the future, ensuring that your content remains secure.

4. Monitor for Unauthorized Access: Periodically check the list of participants on your Whiteboard to ensure that only authorized users have access. If you notice any unfamiliar names, revoke their access immediately.

Conclusion

Setting permissions in Microsoft Whiteboard is a crucial step in managing collaboration effectively. By understanding the different permission levels and applying best practices, you can ensure that your Whiteboard is used efficiently and securely. Whether you're working on a team project, leading a classroom, or presenting to a large audience, setting the right permissions will help you maintain control over your content and enhance the overall collaboration experience.

3.1.3 Collaborating Anonymously

One of the most versatile features of Microsoft Whiteboard is the ability to collaborate with others, even if those individuals do not have a Microsoft account or are not within the same organization. This is particularly useful in situations where you are working with external stakeholders, clients, or team members who may not have access to your organization's infrastructure. In this section, we will explore how anonymous collaboration works, its advantages, potential limitations, and the best practices for ensuring security and productivity while working with anonymous collaborators.

Understanding Anonymous Collaboration in Microsoft Whiteboard

In many collaboration tools, the primary way to involve others is by inviting them through an official platform, requiring them to log in or authenticate themselves using a company email or account. However, Microsoft Whiteboard introduces the ability to collaborate anonymously, which allows you to share your Whiteboard with people outside your immediate network without them having to sign in.

Anonymous collaboration means that anyone who has access to the link can join the Whiteboard session, make edits, add content, and participate in discussions without being identified by their name or email. This offers an easy way to invite external collaborators, partners, or clients to participate in brainstorming sessions, creative collaborations, and strategic planning.

How to Enable Anonymous Collaboration

Enabling anonymous collaboration on Microsoft Whiteboard is a simple process that only requires a few steps. The first thing to remember is that anonymous collaboration is only available when you share a Whiteboard through a specific sharing link. Let's walk through the process of setting up anonymous collaboration:

1. Open Your Whiteboard: Launch Microsoft Whiteboard and open the board you want to share.

2. Click the Share Button: At the top right corner of your screen, you will find the "Share" button, which is the gateway to all collaborative features. Click on this button to open the sharing options.

3. Generate a Sharing Link: In the sharing options window, you will see the option to generate a sharing link. Here, you can configure whether the link will allow anyone to edit or view the Whiteboard. Select the "Anyone with the link can edit" option if you want anonymous users to make changes. If you only want them to view the content, select the "Anyone with the link can view" option.

4. Copy and Share the Link: Once the sharing link is generated, copy it and send it to the collaborators via email, messaging apps, or other communication channels.

Advantages of Anonymous Collaboration

1. Quick and Simple Access:

One of the most significant advantages of anonymous collaboration is the speed and simplicity with which it allows people to access your Whiteboard. There is no need for lengthy registration processes or waiting for approvals from your organization's IT department. This makes it a convenient solution for spontaneous brainstorming sessions or quick feedback from external parties.

2. Ideal for Short-Term Collaboration:

For projects that involve clients, freelancers, or external consultants who may only be working with you for a short period, anonymous collaboration is an ideal choice. Rather than setting up complex permissions or granting long-term access, you can provide the link, collaborate effectively, and close the session when the work is complete.

3. Collaboration Across Different Platforms:

Anonymous collaboration also opens the door to working across various platforms and devices. Since collaborators do not need to sign in using specific credentials, they can easily access the Whiteboard on any device—be it Windows, iOS, Android, or web-based—without compatibility issues.

4. Reduced Administrative Overhead:

Because you don't need to add users individually or manage accounts, anonymous collaboration reduces the administrative burden. This is especially useful when working with large groups or external audiences, such as during virtual workshops, webinars, or online classes.

Potential Limitations and Considerations

While anonymous collaboration offers numerous benefits, there are some important considerations and potential limitations that you should keep in mind.

1. Lack of Accountability:

Since anonymous users are not required to log in, it becomes difficult to track who is making which changes. This lack of accountability can be problematic in situations where it's important to know who contributed specific content or edits. In collaborative environments where accountability is key—such as project management or legal documentation—this feature may not be appropriate.

2. Limited Access Control:

When you share a Whiteboard with anonymous collaborators, anyone with the link can access it. This can lead to security risks if the link is inadvertently shared with individuals who should not have access. While Microsoft Whiteboard allows you to revoke sharing permissions at any time, it's important to be cautious about how widely the link is distributed.

3. No Granular Permissions:

With anonymous collaboration, you cannot assign different levels of permissions (e.g., view-only, comment-only) to specific individuals. Everyone with the link has the same level of access. For teams or organizations that require granular control over who can edit, comment, or view content, it may be better to use more structured collaboration features.

Ensuring Security in Anonymous Collaboration

When engaging in anonymous collaboration, security should always be a top priority, especially when working on sensitive projects or sharing proprietary information. Here are some best practices to ensure that your collaboration remains secure:

1. Use Expiring Links:

Whenever possible, set expiration dates for your sharing links. This ensures that once the collaboration period is over, no one can continue to access the Whiteboard. While this feature is available in other Microsoft tools like OneDrive and SharePoint, it's a helpful practice to apply to any project that involves external collaborators.

2. Revoke Access When Necessary:

If you suspect that the link has been shared with unintended parties or that someone is misusing their access, you can revoke the link and disable collaboration immediately. Microsoft Whiteboard allows you to turn off sharing at any time, which will block further access for anyone using the link.

3. Limit the Scope of Collaboration:

If possible, avoid sharing sensitive information through anonymous Whiteboard sessions. Keep the content limited to brainstorming, creative ideas, or general concepts. For more detailed and sensitive projects, require collaborators to sign in or use more controlled environments like Microsoft Teams or SharePoint.

4. Monitor Changes Closely:

Although you can't track specific anonymous users, it's still important to monitor any changes made to the Whiteboard during the session. Be proactive in reviewing edits, additions, and deletions to ensure that the collaboration remains on track and that no critical content is lost or misinterpreted.

Best Practices for Anonymous Collaboration

To maximize the benefits of anonymous collaboration while mitigating its risks, here are some recommended best practices:

1. Clear Communication:

When inviting anonymous collaborators, ensure that everyone understands the goals of the Whiteboard session, the types of contributions expected, and any ground rules for participation. Clear communication can help prevent confusion and ensure that everyone is on the same page.

2. Assign a Moderator:

To maintain order and productivity in larger anonymous collaborations, consider assigning a moderator. The moderator can help guide discussions, keep the Whiteboard organized, and ensure that all participants have a chance to contribute. They can also monitor for inappropriate changes or off-topic contributions.

3. Use Templates for Structure:

If you're leading a collaborative session, using templates can provide structure and ensure that the discussion stays focused. Microsoft Whiteboard offers a variety of templates for brainstorming, planning, and strategy, which can be customized to suit your needs. Templates help anonymous collaborators know where to add their input, reducing confusion and disorganization.

4. Periodic Check-ins:

During an extended Whiteboard session, consider pausing periodically to review progress, address any questions, and refocus the collaboration. Check-ins help keep everyone aligned and can prevent misunderstandings or repetitive work.

5. Close the Whiteboard Session When Finished:

Once the collaboration is complete, close the session by revoking the sharing link. This ensures that no further edits can be made after the project has wrapped up, and it helps secure the content from unauthorized access. If you need to continue work on the Whiteboard later, you can always re-enable sharing or create a new session.

Conclusion

Anonymous collaboration on Microsoft Whiteboard opens up new opportunities for flexible, inclusive, and dynamic teamwork. Whether you're working with external clients, holding virtual workshops, or simply brainstorming with a diverse group of participants, this feature allows you to invite contributions quickly and easily.

By understanding the advantages and potential risks of anonymous collaboration, and by applying best practices for security and productivity, you can ensure that your collaboration sessions are both successful and secure. In the next section, we will explore how to work simultaneously with others in real-time, taking your collaborative experience even further.

3.2 Working Simultaneously with Others

Collaboration in the digital era is a vital aspect of how teams and individuals work together. Microsoft Whiteboard was designed with collaboration at its core, offering tools and features that facilitate real-time interactions. This section explores the nuances of working simultaneously with others, ensuring a seamless experience even when team members are working from different locations, time zones, or devices. When used effectively, these tools enhance communication, boost productivity, and foster creativity.

3.2.1 Real-Time Collaboration Features

One of the standout features of Microsoft Whiteboard is its capability for real-time collaboration. Unlike traditional whiteboards that are bound by physical presence, Microsoft Whiteboard allows multiple users to interact, contribute, and brainstorm together on the same canvas from various locations. This real-time collaboration is not only practical for team meetings and brainstorming sessions but also for project management, design work, education, and creative thinking.

Understanding Real-Time Collaboration

At its core, real-time collaboration means that when multiple users are working on a single Whiteboard, every action—whether it's drawing, typing, adding sticky notes, or moving objects—can be seen by all participants instantly. This synchronized environment allows teams to work together as though they were in the same room, despite geographical distances.

When a participant updates a Whiteboard (e.g., by adding a new sticky note or drawing a shape), that change is reflected immediately on everyone's screen. There's no need to refresh the page or wait for updates. This instantaneous interaction allows for more dynamic and fluid teamwork, where ideas can be built upon quickly without delays.

Adding Participants to Your Whiteboard

Before diving into the collaborative features, it's essential to understand how to add participants to your Whiteboard. You can invite others by sharing a link or sending an email invitation (which we explored in section 3.1). Once participants join, they gain access to all the tools within the Whiteboard, enabling them to contribute in real time.

One important aspect of real-time collaboration is setting permissions. As the Whiteboard owner, you can control whether participants can edit or view the content. For fully interactive collaboration, editing permissions should be enabled for all participants.

Real-Time Feedback and Interaction

One of the most significant advantages of real-time collaboration in Microsoft Whiteboard is the ability to provide instant feedback. For instance, if a team member is drawing a diagram or organizing sticky notes, others can observe these actions in real-time and suggest changes, additions, or improvements on the spot. This avoids the need for back-and-forth email exchanges or waiting for updated documents to review.

Moreover, this real-time feedback fosters a dynamic workflow. Team members can build on each other's ideas fluidly, combining their individual insights to create something that is more than the sum of its parts. For example, during a brainstorming session, one person can start by adding an idea to the board, and another can quickly add on to that idea, resulting in a more comprehensive concept.

Color-Coded Participants

To make collaboration even more intuitive, Microsoft Whiteboard automatically assigns a unique color to each participant. This color coding allows all contributors to see who is adding or editing specific content on the board. For instance, if someone adds a new sticky note, that note will be outlined in the color associated with their name, making it clear who contributed the content.

This feature adds transparency to the collaboration process, making it easy to track contributions without confusion. It also encourages accountability, as each team member's actions are clearly visible to the group. Additionally, the color-coded participants can help manage large groups by allowing facilitators or moderators to easily see who is most active and who might need encouragement to participate more.

Visualizing Changes in Real Time

In real-time collaboration, every change is visualized as it happens. Whether a team member is moving a shape, changing the color of a note, or highlighting important information, all participants see these actions immediately. This instantaneous reflection of changes ensures that everyone stays on the same page throughout the session.

For instance, imagine a project planning meeting where one person is responsible for drawing out the project's timeline, while another is adding milestones, and a third is assigning tasks. With real-time collaboration, each participant's contributions are immediately visible to everyone, allowing for on-the-fly adjustments and ensuring a cohesive final product.

This capability can be especially valuable in design and creative fields, where visual brainstorming and feedback are critical. Designers, architects, or artists can share ideas on the Whiteboard and receive immediate input, making it easier to refine concepts and work towards a final design.

Synchronization Across Devices

Microsoft Whiteboard's real-time collaboration extends across all devices—desktop, laptop, tablet, or smartphone. Whether a team member is contributing from a PC in the office or a mobile device while on the go, the experience remains consistent. All changes are synced seamlessly, so no one misses any updates.

This cross-device synchronization is crucial for today's increasingly mobile workforce. It ensures that team members can participate in collaborative sessions no matter where they are or what device they're using. The flexibility to switch between devices without losing any progress or updates makes Microsoft Whiteboard a practical tool for remote work environments.

Real-Time Audio and Video Integration

Although Microsoft Whiteboard itself doesn't include native audio or video capabilities, it integrates smoothly with Microsoft Teams. This integration allows teams to collaborate in real-time on the Whiteboard while simultaneously engaging in voice or video calls.

For example, a team can hold a video meeting via Microsoft Teams while using Microsoft Whiteboard to visually capture ideas, make diagrams, or outline action plans. This combination of visual and auditory collaboration helps create a more immersive and interactive experience, making it easier to discuss, debate, and refine ideas as a team.

The audio and video integration also helps remote teams maintain a personal connection while working on shared projects. Hearing someone's voice or seeing their reactions in real-time while collaborating on the Whiteboard fosters a stronger sense of teamwork and can help bridge the gap created by physical distance.

Managing Multiple Contributors

In a collaborative environment, it's essential to manage the input of multiple contributors effectively. While Microsoft Whiteboard allows unlimited participants to collaborate, there are times when too many simultaneous actions can create confusion or clutter.

To mitigate this, it's helpful to set ground rules or assign roles within the team before beginning a collaborative session. For example, one person could be in charge of organizing the Whiteboard while others contribute content. Alternatively, the team could designate specific areas of the Whiteboard for different contributors to work in, ensuring that everyone has space to add their input without overlapping or conflicting with others.

Microsoft Whiteboard also includes a handy undo feature, so if a participant accidentally moves or deletes an important item, the change can be quickly reversed without disrupting the flow of collaboration. This ensures that mistakes are easily corrected, and the team can focus on working together.

Collaboration Etiquette

Successful real-time collaboration requires not only effective tools but also thoughtful communication and etiquette. To get the most out of Microsoft Whiteboard's real-time features, it's essential to encourage a few best practices among collaborators:

1. Clear Communication: Encourage team members to communicate clearly about their actions on the Whiteboard. For example, if someone is reorganizing content, they should let the group know, so no one is confused about sudden changes.

2. Respect for Others' Contributions: In a collaborative space, it's vital to respect the input of others. Avoid deleting or significantly altering content without group consensus, as this can disrupt the flow of ideas.

3. Balancing Participation: Ensure that all participants have an opportunity to contribute. In large groups, some members may dominate the Whiteboard, while others might feel hesitant to participate. Encouraging equal participation leads to a more balanced and productive collaboration session.

4. Establishing Ground Rules: Before starting a collaborative session, set some basic ground rules, such as how the space will be used, what the objectives are, and any specific roles that participants might have. This ensures that everyone is aligned and that the session proceeds smoothly.

Real-Time Collaboration Use Cases

Microsoft Whiteboard's real-time collaboration features can be applied to various use cases across different fields and industries:

- Brainstorming Sessions: Teams can gather on a Whiteboard to throw out ideas, organize thoughts with sticky notes, and refine concepts collaboratively. The fluid nature of real-time updates allows for dynamic brainstorming.

- Project Planning: Project managers can outline timelines, assign tasks, and track progress in real time, with team members contributing their parts of the plan directly on the Whiteboard.

- Education and Teaching: Teachers can use real-time collaboration to engage students during virtual classes, allowing them to contribute answers, ideas, or diagrams directly onto a shared Whiteboard.

- Creative Design: Design teams can collaborate on visual projects by sketching ideas, adding annotations, and receiving immediate feedback from other team members.

- Remote Meetings: Teams working remotely can use the Whiteboard during meetings to visualize ideas, plan strategies, and document action points in real time.

Real-time collaboration in Microsoft Whiteboard fosters an environment of creativity, cooperation, and productivity. By leveraging its powerful tools and features, teams can work together more effectively, regardless of where they are or what devices they are using. The next section will explore how to utilize the "Ink Together" option to further enhance collaboration.

3.2.2 Using the Ink Together Option

In today's dynamic work environment, collaboration is key to success, whether you're working with colleagues in the same room or across different time zones. Microsoft Whiteboard has been designed with this principle in mind, offering tools that make real-time interaction seamless and productive. One such powerful feature is the Ink Together option, which allows multiple participants to draw, annotate, and contribute to the same whiteboard simultaneously, fostering teamwork and enabling creative synergy in a virtual environment. In this section, we will explore the details of the Ink Together option, covering its use cases, how to activate it, and best practices for making the most of this collaboration feature.

What is the Ink Together Option?

The Ink Together option is a feature within Microsoft Whiteboard that enables multiple users to draw or ink on the whiteboard simultaneously, without the limitations of taking turns. This real-time collaborative capability transforms Microsoft Whiteboard into a highly interactive platform, ideal for brainstorming, problem-solving, planning, and other tasks that require immediate input from multiple team members.

This feature is especially useful in scenarios where teams are remotely located but need to visually communicate ideas or concepts. With the Ink Together option, everyone can contribute to the whiteboard as if they were working side by side on a physical whiteboard in the same room. Whether you're using a stylus on a tablet, your mouse, or even your finger on a touch device, the Ink Together option ensures that all participants can see and contribute to the board in real time.

How to Activate the Ink Together Option

Activating the Ink Together option in Microsoft Whiteboard is a straightforward process. The feature is typically enabled by default when multiple users are collaborating on a shared whiteboard. However, it's important to ensure that all users have the necessary permissions and are working in a supported environment (such as having access to Microsoft Whiteboard via Microsoft Teams, the web app, or the desktop app).

Here's how you can activate and make sure the Ink Together option works smoothly:

1. Share the Whiteboard:

- First, you need to share your whiteboard with other collaborators. You can do this by clicking on the "Share" button located in the toolbar and either sending an invitation link or adding collaborators via email.

- Ensure that collaborators have editing permissions to the whiteboard. This will enable them to draw, annotate, and make changes in real-time alongside you.

2. Ensure Permissions are Set Correctly:

- After sharing the whiteboard, verify that permissions are set to "Can Edit" for all participants. This setting allows them to actively engage in the collaboration process, enabling the Ink Together feature.

- You can manage permissions by clicking the "Share" button again and adjusting the settings under the permissions section. Make sure the "Can View" permission is not selected, as this will restrict participants from interacting with the whiteboard.

3. Activate Ink Together:

- When multiple users join the whiteboard with editing permissions, the Ink Together feature is automatically enabled.

- Each participant can then start inking simultaneously, with their cursor or stylus appearing live on the screen for all other users to see.

4. Use Ink Tools:

- Each participant has access to the full range of inking tools, including pens, highlighters, erasers, and the ruler for precision drawing.

- You can customize the color, thickness, and style of your ink tools to differentiate each participant's contributions, making it easier to follow multiple inputs on the board at the same time.

5. Device Support:

- The Ink Together option is supported on a variety of devices, including tablets with stylus support, desktop computers with a mouse, and touchscreens.

- For the best experience, using a touch-enabled device with a stylus will provide the most natural feel for drawing and sketching on the whiteboard.

Use Cases for the Ink Together Option

The Ink Together option offers a wide range of applications in both business and education. Below are some practical use cases where this feature can significantly enhance collaboration and productivity.

1. Brainstorming Sessions:

- During brainstorming sessions, having all participants contribute ideas simultaneously can lead to more diverse and creative solutions. Instead of waiting for one person to finish their input, everyone can draw or write their thoughts on the whiteboard at the same time.

- For example, in a marketing team brainstorming session, different team members can simultaneously sketch ideas for an ad campaign, while another team member writes down key objectives and target audiences.

2. Project Planning and Mind Mapping:

- The Ink Together option is excellent for collaborative project planning and mind mapping. Teams can create mind maps or Gantt charts, with each member contributing to different parts of the project plan simultaneously.

- This method of co-authoring visual elements streamlines the planning process and ensures that all team members are on the same page regarding the project's timeline, goals, and tasks.

3. Problem-Solving and Diagramming:

- Whether you're working on engineering designs, software architecture, or troubleshooting technical issues, real-time collaboration on diagrams and sketches is invaluable. The Ink Together option allows teams to collaboratively work through complex problems, sketching solutions and refining designs in real-time.

- For instance, a software development team can draw flowcharts and system diagrams, with each developer contributing to different sections, identifying bottlenecks, and proposing optimizations.

4. Education and Learning:

- Educators and students can use the Ink Together feature for interactive lessons. Teachers can pose questions or problems, and students can respond by writing or drawing directly on the shared whiteboard.

- For example, in a math class, students can work on different steps of a problem at the same time, allowing the teacher to track progress and correct mistakes in real-time.

5. Design Collaboration:

- Graphic designers, architects, and product teams often require real-time feedback on visual designs. The Ink Together option enables multiple users to annotate and modify designs during collaborative design sessions.

- For example, product managers and designers can use the whiteboard to refine product prototypes, with each participant adding their notes or modifications simultaneously.

Best Practices for Using the Ink Together Option

While the Ink Together option enhances collaboration, using it effectively requires some coordination to ensure that everyone is on the same page. Here are some best practices to help you make the most of this powerful feature.

1. Establish Clear Roles and Zones:

- In larger teams, it's helpful to assign specific roles or zones to each participant. For instance, one person can be responsible for adding shapes and diagrams, while another takes notes or outlines the discussion points.

- You can also divide the whiteboard into sections, with each participant working on a specific part. This approach avoids overcrowding and ensures that each team member has space to contribute without interfering with others' input.

2. Use Different Colors for Clarity:

- When multiple users are contributing at the same time, it can be challenging to track who added which content. Encourage team members to use different ink colors for their input. This not only makes it easier to follow contributions but also helps organize thoughts and ideas visually.

3. Communicate Verbally While Inking:

- While using the Ink Together feature, it's a good idea to maintain verbal communication, especially if you're collaborating in real-time via Microsoft Teams or another video conferencing tool.

- As you contribute to the whiteboard, explain your actions to your team. This real-time communication helps ensure that everyone is on the same page and understands the rationale behind each contribution.

4. Review and Organize Content:

- After an Ink Together session, it's essential to take time to review and organize the whiteboard. Group related ideas, delete unnecessary elements, and ensure that the board is easy to navigate and understand for future reference.

- This review process also helps capture key decisions and ensures that the output of the session is actionable and well-structured.

5. Save Frequently:

- Although Microsoft Whiteboard saves content automatically, it's always a good idea to periodically check that all contributions are being saved correctly, especially if you're working with a large number of participants. Ensure everyone's work is preserved, and that the whiteboard is available for future editing or sharing.

In conclusion, the Ink Together option is a powerful tool for fostering collaboration and creativity in real-time. By enabling multiple participants to work together on a shared canvas, Microsoft Whiteboard enhances teamwork, whether in business settings, classrooms, or remote working environments. The feature's intuitive interface and seamless integration with other Microsoft 365 tools make it an invaluable asset for anyone looking to collaborate visually and interactively.

3.2.3 Tracking Changes by Team Members

Collaboration is one of the key benefits of using Microsoft Whiteboard, especially in environments where team members contribute to a project in real-time or over extended periods. One of the most important aspects of teamwork is knowing who has made changes to the shared workspace. Tracking changes by team members in Microsoft Whiteboard allows users to monitor contributions, maintain accountability, and ensure that the project stays on track.

Understanding How Microsoft Whiteboard Tracks Changes

Microsoft Whiteboard doesn't have an explicit change-tracking system similar to traditional document editors like Microsoft Word, where each revision or change is marked with the editor's name. Instead, changes are reflected in real-time without detailed revision history. However, Whiteboard provides several indirect ways to understand and monitor the contributions of each team member during a collaboration session.

When working with multiple users on a shared Whiteboard, every change appears as it happens. Whether it's a new drawing, text, shape, or sticky note, all team members will see these updates instantaneously, assuming they are viewing the same board. These real-time updates provide a dynamic, visual sense of who is working on what aspect of the project at any given time.

Each participant can observe updates visually in two main ways:

1. Real-Time Visual Cues: When someone is actively drawing, writing, or making adjustments, you can see the changes appear on the screen in real-time. You can also identify the location of other users' cursors or focus areas when they're active.

2. Identifying Specific Contributions: While there isn't a formal audit trail, the nature of Whiteboard's collaborative space allows team members to add their own "signature" by color-coding sticky notes, texts, or annotations to differentiate their input from others. Each user has access to a personal pen or writing tool color, which can help differentiate who contributed specific elements.

Though Whiteboard doesn't track detailed histories of actions like editing text or moving objects, the following strategies can help teams organize and track contributions more efficiently:

Using Names and Labels to Clarify Ownership

One way to make team collaboration more structured is by explicitly labeling each contribution. For example, each team member can add their name next to the content they are responsible for. By making use of the Sticky Notes or Text Box features, individuals can tag different areas of the Whiteboard with their initials or names. This method is particularly useful when several people are working on similar tasks or when multiple items might overlap.

For instance, if your team is brainstorming and adding sticky notes, you could assign each person a different color sticky note, or ask everyone to label their notes with their name or initials. This not only helps identify who added each note but also makes it easier to follow up on certain ideas or tasks with the right person later on.

The Role of the Ink Together Feature

The Ink Together feature is another useful tool for team collaboration, especially when multiple members are working on different parts of a project at the same time. Ink Together allows users to draw simultaneously on the same section of the board, and this can be a great way to split work responsibilities. For example, in a design session, one person might outline a structure while another adds details or annotations.

Although Ink Together does not provide individual labels, teams can pair it with the strategies mentioned above to clarify contributions. By combining real-time drawing with color-coded pens and specific areas of focus, the team can keep track of changes efficiently even without a formal change-tracking tool.

Reviewing Changes through Version Control Outside of Whiteboard

For teams looking for more formal version control, an option is to periodically export the Whiteboard as an image or PDF and save it as a versioned file. This process, while manual, allows for tracking progress at specific points in time. Teams could agree on key checkpoints during their project and save the Whiteboard state at those moments.

For example, after each team meeting or milestone, the project lead could export the Whiteboard and store it in a shared location (like Microsoft OneDrive or SharePoint) with a timestamp and version number. This method helps track overall project progress and maintain a record of how the Whiteboard evolves over time.

Tracking Changes in Large Teams

In larger teams where multiple people may be working on a Whiteboard simultaneously, keeping track of changes can become more complex. However, Microsoft Whiteboard integrates with other Microsoft 365 tools, like Microsoft Teams, that offer additional collaboration features.

When a Whiteboard is shared in a Teams meeting or workspace, each participant's actions are synchronized across all devices. Although Whiteboard itself doesn't track individual changes, the surrounding Microsoft ecosystem provides opportunities to better track and organize contributions. For example, using the chat or comments section in Microsoft Teams while working on a Whiteboard allows team members to discuss changes, provide feedback, and document decisions made during a session.

Each time someone contributes to a Whiteboard in a Teams meeting, they can add context to their changes in the chat. This helps keep everyone informed and creates a documented record of decisions. Combined with exporting Whiteboards at regular intervals, this can provide a more comprehensive overview of contributions and changes over time.

Keeping Teams Accountable through Tasks and Responsibilities

Another key aspect of tracking changes in a collaborative Whiteboard environment is maintaining accountability for tasks and responsibilities. While Whiteboard doesn't provide a task management feature, teams can use the following strategies to manage contributions effectively:

- Assigning tasks within the Whiteboard: Each member can label sections of the Whiteboard that they're responsible for completing. This can be done through sticky notes, text boxes, or even drawing boxes around sections with a label like "John's section" or "Sarah's ideas."

- Using Microsoft Planner or To Do in conjunction with Whiteboard: For more detailed task tracking, teams can create tasks in Microsoft Planner or To Do, linking specific sections of the Whiteboard to each task. This allows teams to track who is responsible for each part of the project while keeping a clear record of what's been completed.

By combining task tracking from external tools with Whiteboard's collaborative features, teams can keep a clearer record of who has contributed to different parts of the project.

Real-Time Collaboration and Feedback Loops

One of the strengths of Microsoft Whiteboard is its ability to support fast, iterative feedback. In a team setting, changes can be tracked through verbal or written communication alongside the Whiteboard session. Teams working together in real time can take advantage of Whiteboard's commenting feature, where individuals can add notes or comments next to their contributions. This can help initiate feedback loops where team members review each other's work and make further suggestions.

For example, during a brainstorming session, team members might each take responsibility for adding their ideas to different sections of the Whiteboard. Afterward, they could review the entire board together, using sticky notes to provide feedback or suggestions next to the original contributions. This method allows for transparent, documented feedback on each person's work and ensures that everyone's input is considered.

Synchronizing Work Across Multiple Sessions

When a team works on a project over several sessions, tracking progress between meetings can be challenging without detailed change-tracking features. To ensure that everyone is on the same page, it's a good idea to create a system for marking what's been done and what still needs attention.

One approach is to use color-coding to show the status of different tasks or areas of the Whiteboard. For example, team members can use:

- Green sticky notes for completed tasks,

- Yellow for tasks in progress,

- Red for items that need immediate attention.

This system allows everyone to quickly see the current status of the project without needing to go through all the content.

Creating a Collaborative Culture in Whiteboard

Tracking changes by team members requires not only technical solutions but also fostering a collaborative culture within the team. Encouraging transparency, open communication, and clear responsibilities helps make the most of Microsoft Whiteboard's capabilities, even without formal change-tracking tools.

Teams should establish ground rules for how to work together on Whiteboard, such as:

- Using specific colors or labels to identify contributions,

- Assigning responsibilities for different sections of the Whiteboard,

- Reviewing and discussing changes together at regular intervals.

By setting these expectations upfront, teams can avoid confusion and make their collaboration in Microsoft Whiteboard smoother and more effective.

Conclusion

Tracking changes by team members in Microsoft Whiteboard is a critical part of maintaining accountability and ensuring that a project stays on track. While Whiteboard does not offer detailed revision history, teams can use color-coding, labels, and external tools like Microsoft Teams to manage collaboration effectively. By combining these strategies with strong communication and task management, teams can create a productive and transparent collaborative environment within Microsoft Whiteboard.

3.3 Communication Tools for Teams

3.3.1 Commenting and Notes

One of the most powerful features of Microsoft Whiteboard is its ability to foster communication and collaboration among team members in real-time. While drawing, sketching, and sharing visual ideas on a digital canvas is at the core of Microsoft Whiteboard, the tool goes beyond just visual communication. The ability to leave comments and notes is essential for creating a more structured and coherent dialogue during collaborative sessions. These features play a crucial role in facilitating communication, providing feedback, and capturing key points without disrupting the flow of ideas.

1. The Importance of Commenting and Notes in Collaboration

In a team setting, especially in virtual environments, the flow of ideas is constant, and clarity is paramount. While sketches and diagrams help visualize ideas, text-based communication such as comments and notes provides context, feedback, and further clarification.

For example, in brainstorming sessions, a team may sketch out a concept for a new product. At the same time, members may use the commenting feature to suggest improvements, identify challenges, or clarify elements of the design. In a business environment, where feedback loops are essential, notes allow for efficient back-and-forth communication without the need for interrupting the person presenting the whiteboard.

Microsoft Whiteboard's commenting and notes feature offers flexibility. Comments can be written on the spot and linked to specific sections of the whiteboard, ensuring that feedback is contextual. For team members who cannot participate in the real-time session, notes can serve as a log of feedback, tasks, or ideas that require further review.

2. Adding Comments to Your Whiteboard

The process of adding comments on Microsoft Whiteboard is intuitive. Here's how you can seamlessly integrate comments into your whiteboarding sessions:

1. Accessing the Comment Tool:

The comment tool can be found in the toolbar, usually represented by a speech bubble icon. When you select this tool, a text box will appear on the whiteboard where you can type your comment. The beauty of this feature lies in its simplicity—just click and type. You can position the comment box anywhere on the whiteboard, which allows for targeted feedback.

2. Formatting Comments for Clarity:

Microsoft Whiteboard allows you to format your comments for better readability. While the text formatting options in Whiteboard are not as comprehensive as a word processor, you can adjust font size, color, and style to make comments stand out. This can be particularly useful in scenarios where certain comments are more critical than others, or if you want to categorize feedback.

3. Tagging and Identifying Users in Comments:

One standout feature of the comments tool is the ability to tag specific team members. Using the "@" symbol followed by a person's name, you can notify team members about specific feedback or tasks related to their responsibilities. For example, if one person is responsible for designing a certain aspect of a project, you can tag them in the comment to ensure they receive direct feedback.

4. Linking Comments to Objects or Areas on the Whiteboard:

Comments in Microsoft Whiteboard can be associated with specific objects or areas, helping team members pinpoint the exact part of the whiteboard the feedback pertains to. Whether you're reviewing a diagram, chart, or a written idea, linking your comment to that object keeps the feedback organized and context-specific.

3. Managing and Responding to Comments

Once comments are added, they become an integral part of the collaborative process. Just as important as leaving feedback is managing and responding to it efficiently. Microsoft Whiteboard offers several tools to help teams manage their comments.

1. Replying to Comments:

Just as in any collaborative platform, Microsoft Whiteboard allows users to reply to specific comments. This helps maintain a dialogue within the context of each feedback item.

Rather than starting a new comment, team members can respond to existing ones, creating a thread of communication that remains attached to the original point of feedback.

2. Resolving and Deleting Comments:

Once feedback is addressed or no longer needed, comments can either be marked as "resolved" or deleted. This ensures that the whiteboard doesn't become cluttered with outdated information. Resolved comments can still be viewed, but they are marked to indicate that the issue has been addressed. This feature helps keep the collaborative space organized and focused on current tasks or feedback.

3. Comment Notifications:

If you've tagged specific team members in comments, they will receive notifications via Microsoft Teams or email, depending on how the whiteboard is set up. This ensures that no feedback goes unnoticed and that tasks can be addressed in a timely manner.

4. Tracking Feedback History:

Since Microsoft Whiteboard is integrated with cloud services, all comments are saved and synced in real-time. This allows team members to track the history of feedback and review older comments if needed. Having a log of all communication ensures transparency and accountability in collaborative work.

4. Using Notes for Long-Form Feedback or Documentation

While comments are ideal for brief feedback or clarifications, Microsoft Whiteboard also provides a Notes feature for more in-depth commentary or documentation.

1. Creating Sticky Notes for Quick Ideas:

Sticky notes are a key feature in Microsoft Whiteboard and are particularly useful when brainstorming. Team members can quickly jot down ideas, to-do lists, or reminders during meetings. These notes can be color-coded, making it easier to categorize and prioritize information.

2. Long-Form Notes for Detailed Information:

Sometimes feedback or instructions require more explanation than a simple comment allows. This is where long-form notes come in handy. Users can create larger text boxes that allow for detailed explanations, project guidelines, or documentation directly on the whiteboard. These notes remain visible alongside the visuals, ensuring all necessary information is available in one place.

3. Organizing Notes on the Whiteboard:

Notes can be easily moved around the whiteboard, grouped, or even layered over images, diagrams, or charts. This flexibility allows teams to organize their ideas in ways that suit their specific needs. For example, during a brainstorming session, a team might place sticky notes in clusters to represent different project phases or task categories.

4. Collaborating with Notes in Real-Time:

Similar to comments, notes in Microsoft Whiteboard can be added and edited by multiple team members in real-time. This allows for seamless collaboration as everyone contributes their thoughts, plans, or questions without waiting for others to finish their input. Real-time updates ensure that the whiteboard reflects the most up-to-date information.

5. Best Practices for Commenting and Note-Taking

To get the most out of the commenting and notes features in Microsoft Whiteboard, it's important to follow some best practices that will help streamline collaboration:

1. Be Clear and Concise:

When leaving comments, ensure they are clear and to the point. Avoid vague feedback that could lead to confusion. Using specific examples or linking the comment to the relevant part of the whiteboard will help prevent miscommunication.

2. Organize Notes and Comments by Priority:

Use color coding or labeling to organize notes and comments by priority. For example, urgent feedback can be in red, while less critical ideas can be in yellow. This makes it easier for team members to prioritize their actions.

3. Follow-Up on Feedback:

Simply leaving a comment is not enough; it's important to follow up on it. Encourage team members to respond to comments and resolve issues quickly. Regularly check the comment section to ensure that nothing is overlooked.

4. Collaborate on Notes in Parallel:

Notes are best used when multiple team members can contribute simultaneously. Encourage everyone to use sticky notes or add text boxes as they brainstorm or discuss ideas. This will help keep the flow of information constant and dynamic.

5. Document Action Items:

Comments and notes are not only for feedback but can also be used to track action items. By writing out specific tasks in notes, assigning them to team members, and marking them as completed, you can use Microsoft Whiteboard as a project management tool.

6. Integrating Notes and Comments with Other Tools

Since Microsoft Whiteboard integrates well with other tools in the Microsoft 365 ecosystem, such as Microsoft Teams and OneNote, the feedback process can extend beyond the whiteboard itself.

1. Syncing Comments with Microsoft Teams:

Comments left on a whiteboard can automatically sync with your Microsoft Teams workspace, allowing team members to view, respond to, or address feedback directly from Teams. This integration keeps communication unified and prevents the need for multiple platforms to track collaboration.

2. Exporting Notes to OneNote or Word:

If long-form notes contain essential documentation, you can export them to OneNote or Word for further editing and sharing. This ensures that important details are retained and organized for future reference.

By mastering the commenting and notes features in Microsoft Whiteboard, teams can ensure that their collaboration is both visual and textually rich. This blend of feedback methods allows for clarity, accountability, and efficient communication, making Whiteboard an indispensable tool for teams working in any environment, whether physical or remote.

3.3.2 Tagging and Assigning Tasks

In any collaborative environment, particularly when working in teams, it is essential to maintain clarity in communication and responsibility. Microsoft Whiteboard offers tools that can help organize the workflow by tagging team members and assigning tasks, making the platform a powerful tool not only for brainstorming but also for project management.

Understanding Tagging in Microsoft Whiteboard

Tagging in Microsoft Whiteboard is a relatively simple yet highly effective feature for organizing collaborative efforts. Tagging allows users to assign names, labels, or categories to various elements within a Whiteboard session, ensuring that everyone in the team is aware of what each element represents and who is responsible for it.

How Tagging Works

Tagging in Microsoft Whiteboard can be applied to a wide range of items, such as sticky notes, drawings, shapes, or text boxes. The idea behind tagging is to provide visual cues that indicate ownership or responsibility. Tags can be used to signify a person, a task, or even a priority level, making it easier for the team to understand what is required and by whom.

- Adding Tags to Objects: To tag an object in Microsoft Whiteboard, you can click on the item and select the option to add a tag. You can then type the name of the team member, project phase, or task category to associate it with the object.

- Tagging for Priority Levels: In addition to identifying team members or departments, tagging can also be used for prioritization. For example, you might use different colors or labels to indicate the urgency of tasks: "High Priority," "Medium Priority," or "Low Priority."

Benefits of Tagging

The ability to tag elements within a Whiteboard serves several important functions in collaborative settings:

1. Clarity of Responsibility: One of the most significant advantages of tagging is the clarity it brings to team tasks. When multiple people are working on the same board, tagging allows everyone to easily see who is responsible for which aspect of the project. This can reduce confusion and ensure that accountability is clear.

2. Enhanced Organization: Large projects often involve many interconnected parts. Tagging helps keep everything organized by categorizing tasks, milestones, or other important elements. For example, a project manager could tag all tasks that belong to a specific project phase, or team members could tag their individual contributions.

3. Improved Communication: By using tags to highlight tasks, questions, or important notes, communication becomes more streamlined. For example, if a task needs further input from a specific person, tagging them directly on the Whiteboard can quickly bring it to their attention without the need for additional emails or meetings.

4. Tracking Progress: Teams often need to monitor the progress of various tasks and activities in real-time. By tagging items with priority levels or statuses (such as "In Progress," "Completed," or "Pending Review"), team members can quickly assess the current state of the project at a glance.

Assigning Tasks in Microsoft Whiteboard

Assigning tasks within Microsoft Whiteboard works in tandem with the tagging feature, enabling team members to designate specific tasks or actions for each individual on the team. This ensures that everyone knows what they need to do, and it centralizes task management within the Whiteboard, eliminating the need for external project management tools.

How to Assign Tasks

While Microsoft Whiteboard does not have a formal task management feature in the way that dedicated project management tools like Microsoft Planner or Trello do, there are still several ways to assign tasks using the tools available in Whiteboard.

- Using Sticky Notes: One of the simplest ways to assign tasks in Microsoft Whiteboard is by using sticky notes. You can create a sticky note for each task, add a description of the task, and then tag the person responsible for completing it. Additionally, you can use color-coding or symbols to indicate the task's priority or deadline.

- Text Boxes for Task Descriptions: If a task requires a more detailed explanation, you can use a text box to outline the task and then assign it to a team member by tagging them directly within the text. This method is especially useful for more complex tasks that may require additional instructions or resources.

- Grouping Tasks by Team Members: Another effective method is to group tasks by team members. For example, you could create a dedicated area of the Whiteboard for each team member and place their assigned tasks in that section. This way, everyone can easily see their individual responsibilities.

Best Practices for Assigning Tasks

1. Be Clear and Specific: When assigning tasks, it's crucial to be as clear and specific as possible. Use detailed descriptions to ensure that the person receiving the task understands exactly what is required. Avoid vague instructions, as they can lead to confusion or delays.

2. Set Deadlines: Even though Microsoft Whiteboard does not include built-in deadline management, you can still include due dates in the task descriptions or create a visual timeline on the Whiteboard. This helps team members stay on track and ensures that tasks are completed in a timely manner.

3. Use Visual Cues: Take advantage of the visual nature of Whiteboard by incorporating arrows, lines, or other symbols to show relationships between tasks, deadlines, or responsibilities. This visual representation can help team members understand how their tasks fit into the larger project.

4. Track Progress Visually: You can also use the Whiteboard to track the progress of tasks. For instance, you might create a column for "To Do," "In Progress," and "Completed," and move tasks between these columns as they progress. This gives the entire team an overview of the project's status at a glance.

Real-World Applications of Tagging and Assigning Tasks

To better understand how tagging and assigning tasks can benefit teams, let's look at a couple of real-world scenarios.

Scenario 1: Brainstorming and Task Assignment in a Marketing Team

A marketing team is using Microsoft Whiteboard to brainstorm ideas for an upcoming campaign. Each team member contributes their ideas, and the team leader uses tagging to identify the person responsible for developing each idea further.

For instance, a sticky note containing an idea for a new social media strategy is tagged with the name of the social media manager, while another note with an idea for a promotional video is tagged with the video production team. The team leader assigns tasks to individuals by creating a to-do list on the Whiteboard and tagging team members next to each task. Throughout the week, team members can update the Whiteboard by moving their tasks to the "Completed" section or adding additional notes and progress updates.

Scenario 2: Project Management in an Engineering Team

An engineering team is working on a complex product development project. The project manager creates a timeline on Microsoft Whiteboard, with each phase of the project represented as a different section. Tasks within each section are tagged with the names of the engineers responsible for them, ensuring that everyone knows what they are working on.

As the project progresses, team members update their tasks by marking them as "In Progress" or "Completed" on the Whiteboard. The project manager uses tags to assign new tasks and monitor overall progress, enabling the team to collaborate efficiently and meet deadlines.

Tagging and task assignment in Microsoft Whiteboard may be relatively simple features, but they provide powerful benefits for teams working in both remote and in-person environments. By incorporating these tools into your workflow, you can enhance communication, streamline collaboration, and ensure that everyone is on the same page. Whether you're managing a project, brainstorming ideas, or tracking the progress of individual tasks, the flexibility of Microsoft Whiteboard makes it an invaluable tool for team collaboration.

3.3.3 Integrating Microsoft Teams with Whiteboard

In today's digital workplace, seamless collaboration between teams is essential, especially in remote or hybrid work environments. Integrating Microsoft Whiteboard with Microsoft Teams brings together visual collaboration and team communication, making it easier for teams to brainstorm, plan, and execute tasks in a cohesive manner. This integration allows users to access and use Microsoft Whiteboard directly within Microsoft Teams, offering a unified space for meetings, real-time ideation, and task management without switching between applications.

Why Integrate Microsoft Whiteboard with Teams?

Microsoft Whiteboard is a dynamic, flexible platform that allows users to visually organize thoughts and ideas. Microsoft Teams, on the other hand, is an essential tool for team communication, file sharing, and project management. By combining the two, you can amplify both tools' strengths, enhancing the way teams collaborate in real-time and across time zones. Teams can work on a shared whiteboard during meetings or asynchronous sessions, which fosters a more creative, organized, and engaged environment.

Benefits of Integration

The integration offers several key benefits:

1. *Real-time collaboration:* Teams can co-edit a whiteboard during a meeting, brainstorming session, or planning event in real-time.

2. *Centralized workspace:* Everything is accessible within Teams, which means team members don't need to leave the app to collaborate visually.

3. *Enhanced communication:* By using Whiteboard within Teams, members can communicate through chat, audio, or video while working on the board, ensuring smooth discussions.

4. *Task delegation and tracking:* Ideas generated on the Whiteboard can quickly be turned into actionable tasks within Teams, streamlining the workflow.

5. *Persistent whiteboards:* Any Whiteboard created in a meeting will remain saved in Teams, making it easy to revisit or build upon ideas later.

How to Use Microsoft Whiteboard in Microsoft Teams

Microsoft Teams provides multiple ways to use Whiteboard. You can either start a new Whiteboard session during a meeting or open an existing Whiteboard for the team to collaborate on. The process is simple and user-friendly, ensuring that even beginners can quickly adopt the functionality.

1. Adding Microsoft Whiteboard to a Teams Meeting

When scheduling a meeting in Microsoft Teams, you can easily add a Whiteboard session that attendees can collaborate on before, during, or after the meeting.

Step-by-Step Guide:

1. Schedule a Meeting: In Microsoft Teams, click on the Calendar tab and select "New Meeting." Set your meeting details, including the participants, date, time, and agenda.

2. Join the Meeting: When the meeting starts, join it as the host or as a participant.

3. Open Whiteboard: Once inside the meeting, click on the "Share" button in the meeting control bar. From the sharing options, select "Microsoft Whiteboard."

4. Collaborate in Real-Time: A blank whiteboard will open, allowing all participants to collaborate. They can draw, type, and add notes, shapes, or images to the shared space.

5. Save Automatically: The Whiteboard is automatically saved in the meeting chat. You can return to it anytime by navigating to the meeting's chat history and opening the Whiteboard again.

2. Creating a Standalone Whiteboard in Teams

Aside from integrating Whiteboard during meetings, you can also create standalone whiteboards in your Teams channels for ongoing collaboration.

Steps to Create a Whiteboard in a Channel:

1. Navigate to the Channel: In Teams, select the channel where you want to create a Whiteboard.

2. Add a Tab: At the top of the channel, click on the "+" icon to add a new tab.

3. Select Whiteboard: In the list of available apps, search for and select "Microsoft Whiteboard."

4. Name Your Whiteboard: Give the Whiteboard a relevant name and click "Save." The Whiteboard is now pinned as a tab in the channel for everyone to access and collaborate on at any time.

Using Microsoft Whiteboard Features in Teams

When using Microsoft Whiteboard in Teams, you have access to the full range of features offered by Whiteboard, which enhances team collaboration. Let's explore these features and how they work within the Teams environment.

1. Drawing Tools and Inking

Whiteboard's inking tools allow users to draw freely on the canvas. Team members can use different pens, colors, and line thicknesses to visualize ideas. This feature is especially useful for brainstorming, as it mimics a traditional whiteboard, but with the added benefit of being stored digitally.

Example Use Case:

In a brainstorming session, participants can use different ink colors to represent different ideas. For instance, each participant may choose a specific color to outline their thoughts, making it easy to identify who contributed what during the discussion.

2. Sticky Notes

Sticky notes are a valuable tool for organizing thoughts and tasks. In a Teams meeting, participants can add sticky notes with key points, ideas, or action items. Sticky notes are great for visually organizing concepts and grouping similar thoughts.

Example Use Case:

During a team retrospective meeting, team members can place sticky notes under various categories, such as "What went well," "Challenges," and "Action items." This visual organization makes it easy to group feedback and prioritize tasks.

3. Text and Shapes

Text boxes and pre-built shapes in Whiteboard help teams create structured diagrams and processes. This is particularly useful for mapping out workflows, creating decision trees, or building simple flowcharts.

Example Use Case:

In a project planning session, the team can create a visual project timeline using shapes for milestones and text boxes for deadlines or task descriptions. This makes it easier to visualize the project at a glance.

4. Images and Attachments

Users can import images and files into the Whiteboard, which can then be annotated or expanded upon. This feature helps teams analyze visual information or discuss documents in real-time.

Example Use Case:

If the team is discussing a marketing plan, they can import product images, campaign mockups, or competitor analysis charts to the Whiteboard. Participants can then draw on or add notes to these images to enhance discussion.

Best Practices for Integrating Whiteboard with Microsoft Teams

While integrating Microsoft Whiteboard with Teams is highly beneficial, following best practices ensures that your team maximizes its potential and avoids common pitfalls.

1. Assign a Facilitator

When using Whiteboard in a Teams meeting, assign a facilitator to guide the session and ensure that everyone is contributing efficiently. The facilitator can manage the Whiteboard, group ideas, and ensure that the session stays on track.

2. Encourage Participation

Whiteboard's collaborative features are most effective when all team members contribute. Encourage everyone to use the tools available, whether it's adding sticky notes, drawing, or contributing to text-based discussions. Ensuring that everyone participates leads to a richer, more comprehensive outcome.

3. Use Whiteboard Templates

For more structured sessions, Whiteboard offers templates for various purposes, such as brainstorming, project planning, and decision-making. These templates provide a framework that speeds up the process and ensures consistency.

4. Revisit the Whiteboard

After a meeting, make it a habit to revisit the Whiteboard. It's easy to leave ideas behind once the meeting is over, but continually revisiting the Whiteboard allows for refining ideas, tracking progress, and ensuring accountability.

Troubleshooting Common Issues

Although integrating Whiteboard with Teams is generally seamless, there are some issues you may encounter.

1. Syncing Problems

If participants notice that changes made to the Whiteboard are not reflecting in real-time, it may be due to syncing issues. Ensure all participants are connected to a stable internet connection, and try refreshing the Whiteboard or Teams session if the problem persists.

2. Access and Permissions

Sometimes, participants may be unable to edit the Whiteboard, especially if permissions were not set correctly. Double-check the sharing settings in Teams and ensure that everyone who needs access has the necessary editing permissions.

3. Whiteboard Doesn't Load

Occasionally, Whiteboard might fail to load within Teams. If this happens, try clearing the Teams cache or restarting the application. If the issue persists, contact IT support or check if there are any ongoing service disruptions with Microsoft Teams or Whiteboard.

Conclusion: The Power of Integration

By integrating Microsoft Whiteboard with Teams, organizations can significantly improve their collaborative processes. Whether working on project plans, brainstorming ideas, or simply visualizing workflows, the combination of these two tools allows teams to communicate more effectively and work together more creatively. As businesses and educational institutions continue to embrace remote and hybrid work environments, leveraging such integrations becomes essential for maintaining productivity and fostering innovation.

In conclusion, Microsoft Whiteboard's seamless integration with Teams provides an all-in-one platform for collaboration, ideation, and execution. Whether for real-time meetings or asynchronous planning, this integration offers numerous features that enhance communication, drive creativity, and ensure that teams stay aligned on their goals.

CHAPTER IV
Advanced Whiteboard Features

4.1 Templates for Brainstorming and Planning

Templates play a vital role in streamlining the creative and organizational processes on Microsoft Whiteboard. They provide structured layouts, helping teams and individuals efficiently manage ideas, plan projects, and collaborate. One of the standout features of Microsoft Whiteboard is the availability of built-in templates that cater to various brainstorming, planning, and organizational needs.

4.1.1 Using Built-in Templates

Built-in templates on Microsoft Whiteboard serve as a starting point for users who want to create organized whiteboards quickly. These templates are pre-designed with specific structures, allowing users to dive straight into their tasks without spending time designing layouts from scratch. Whether you're planning a project, brainstorming new ideas, or structuring team tasks, built-in templates make the process smoother and more efficient.

1. Why Use Built-in Templates?

Microsoft Whiteboard's built-in templates simplify the creative and organizational processes in several ways:

- Time-saving: Templates provide a quick and easy starting point, reducing the need for manual setup.

- Consistency: Teams working on the same projects can ensure consistency by using the same templates.

- Guidance: Templates are designed for specific tasks like brainstorming or planning, guiding users through structured activities that might otherwise seem overwhelming.

Using a template helps users focus on content rather than structure, which can be especially helpful for beginners unfamiliar with Whiteboard's features.

2. How to Access Built-in Templates

Accessing built-in templates in Microsoft Whiteboard is straightforward:

- *Step 1: Open Microsoft Whiteboard*

Start by creating a new whiteboard or opening an existing one where you'd like to use a template.

- *Step 2: Open the Templates Library*

On the toolbar, you'll see an icon for templates. Clicking this will open the template library, displaying a variety of options for different use cases.

- *Step 3: Browse and Select a Template*

Browse the template library to find one that suits your needs. Templates are typically grouped into categories like "Brainstorming," "Project Planning," "Meetings," and more. You can preview each template before selecting one.

- *Step 4: Insert and Customize*

Once you've selected a template, click to insert it into your whiteboard. The template will appear, and you can begin customizing it. Templates are fully interactive, meaning you can edit text, move elements around, and even add additional features like sticky notes or images.

3. Types of Built-in Templates

Microsoft Whiteboard offers various templates designed for different purposes. Here's an overview of the most common ones:

- *Brainstorming Templates:*

Ideal for capturing and organizing ideas during brainstorming sessions. These templates often feature areas for participants to write down their thoughts, group related ideas, and prioritize actions. Common brainstorming templates include mind maps and idea boards.

- *Project Planning Templates:*

These templates are tailored for teams working on complex projects. They typically include sections for project timelines, tasks, responsibilities, and deliverables. Gantt charts and task boards are some examples of project planning templates.

- *Meeting Templates:*

Meeting templates help structure team discussions. They include sections for agendas, action items, and notes. These templates are great for keeping meetings organized and ensuring that important points are captured.

- *SWOT Analysis Template:*

For businesses or teams conducting a SWOT analysis (Strengths, Weaknesses, Opportunities, and Threats), Whiteboard's built-in SWOT template provides a structured framework for listing each element, making it easier to visualize and analyze.

- *Retrospective Templates:*

These templates are often used at the end of a project to reflect on what went well and what didn't. They include areas for participants to give feedback on successes, challenges, and lessons learned.

4. Customizing Built-in Templates

While the built-in templates provide a ready-made structure, customization is key to tailoring them for specific needs. Here are some ways you can customize templates in Microsoft Whiteboard:

- *Modifying Text:* Each template comes with text boxes or sticky notes that you can edit to reflect your own content. Whether it's the title of a section or individual action items, simply click on the text to modify it.

- *Adding More Elements:* Templates are not static; you can always add more elements such as images, sticky notes, or diagrams. This flexibility allows you to expand upon the template's original design to suit the evolving needs of your project or brainstorming session.

- *Resizing and Moving Template Components:* All components within a template can be resized or moved around. This can help you emphasize certain sections of the template or make space for additional information.

- *Changing Colors and Themes:* Microsoft Whiteboard allows you to change the color scheme of templates. This is useful for branding purposes or for distinguishing between different sections. You can apply different colors to sticky notes, text boxes, or shapes to make your whiteboard more visually appealing and easier to navigate.

5. Best Practices for Using Built-in Templates

While using templates, there are some best practices you can follow to ensure you get the most out of them:

- *Choose the Right Template for the Task:* Not all templates are suited for every task. Make sure you select a template that aligns with your goals. For example, a project planning template is better suited for task management than a brainstorming template.

- *Don't Overcrowd the Template:* Templates provide structure, but they can become cluttered if too much information is added. Be mindful of the balance between content and space. Use multiple whiteboards if necessary.

- *Collaborate with Others on Templates:* Templates can be shared with team members to ensure everyone is on the same page. Invite others to contribute their ideas, and allow them to interact with the template to co-create the content.

6. Advantages of Using Built-in Templates

Using built-in templates offers numerous advantages that can greatly enhance productivity and creativity:

- *Ease of Use:* Templates simplify complex tasks, allowing users to dive right into the creative or planning process without getting bogged down by the details of structuring their whiteboard.

- *Enhanced Collaboration:* Teams can work together on a single whiteboard using a shared template. This not only keeps everyone focused but also ensures that all team members are contributing to the same framework, fostering clearer communication and collaboration.

- *Scalability:* As projects grow in scope, templates can easily be modified to accommodate new elements. Whether it's adding more sections, changing layouts, or integrating other tools, templates are versatile enough to scale with your project.

- *Visual Organization:* Templates provide visual clarity, making it easier to see how different components of a project or brainstorming session connect. The organized structure helps users focus on the content, leading to more productive outcomes.

7. Real-Life Scenarios of Using Built-in Templates

To better understand the power of built-in templates, here are a few real-life scenarios where they can be utilized:

- *Brainstorming Session with a Remote Team:*

A team working remotely needs to generate ideas for a new marketing campaign. Using the brainstorming template, they can quickly jot down ideas in real-time, group similar thoughts, and prioritize which concepts to explore further.

- *Project Management for a Software Development Team:*

A software development team uses the project planning template to outline key deliverables, assign tasks to team members, and track progress. This structure helps ensure that everyone knows their responsibilities and timelines.

- *SWOT Analysis for a Small Business:*

A small business conducts a SWOT analysis to evaluate its position in the market. Using the SWOT template, the team can collaboratively identify strengths, weaknesses, opportunities, and threats, leading to more informed strategic decisions.

8. Final Thoughts on Using Built-in Templates

Built-in templates in Microsoft Whiteboard are powerful tools for enhancing productivity, creativity, and collaboration. Whether you're working alone or as part of a team, templates provide structure, saving time and ensuring a more organized approach to tasks. From brainstorming new ideas to managing complex projects, templates offer the flexibility needed to adapt to a wide range of scenarios.

By mastering the use of built-in templates, you can leverage Microsoft Whiteboard's full potential and unlock new levels of creativity and efficiency in your work. In the next section, we will explore how to further customize templates to suit specific needs, ensuring that your Whiteboard experience is as effective as possible.

4.1.2 Customizing Templates for Your Needs

One of the most powerful features of Microsoft Whiteboard is its ability to adapt and conform to various workflows through customizable templates. While built-in templates provide a quick way to get started with brainstorming or planning, the ability to personalize these templates can dramatically improve your productivity and tailor the tool to suit specific project requirements, team structures, or individual preferences.

Customizing templates within Microsoft Whiteboard involves altering their structure, layout, and content to meet your exact needs. This allows you to take a pre-designed framework and make it uniquely yours, enhancing the collaborative and visual nature of the tool.

The Benefits of Customizing Templates

Customizing templates offers several advantages that can improve both the efficiency and effectiveness of your work. Below are a few reasons why it's worth investing time in tailoring templates to your workflow:

1. *Tailored to Specific Projects:* Every project has its own set of goals, processes, and stakeholders. A customized template ensures that your Whiteboard workspace reflects these needs. Whether you are planning a marketing campaign or laying out a product roadmap, customizing templates helps you keep focus on your specific deliverables.

2. *Enhanced Team Collaboration:* By tailoring templates to match your team's style of work, you encourage smoother collaboration. Customized templates can help guide conversations, define roles more clearly, and provide visual cues that make it easier for everyone to contribute and stay on the same page.

3. *Improved Workflow:* Pre-made templates are useful, but they might not always align with how you or your team work best. Modifying them can streamline workflows, removing

unnecessary steps, adding useful markers, or even creating sections for brainstorming and detailed analysis side by side.

4. Branding and Consistency: If you're working in an organization, customizing templates can help you incorporate branding elements, such as specific color schemes or font choices, ensuring a consistent look and feel across all projects. This also helps create familiarity when different departments collaborate on shared boards.

Steps for Customizing Templates

Customizing templates in Microsoft Whiteboard is a straightforward process, allowing you to easily adapt the tool to suit your needs. Here's a step-by-step guide to help you get started:

1. Choose the Right Template

The first step in customizing a template is to start with one that is closest to your intended purpose. Microsoft Whiteboard offers several built-in templates for brainstorming, problem-solving, project planning, and more. It's essential to select a base template that already includes many of the elements you need, so you don't have to build everything from scratch.

For example, if you're conducting a brainstorming session with your team, a brainstorming template will likely have sections for ideas, feedback, and prioritization. However, you may want to add additional areas for further discussion or custom categories for different types of ideas.

2. Modify Content and Labels

Once you've chosen a template, begin customizing the content. This can involve modifying the labels in the template, such as renaming sections, altering text to reflect your goals, or replacing placeholders with your specific project data. This is particularly useful if you're working on an ongoing project where different phases or milestones need to be identified and tracked.

For instance, a generic project planning template might have sections labeled "Milestones," "Resources," and "Deadlines." If you're working on a product launch, you can change these labels to reflect the specific phases of your launch, such as "Design," "Marketing Plan," and "Launch Date."

3. Add or Remove Sections

Not every template will have exactly what you need, and some might have extra sections that aren't relevant to your project. To customize the template further, you can easily add or remove sections.

For example, a project management template might include a timeline that's useful for long-term planning but irrelevant for short-term projects. You can remove the timeline and replace it with a more focused section for immediate action items or daily tasks. Conversely, if a section for "Team Roles" is missing, you can create one to ensure that everyone knows their responsibilities during the project.

4. Customize Visual Elements

Microsoft Whiteboard allows you to customize not only the content but also the visual aspects of templates. This can include changing the colors of text boxes or shapes, altering the line thickness, or adjusting font sizes. By playing with these visual elements, you can make your template easier to understand and more visually appealing.

For example, you can color-code different sections of your Whiteboard for better clarity—using one color for deadlines, another for high-priority tasks, and a third for low-priority tasks. You can also use different shapes and icons to represent various action items, making the Whiteboard intuitive and engaging for everyone involved.

5. Insert Additional Media

One of the most powerful features of Microsoft Whiteboard is the ability to insert external media such as images, documents, and files. When customizing a template, consider adding visual elements that enrich your Whiteboard and provide more context.

For example, in a project management template, you can insert a Gantt chart, product mockups, or important files like the project brief. Adding these types of media enhances the overall effectiveness of the template and gives all stakeholders easy access to the most relevant documents.

6. Save and Reuse Custom Templates

After you've spent time customizing a template, you don't want to repeat the process for each new project. Microsoft Whiteboard allows you to save customized templates so that you can reuse them in future sessions.

To do this, once you've completed your customizations, make sure to save the Whiteboard with a clear name that reflects its purpose, like "Marketing Campaign Template" or

"Product Launch Template." This way, when you start a new project, you can quickly access the template and adapt it with minimal effort.

Best Practices for Customizing Templates

Customizing templates in Microsoft Whiteboard can significantly improve your workflow, but it's essential to follow a few best practices to make the most of this feature:

1. *Keep it Simple:* While it's tempting to add many sections, shapes, and colors to your templates, it's essential to keep them simple and easy to navigate. A cluttered Whiteboard can quickly become overwhelming and difficult to manage.

2. *Be Consistent:* If you plan to use templates across different teams or departments, ensure that there is consistency in the layout and design. This makes it easier for people to use and understand the Whiteboard, regardless of the project they're working on.

3. *Iterate and Improve:* Don't be afraid to continually modify and improve your templates as you discover new needs or ways of working. What works for one project might need slight alterations for another, and staying flexible ensures that your templates evolve alongside your workflows.

4. *Use Visual Hierarchy:* To make your Whiteboard more intuitive, use visual hierarchy to prioritize content. Larger, bolder fonts can be used for important sections, while smaller text can signify less urgent or secondary information. Different shapes or symbols can also help to distinguish between tasks, goals, and deadlines.

5. *Solicit Team Feedback:* Since Whiteboards are often used collaboratively, it's a good idea to get input from your team when customizing templates. Ask for feedback on what's working, what could be improved, and any specific sections they might find helpful. This collaborative approach ensures the template serves the entire team effectively.

Real-Life Examples of Customizing Templates

Marketing Campaign Template

A marketing team working on a new product launch might start with a pre-designed brainstorming template but customize it to include sections for target audience research, marketing channels, key messaging, and launch timeline. The team could add sticky notes for each phase of the campaign, include links to relevant design files, and use color coding to highlight the most critical deadlines.

Project Management Template

A project manager overseeing a multi-department initiative could take a project planning template and adjust it to include milestones for each team, such as design, engineering, and quality assurance. The manager could also add a section for risks and mitigation strategies, customize the color scheme to distinguish between completed and pending tasks, and integrate a timeline that fits the project's overall deadline.

Team Collaboration Template

For teams working on continuous improvement processes, a feedback template might be customized to reflect specific areas of the business, such as customer service, product development, or marketing. Team members can leave comments and suggestions in different sections, and the template can include follow-up actions, responsible parties, and deadlines for implementation.

Conclusion

Customizing templates in Microsoft Whiteboard is a game-changer for anyone looking to enhance their visual collaboration experience. By following these steps and best practices, you can adapt Whiteboard templates to fit your specific needs, whether you're working alone or with a team. The flexibility offered by Microsoft Whiteboard ensures that it can be shaped to reflect your unique workflow, ultimately leading to more efficient, creative, and collaborative outcomes.

4.1.3 Saving Custom Templates

Templates play an essential role in speeding up workflows and ensuring consistency in brainstorming, planning, and team collaboration. Microsoft Whiteboard provides built-in templates for a variety of tasks, but one of its greatest advantages is the ability to create and save your own custom templates tailored to your specific needs. This section will walk you through how to create, customize, and save templates in Microsoft Whiteboard, allowing you to streamline your work and avoid repetitive setups.

The Importance of Custom Templates

When you work with a team or collaborate on multiple projects, having a template that fits your specific workflow is a game-changer. While pre-built templates are useful for general purposes, they might not always suit the exact needs of your task or team. By creating and saving your custom templates, you:

- *Increase Efficiency:* Instead of starting from scratch every time, a custom template provides a pre-organized structure, helping you begin work faster.

- *Ensure Consistency:* If you're managing a project or working with a team, a custom template ensures that everyone is working with the same structure, guidelines, or layout.

- *Tailor to Specific Needs:* Custom templates allow you to integrate personal preferences, company standards, or project-specific requirements.

Now, let's dive into how to create and save custom templates in Microsoft Whiteboard.

Step 1: Designing Your Custom Template

The first step in creating a custom template is designing the structure and elements that will serve as the foundation for future projects. You'll want to carefully consider which components are essential and repeatable across your projects.

Choosing the Right Elements

When designing your custom template, consider including the following:

1. Headings and Subheadings: Use text boxes or sticky notes to define key areas like project titles, phases, or sections.

2. Shapes and Diagrams: If you often use specific shapes or diagrams, include placeholders for them. You can easily adjust their size and position later as needed.

3. Flowcharts: For tasks that involve processes or step-by-step workflows, including flowchart elements such as arrows and lines ensures you're always ready to outline a plan of action.

4. Color Coding: If you're working with a team or managing multiple elements, use color coding to differentiate sections, tasks, or priorities. This visual distinction can help you stay organized and communicate more effectively.

5. Sticky Notes for Input: Create sections where team members can easily add their thoughts or feedback using sticky notes. You can even pre-assign different colored sticky notes for different departments or roles within your team.

6. Placeholders for Images or Files: If you often need to import visuals or documents, leave room in your template to insert images or PDFs without disrupting the layout.

Layout and Structure

A clean and structured layout will be key to the usefulness of your custom template. Here are a few layout tips to consider:

- Alignment: Use the alignment tools within Microsoft Whiteboard to make sure your shapes, text boxes, and diagrams are lined up properly. This not only makes your board look professional but also ensures clarity when collaborating with others.

- Sections and Spacing: Dividing your whiteboard into clearly defined sections can make it easier to follow. Use shapes to create boundaries between different parts of the board, and leave enough space to ensure everything is readable.

- Clear Labels: Every element should have a clear label or title so that users understand its purpose. This is especially important for team collaborations or large projects with many moving parts.

Once you've designed the perfect layout, you're ready to save your custom template.

Step 2: Saving Your Custom Template

Saving your custom template in Microsoft Whiteboard is a simple process, but it's important to do it properly so that you can easily access it in the future. Microsoft Whiteboard doesn't have a specific "Save as Template" function yet, but you can effectively save your board as a template by following the steps outlined below.

Option 1: Save a Copy of Your Template

The simplest way to save your custom template is by duplicating the whiteboard you've created. This method allows you to create a template that you can reuse whenever needed without altering the original.

1. Create Your Template: Once you've finished designing your whiteboard with the desired elements, make sure everything is properly aligned and labeled.

2. Save the Whiteboard: By default, Microsoft Whiteboard saves all whiteboards to your cloud storage (Microsoft OneDrive or other Microsoft 365 accounts). However, it's important to name your whiteboard clearly to indicate that it's a template. For example, you could name it "Project Planning Template" or "Brainstorming Template."

3. Duplicate the Template: When you're ready to use the template for a new project, navigate to your saved whiteboard and create a duplicate by clicking on the three-dot menu on the board's tile. Select "Duplicate" to create a copy of the board. Now, you have a fresh version of the template, ready to be filled in with new content.

Option 2: Saving and Sharing Templates for Team Use

If you're working in a team environment, it can be useful to create a central repository of templates that everyone can access. This ensures that all team members are working from the same foundational materials and following consistent guidelines.

1. Create a Shared Folder: Within your organization's Microsoft 365 or OneDrive account, you can create a shared folder specifically for templates. By storing your custom templates here, everyone on the team can easily access and duplicate them.

2. Save Your Whiteboard to the Shared Folder: After creating your custom template, make sure it's saved to the shared folder. You can do this by selecting "Share" from the Whiteboard interface and choosing the shared folder from your OneDrive.

3. Set Permissions: To ensure that no one accidentally edits the original template, set the permissions to "view only." This will allow team members to view the template and create their own copies, but prevent them from making changes to the original.

4. Sharing Templates via Link: Another option is to share the whiteboard template via a link. You can generate a shareable link from the Whiteboard and distribute it to team members. They can then duplicate the board and use it as a template for their individual projects.

Step 3: Using Your Custom Template

Once you've saved your custom template, the next step is to integrate it into your workflow. The beauty of custom templates lies in their reusability. Here's how you can effectively use them across different projects and teams:

Reusing and Modifying the Template

When you open a copy of your template for a new project, you'll likely need to make some adjustments depending on the specific needs of the task. Fortunately, Microsoft Whiteboard makes it easy to modify any element of the template. Here are a few key tips:

- Adjust Placeholder Text: If your template includes text boxes or headings, make sure to customize them with relevant information. You can replace placeholder text like "Project Title" or "Phase 1" with real project data.

- Add New Elements: While the template serves as the foundation, don't be afraid to add new elements as the project evolves. Templates are designed to be flexible, allowing you to add, move, or remove elements as needed.

- Reshape Diagrams or Charts: If your project requires different diagrams than those provided in the template, use Microsoft Whiteboard's shape and drawing tools to modify existing diagrams or add new ones.

Collaborating with Others Using Templates

One of the biggest advantages of using custom templates is the ability to collaborate efficiently with others. When working with a team, you can assign different sections of the template to different team members, ensuring that everyone knows their responsibilities. Here's how to enhance collaboration using templates:

- Assign Sections: If your template includes sections for different tasks or departments, clearly label those areas and assign them to specific team members. This avoids confusion and ensures that everyone is on the same page.

- Use Comments: If your team needs to discuss or provide feedback on certain elements of the whiteboard, take advantage of the comment feature in Microsoft Whiteboard. Team members can leave comments directly on the board, making it easy to collaborate asynchronously.

- Track Progress: As your project progresses, you can update your whiteboard template to reflect the current status. Use sticky notes or labels to mark completed tasks or indicate what still needs to be done.

Step 4: Maintaining and Updating Templates

Once you've used your custom template for several projects, you might find that some elements need to be updated or improved. Microsoft Whiteboard allows you to easily make changes to your template and save the updated version. Here are a few tips for maintaining your custom templates:

1. Review After Every Project: After each project, take a moment to review the template and see if there are any areas for improvement. This could include adding new sections, removing outdated elements, or improving the overall layout.

2. Version Control: If you're making significant changes to your template, it's a good idea to save it as a new version. For example, you could save it as "Project Planning Template v2" to keep track of updates and ensure that older projects still reference the correct version.

3. Solicit Feedback from Team Members: If you're using templates in a team environment, ask your colleagues for feedback. They might have suggestions for improving the template based on their experiences.

In conclusion, saving and using custom templates in Microsoft Whiteboard is a powerful way to boost productivity, ensure consistency, and streamline collaboration. Whether you're managing projects, leading brainstorming sessions, or collaborating with a remote team, custom templates provide a foundation that you can rely on time and time again. By taking the time to create and refine templates tailored to your specific needs, you'll unlock the full potential of Microsoft Whiteboard as a collaborative tool.

4.2 Integrating Microsoft Whiteboard with Other Tools

One of the most powerful features of Microsoft Whiteboard is its ability to integrate with other Microsoft 365 applications. These integrations allow users to leverage the tools they are already familiar with while enhancing collaboration and productivity across platforms. This section explores how to embed Microsoft Whiteboard into other tools such as Microsoft Teams, OneNote, PowerPoint, and other Microsoft 365 applications. This capability streamlines workflows, facilitates team collaboration, and makes it easier to share and present information across different platforms.

4.2.1 Embedding in Microsoft Teams

Microsoft Teams is a widely used platform for collaboration, especially in business and educational settings. By embedding Microsoft Whiteboard within Teams, you create a seamless environment where users can collaborate on a whiteboard without leaving the Teams interface. Whether it's a brainstorming session, a virtual meeting, or a project planning exercise, Whiteboard within Teams provides an interactive space where ideas can flow freely.

Setting Up Microsoft Whiteboard in Teams

Integrating Microsoft Whiteboard into Teams is straightforward and can be done during or before a meeting. Here are the steps to set up and use Whiteboard in Teams:

1. During a Teams Meeting:

When you're in a Microsoft Teams meeting, you can access Whiteboard by following these steps:

- In the meeting toolbar, click on the Share button.

- From the sharing options, select Microsoft Whiteboard. This will launch a blank whiteboard that everyone in the meeting can interact with.

At this point, all participants can draw, write, and add content to the whiteboard in real time. This is especially useful during brainstorming sessions or when you need to visualize concepts during discussions.

2. Before or After a Teams Meeting:

You can also prepare a Whiteboard ahead of a meeting or continue working on it after the meeting ends. To do this:

- Open the relevant Teams channel or chat where you want to embed the whiteboard.

- In the top navigation bar, click on the Whiteboard tab (you may need to add the tab by clicking on the "+" icon and selecting Microsoft Whiteboard from the list of apps).

- A new or existing whiteboard will open, allowing you to work on it before or after the meeting.

This functionality is particularly beneficial for project planning, as it lets teams build on ideas after a meeting has concluded, ensuring that nothing is missed.

Collaborative Features of Whiteboard in Teams

When embedded in Teams, Microsoft Whiteboard offers a range of collaborative features that make teamwork more efficient and creative. Some key features include:

- *Real-time Co-authoring:* Multiple team members can work on the whiteboard simultaneously. As they contribute, all updates are visible in real-time, making it easy to follow the flow of ideas.

- *Inking and Drawing:* Participants can use the inking tools to draw or write on the whiteboard. This is particularly useful during brainstorming sessions, as team members can quickly sketch out ideas or write notes.

- *Sticky Notes and Text Boxes:* Just like in the standalone Whiteboard app, users can add sticky notes and text boxes to organize their thoughts. Sticky notes are especially useful for virtual brainstorming sessions, as they can be used to jot down quick ideas, action items, or feedback.

- *Shapes and Templates:* Built-in shapes, flowcharts, and templates can be used to structure discussions. These features are invaluable for process mapping, visualizing workflows, or laying out complex diagrams.

- *Reactions and Annotations:* Users can react to different ideas or annotations using emojis or by drawing attention to specific parts of the whiteboard. This is helpful in collaborative environments where feedback is crucial.

Best Practices for Using Whiteboard in Teams

While the integration of Whiteboard in Microsoft Teams is designed to be user-friendly, following some best practices can help you and your team make the most of this feature:

1. *Define Roles and Guidelines:* Before starting a collaborative session on the whiteboard, it's helpful to define roles or guidelines for how the whiteboard will be used. For instance, one person might act as the facilitator, guiding the flow of the discussion, while others contribute ideas or comments. This helps avoid clutter and ensures that the whiteboard remains organized and focused.

2. *Use Templates for Structured Sessions:* If your team is working on a specific task, such as project planning or process mapping, consider using built-in templates to structure the session. Templates help keep the session focused and ensure that all key areas are covered.

3. *Keep It Simple:* While it's tempting to add lots of content to the whiteboard, simplicity is key to maintaining clarity. Try to limit the number of shapes, drawings, and text boxes on the screen to avoid overwhelming participants.

4. *Follow Up After Meetings:* Once the meeting is over, share the whiteboard with participants and encourage them to review it or add additional thoughts. This ensures that important ideas aren't lost and that the whiteboard serves as an ongoing resource for the team.

Practical Use Cases for Whiteboard in Teams

The integration of Microsoft Whiteboard with Teams opens up numerous possibilities for businesses, educators, and organizations. Here are some practical use cases for this feature:

- *Virtual Brainstorming Sessions:* Teams can use the whiteboard to collaborate in real-time, brainstorming ideas, sketching out concepts, and visually mapping out strategies. This is particularly useful for remote teams who need a shared visual space to work on ideas together.

- *Project Planning and Task Management:* Whiteboard in Teams can be used to outline project plans, create task lists, and assign responsibilities. Sticky notes can represent individual tasks, and templates like Kanban boards can be used to track project progress.

- *Teaching and Learning:* In educational settings, instructors can use Whiteboard to present visual lessons, illustrate complex concepts, or collaborate with students. The interactive nature of Whiteboard makes it easier for students to engage with the material and participate in discussions.

- *Workshops and Training:* Whiteboard is a powerful tool for workshops and training sessions, where visual aids and interactive exercises are essential. Teams can participate in exercises such as role-playing, mind mapping, or process mapping, all within the Whiteboard interface.

- *Feedback and Review Sessions:* Whiteboard can also be used during feedback sessions, where team members can annotate documents, add sticky notes, or draw attention to specific areas for improvement.

Benefits of Using Whiteboard in Teams

There are several benefits to integrating Microsoft Whiteboard within Teams, particularly in the areas of collaboration, productivity, and engagement:

- *Enhanced Collaboration:* Whiteboard fosters a collaborative environment where all team members can contribute ideas, regardless of their location. This is especially important for remote teams who need tools that facilitate seamless collaboration.

- *Improved Productivity:* By integrating Whiteboard with Teams, users can streamline their workflows, eliminating the need to switch between different apps. Everything from brainstorming to project planning can be done within a single platform, saving time and effort.

- *Increased Engagement:* The interactive nature of Whiteboard makes it easier for team members to engage with the content and participate in discussions. This leads to more creative and productive meetings, where all participants can contribute equally.

- *Visualizing Ideas:* Whiteboard allows teams to visualize their ideas in a way that traditional documents or spreadsheets can't. This is especially useful for brainstorming sessions, process mapping, and problem-solving exercises, where visual aids can clarify complex concepts.

Limitations and Considerations

While Microsoft Whiteboard in Teams offers many advantages, there are a few limitations and considerations to keep in mind:

- *Limited Features in the Teams Version:* The Whiteboard available within Teams may not have all the advanced features of the standalone Whiteboard app. For example, some users have noted that certain templates and tools are not available when accessing Whiteboard through Teams.

- *Screen Size and Visibility:* In larger meetings, it can be difficult for participants to view all parts of the whiteboard, especially if the content is spread out. It's important to keep the whiteboard organized and avoid clutter to ensure that everyone can follow along.

- *Performance Issues:* Depending on the size of the whiteboard and the number of participants, there may be occasional performance issues, such as lag or delays in updating. To minimize these issues, try to keep the whiteboard content manageable and avoid overloading it with too many elements.

In summary, embedding Microsoft Whiteboard in Microsoft Teams provides a versatile and powerful tool for collaboration, brainstorming, and planning. By leveraging the integration between these two platforms, teams can enhance their productivity, foster creative thinking, and work together more effectively.

4.2.2 Using with OneNote and PowerPoint

One of the key advantages of Microsoft Whiteboard is its seamless integration with other Microsoft 365 applications, especially OneNote and PowerPoint. Both of these tools are widely used for note-taking, presentations, and organizing information, and by combining their functionality with Microsoft Whiteboard, you can elevate the effectiveness of your meetings, brainstorming sessions, and collaborative efforts. This section will explore the integration between Whiteboard and these two essential tools, showing you how to leverage their combined capabilities to maximize productivity.

Using Microsoft Whiteboard with OneNote

OneNote is an excellent tool for capturing notes, ideas, and research. It allows users to organize their content in notebooks, sections, and pages. When used alongside Microsoft Whiteboard, it enhances the brainstorming process by providing a structured environment where ideas can be expanded and categorized while still allowing for creative free-form thinking on the Whiteboard itself.

1. Inserting a Whiteboard into OneNote

One of the most efficient ways to use Microsoft Whiteboard with OneNote is by embedding a Whiteboard directly into a OneNote page. This is useful for users who want to combine structured note-taking with a visual and collaborative brainstorming process.

Here's how you can embed a Whiteboard into OneNote:

- Step 1: Open OneNote and navigate to the page where you want to insert the Whiteboard.

- Step 2: Click on the "Insert" tab in the OneNote ribbon.

- Step 3: Select "File" and then choose "Insert as Printout" to insert a Whiteboard image. You can export the Whiteboard as an image or PDF (explained in a later section) and then embed it into OneNote.

- Step 4: The Whiteboard will appear as an image or document within your OneNote page. You can annotate or add notes directly onto the page in addition to the embedded Whiteboard content.

This method allows you to keep your visual brainstorming content within your more structured notes. OneNote's search functionality makes it easy to retrieve this content later, even if you've added layers of other information and notes on the page.

2. Creating a Workflow Between Whiteboard and OneNote

Another useful method is to create a workflow between Whiteboard and OneNote. This workflow can be used to manage projects, track brainstorming sessions, and develop ideas into more detailed plans.

- Brainstorm in Whiteboard: Start by using Whiteboard for free-form brainstorming. This could involve sketching out ideas, creating diagrams, or using sticky notes to organize thoughts.

- Document in OneNote: After the brainstorming session, you can transfer the key ideas into OneNote for more detailed planning. Use the structured organization features of

OneNote, such as notebooks, sections, and pages, to categorize your ideas and flesh them out further.

- Syncing Between Tools: While there is no direct automatic syncing between OneNote and Whiteboard, you can manually update your OneNote with new versions of your Whiteboard sketches and diagrams. This ensures that both tools are used to their full potential—Whiteboard for creativity and free-form collaboration, and OneNote for detailed planning and documentation.

3. Annotating Whiteboards with OneNote

After importing a Whiteboard into OneNote, you can use OneNote's annotation features to add additional comments, insights, or explanations. This is particularly useful in educational settings where a teacher may want to provide extra commentary on a Whiteboard used during a lesson, or in business meetings where you might need to expand on ideas after a brainstorming session.

- Step 1: Click on the image or printout of the Whiteboard in OneNote.

- Step 2: Use OneNote's pen, highlighter, or text tools to add annotations.

- Step 3: You can also use OneNote's voice recording features to add an audio note explaining the Whiteboard content.

This combination of visual content and detailed annotations enhances the overall value of your notes, providing a comprehensive record of your brainstorming and planning sessions.

4. Sharing Whiteboard and OneNote Content

Once you've integrated Whiteboard with OneNote, sharing the content with colleagues, students, or team members is simple. OneNote allows you to share notebooks or individual pages with others, making it easy to collaborate on ideas and projects.

To share your OneNote page that includes Whiteboard content:

- Step 1: Click the "Share" button in OneNote.

- Step 2: Choose whether to share the entire notebook or just specific pages.

- Step 3: Send an email invitation to collaborators, or generate a shareable link that can be sent via email or chat.

With Whiteboard embedded into OneNote, your collaborators can see both the visual brainstorming from Whiteboard and the more structured notes from OneNote in one place.

Using Microsoft Whiteboard with PowerPoint

PowerPoint is the go-to tool for creating and delivering presentations. When used together with Microsoft Whiteboard, it can help transform brainstorming sessions, visual collaboration, and team discussions into polished presentations. The integration between Whiteboard and PowerPoint is particularly helpful for taking raw ideas from the Whiteboard and turning them into organized, visually appealing slides.

1. Exporting Whiteboard Content to PowerPoint

The most straightforward way to integrate Whiteboard content into PowerPoint is by exporting your Whiteboard as an image or PDF and then importing it into a PowerPoint presentation. This allows you to present brainstorming results, diagrams, or collaborative ideas visually within a more structured format.

Here's how you can do it:

- Step 1: In Microsoft Whiteboard, click on the "Export" button (usually found under the settings menu).

- Step 2: Choose whether you want to export the Whiteboard as an image (PNG, JPG) or as a PDF file.

- Step 3: Open PowerPoint and navigate to the slide where you want to insert the Whiteboard content.

- Step 4: Click on the "Insert" tab and select "Pictures" or "Object" (for PDF).

- Step 5: Browse for the exported Whiteboard file and insert it into the slide.

This method is particularly useful for project planning sessions, brainstorming meetings, and workshops where the Whiteboard was used as a tool to generate and organize ideas, and now the content needs to be presented to a broader audience.

2. Using PowerPoint with Whiteboard During Presentations

Another powerful use of Whiteboard with PowerPoint is to use the Whiteboard during a live presentation. While PowerPoint is great for structured slides, Whiteboard can be used during the presentation to make annotations, sketch out ideas in real-time, or answer audience questions visually.

Here's how to use Whiteboard during a PowerPoint presentation:

- Step 1: Begin your PowerPoint presentation as usual.

- Step 2: When you need to illustrate something that isn't included on the slides, open Microsoft Whiteboard.

- Step 3: Use Whiteboard to sketch, write, or visually explain concepts as you present.

- Step 4: You can switch between PowerPoint slides and Whiteboard as needed, making your presentation more interactive and engaging.

This is especially useful in educational or workshop settings where the audience might have questions that require visual explanations. The flexibility to switch between PowerPoint and Whiteboard ensures that you can adapt your presentation to the needs of the audience in real-time.

3. Collaborating with Teams in PowerPoint and Whiteboard

When working in teams, you can leverage both PowerPoint and Whiteboard to develop ideas collaboratively. For example, if your team is preparing a presentation, you can first brainstorm on the Whiteboard,

then transition to PowerPoint to structure the ideas into a formal presentation. This workflow helps ensure that the creative process remains fluid, while the final output is polished and professional.

Here's how you can collaborate effectively:

- Step 1: Brainstorm with Whiteboard

Start with a brainstorming session in Microsoft Whiteboard. Here, your team can sketch out ideas, create diagrams, or jot down key points. Everyone can contribute to the Whiteboard simultaneously in real-time, making it a highly interactive way to gather input.

- Step 2: Transfer Ideas to PowerPoint

Once the brainstorming is complete, select the key ideas or diagrams from Whiteboard and export them. These can then be integrated into PowerPoint slides to form the core content of your presentation. You can import Whiteboard images directly into relevant slides to visually represent the brainstorming process.

- Step 3: Finalize the Presentation in PowerPoint

After transferring the visual content, work together to organize the slides, ensuring that each key point is clearly presented. PowerPoint's tools for creating text, graphs, and transitions allow you to turn the collaborative ideas from the Whiteboard into a polished, cohesive presentation.

- Step 4: Present with Whiteboard as an Interactive Tool

During the actual presentation, you can switch back to Whiteboard at any point to engage the audience with live drawings or annotations. This flexibility ensures that if any new ideas or feedback arise during the presentation, you can visually illustrate and incorporate them in real-time.

4. Tips for Maximizing Whiteboard and PowerPoint Integration

- Use Whiteboard for Initial Ideation: PowerPoint is great for structured presentations, but Whiteboard excels in unstructured creativity. Start with Whiteboard to brainstorm, and once you have the ideas fleshed out, use PowerPoint to organize them into slides.

- Enhance Visual Impact: PowerPoint slides can be enhanced by the spontaneous drawings and sketches from Whiteboard. These help to break the monotony of structured text and charts, giving the audience a more dynamic and engaging experience.

- Encourage Collaboration with Teams: Whether in remote meetings or in-person, Whiteboard's collaborative tools paired with PowerPoint's presentation abilities create a more dynamic team working environment. Use Whiteboard during meetings to encourage idea generation, then structure and assign tasks using PowerPoint for more formal communication.

- Annotate PowerPoint Slides with Whiteboard: After you've created your PowerPoint slides, open them in Whiteboard to add annotations or make real-time notes during a meeting. This can be especially useful for training sessions or interactive presentations where feedback from participants is encouraged.

By combining the creative, freeform aspects of Microsoft Whiteboard with the structured presentation capabilities of PowerPoint and the organization strengths of OneNote, you can enhance collaboration and presentation processes. Each tool complements the other, helping users go from brainstorming to polished output, all within the Microsoft ecosystem. This integration empowers teams to brainstorm, collaborate, and present with more efficiency and clarity.

4.2.3 Exporting to Other Microsoft 365 Apps

Microsoft Whiteboard is a powerful visual collaboration tool, but its full potential is realized when integrated with other applications within the Microsoft 365 ecosystem. Exporting content from Microsoft Whiteboard to other Microsoft 365 apps allows for seamless sharing, enhanced collaboration, and extended functionality across teams, departments, and projects. Whether you're moving visual concepts to documentation, embedding diagrams in presentations, or integrating planning sessions into task management tools, exporting from Whiteboard to other Microsoft apps ensures that your work flows smoothly across different platforms.

This section explores how to export your whiteboard content to several key Microsoft 365 applications—Microsoft Word, PowerPoint, OneNote, and Excel—each offering unique ways to extend and refine your ideas.

Exporting to Microsoft Word

Microsoft Word is a leading word processing application that enables users to create text-based documents. Exporting content from Microsoft Whiteboard to Word can transform visual ideas into detailed reports, meeting summaries, or project plans. The integration between Whiteboard and Word makes it easy to capture and articulate the insights that emerge from collaborative sessions, brainstorming meetings, and planning activities.

Steps to Export to Microsoft Word:

1. Select the Content to Export:

To export specific content, start by highlighting the area of the whiteboard that you want to transfer to Word. You can either select individual elements like sticky notes, text boxes, shapes, or opt to export the entire whiteboard.

2. Choose the Export Format:

Once the content is selected, click on the ellipsis menu (three dots) located in the toolbar. From the dropdown menu, choose the "Export" option, and select the file format compatible with Microsoft Word—commonly JPEG, PNG, or PDF. While these formats capture the visual content, you may need to manually input the text content from sticky notes and other annotations directly into Word.

3. Insert into Microsoft Word:

After saving your export, open Microsoft Word. Navigate to the location where you want to insert the Whiteboard content, such as a report section or project outline. Click on "Insert," choose "Pictures" or "Object," and then upload the exported image file of your whiteboard content. Alternatively, if you exported as a PDF, you can insert the PDF or extract images from it for placement in Word.

4. Enhancing Your Document:

With the Whiteboard content now in Word, enhance your document by adding additional text explanations, formatting, and structure. You can use Word's editing tools to add bullet points, explanations, and references to give context to the visual content exported from Whiteboard. This is especially useful for team reports, where detailed descriptions accompany visual elements.

Use Cases:

- Meeting Summaries: After a collaborative whiteboard session, export the content to Word to create a clear, concise meeting summary. The whiteboard visuals can serve as illustrations, while the accompanying text provides detailed notes and action items.

- Project Plans: Use Whiteboard to outline project workflows visually, then export the designs to Word to draft formal project plans. The combination of visual flowcharts and descriptive text helps stakeholders understand complex projects at a glance.

- Research Papers or Proposals: For academic or business research, brainstorm ideas and concepts on Whiteboard, then export to Word to incorporate the visuals into your written research or proposal drafts.

Exporting to Microsoft PowerPoint

Microsoft PowerPoint is a widely-used tool for creating presentations, and integrating Whiteboard content into PowerPoint allows for a more dynamic and visually engaging experience. Whiteboard's drawing, annotation, and diagramming features make it an excellent companion for PowerPoint, providing a way to visually represent concepts that complement your slides.

Steps to Export to PowerPoint:

1. Capture Key Whiteboard Elements:

Similar to exporting to Word, start by selecting the relevant parts of your whiteboard that you want to include in your PowerPoint presentation. Whether it's a process flow, a mind map, or a series of images, choose the most relevant visual elements.

2. Export as Image or PDF:

After selecting your content, export it as an image (JPEG or PNG) or PDF by using the export function from the toolbar. PowerPoint supports both formats, making it easy to embed Whiteboard visuals into slides.

3. Inserting into PowerPoint:

Open PowerPoint and navigate to the slide where you want to insert the Whiteboard content. Click on "Insert," then choose "Picture" for images or "Object" for PDFs. Place the exported content on your slide, and resize or adjust the layout as needed.

4. Enhancing Presentations with Annotations:

PowerPoint allows for additional customization, such as adding text boxes, shapes, and animations to your Whiteboard content. You can highlight key areas, add captions, or use transitions to create engaging, interactive presentations.

Use Cases:

- Visualizing Project Timelines: During project kick-off meetings, create timelines or process flows in Whiteboard and export them into PowerPoint to present the project's next steps visually.

- Presenting Brainstorming Sessions: Use Whiteboard for brainstorming ideas with your team, then export and embed the brainstorming results into PowerPoint to present during follow-up meetings. This ensures everyone can see how ideas evolved.

- Interactive Presentations: PowerPoint presentations often need visuals that explain complex concepts. Whiteboard can help you create diagrams, mind maps, or models that you can integrate into your slides for a more interactive and engaging presentation.

Exporting to Microsoft OneNote

Microsoft OneNote is a powerful note-taking application that is perfect for storing and organizing information from various sources. Exporting content from Whiteboard to OneNote allows you to integrate visual brainstorming and diagrams into your notes, ensuring that all ideas and concepts from Whiteboard sessions are stored alongside written content in an organized manner.

Steps to Export to OneNote:

1. Prepare the Whiteboard for Export:

Like other apps, start by selecting the content from your whiteboard that you want to move to OneNote. This might include sticky notes, diagrams, drawings, and annotations.

2. Export as Image or PDF:

Once you've selected the relevant content, export it as an image (JPEG or PNG) or a PDF file. OneNote supports these formats, making it easy to incorporate visual elements into your notebooks.

3. Inserting into OneNote:

Open your OneNote notebook and navigate to the section where you want to add the Whiteboard content. Click on "Insert," then choose either "Picture" for images or "File Printout" for PDFs. Place the exported Whiteboard content into your notebook, and position it next to relevant notes or text entries.

4. Organizing Your Notes:

OneNote allows you to group visual and textual content together seamlessly. After inserting your Whiteboard content, you can add text annotations, additional notes, or tags to help organize and categorize your information.

Use Cases:

- Collaborative Meeting Notes: During a brainstorming or project planning session, capture your Whiteboard visuals and integrate them into OneNote. Add meeting notes, action items, and to-dos next to the visual content for a complete record of the meeting.

- Personal Study and Learning: Whiteboard is an excellent tool for visual learners. Export mind maps, diagrams, or flowcharts from Whiteboard into OneNote to complement your study notes, making it easier to review and understand concepts.

- Project Documentation: Use OneNote to document your project lifecycle by combining visual planning from Whiteboard with text-based project updates. This creates a comprehensive view of the project's progress.

Exporting to Microsoft Excel

While Microsoft Excel may not seem like an obvious partner for Microsoft Whiteboard, exporting Whiteboard content to Excel can be highly beneficial for teams who need to combine visual planning with data analysis or tracking. Whether you're exporting charts, diagrams, or process flows, Excel can integrate these visuals alongside numerical data and formulas, offering a more holistic approach to project management and planning.

Steps to Export to Excel:

1. Select and Export Content:

Choose the visuals from your Whiteboard that you want to include in Excel, such as flowcharts or planning diagrams. Export the content as an image (JPEG or PNG) or PDF, which Excel supports for inserting.

2. Insert into Excel Spreadsheet:

Open your Excel file and navigate to the sheet where you want to add the Whiteboard content. Click on "Insert," then choose "Pictures" or "Object," depending on whether you're using an image or PDF. Place the visual content next to relevant data points or tracking tables.

3. Enhancing with Data:

Excel's strength is in handling data. After adding your Whiteboard content, you can organize accompanying data, add tables, or use charts and graphs to complement the visuals. This is especially useful for project managers or analysts who need to visualize processes alongside data.

Use Cases:

- Visualizing Data Workflows: Use Whiteboard to create process diagrams, then export them to Excel to complement tracking sheets or workflow data.

- Project Tracking and Updates: For teams using Excel to manage project timelines, exporting Whiteboard diagrams or timelines into Excel can help contextualize the data, offering a clearer picture of the project's stages.

- Brainstorming with Data: During brainstorming sessions, ideas and visual concepts often need to be quantified or backed up with data. Export Whiteboard visuals into Excel, where you can further analyze, refine, and track the results.

Conclusion

Exporting content from Microsoft Whiteboard to other Microsoft 365 applications extends the capabilities of your collaborative efforts. By moving content into Word, PowerPoint, OneNote, and Excel, you can leverage the strengths of each tool to document, present, and analyze your work. The seamless integration between Whiteboard and these apps ensures that visual ideas are never confined to one space, but instead, become part of a broader workflow that enhances productivity and collaboration across teams and projects.

4.3 Advanced Drawing and Diagramming Techniques

One of the strengths of Microsoft Whiteboard is its ability to help users visualize complex processes, structures, and workflows. Advanced drawing and diagramming techniques such as creating flowcharts, mind maps, and using icons and symbols can enhance collaboration, planning, and brainstorming sessions. In this section, we'll explore how to utilize Microsoft Whiteboard's tools to create effective and visually appealing flowcharts.

4.3.1 Creating Flowcharts

Flowcharts are a fundamental tool for visualizing processes and workflows, making them an essential asset for business planning, software development, project management, and education. They represent a step-by-step sequence of actions or decisions, allowing users to easily understand and communicate complex ideas. Microsoft Whiteboard provides a set of intuitive tools that simplify the creation of flowcharts.

Symbol	Name	Function
	Oval	Represents the start or end of a process
	Rectangle	Denotes a process or operation step
	Arrow	Indicates the flow between steps
	Diamond	Signifies a point requiring a yes/no
	Parallelogram	Used for input or output operations

1. Understanding Flowchart Symbols

Before diving into creating a flowchart, it's essential to understand the most common symbols used in flowchart diagrams. In Microsoft Whiteboard, you can draw these symbols by hand or use shape recognition to create precise shapes. Here are the basic symbols commonly used:

- Oval (Start/End): Represents the start or end of a process.

- Rectangle (Process): Used to show a task or action in a process.

- Diamond (Decision): Indicates a decision point, typically yes/no or true/false.

- Arrow: Shows the direction of flow from one step to the next.

- Parallelogram (Input/Output): Used to represent inputs or outputs within a process, such as data entry or the result of a calculation.

These shapes form the foundation of flowchart design. In Whiteboard, you can manually draw these shapes or use the shape tool for more precision. Knowing how and when to use these shapes will help you build a clear and effective flowchart.

2. Step-by-Step Guide to Creating a Flowchart

Let's now go step-by-step through the process of creating a flowchart in Microsoft Whiteboard.

1. Define the Purpose of the Flowchart

Before you begin, clarify what process you want to visualize. Whether it's a business workflow, a decision-making process, or a software algorithm, the clearer the purpose, the easier it will be to construct the flowchart.

2. Start with a New Whiteboard

Open Microsoft Whiteboard and create a new board. It's often helpful to have a blank canvas so you can freely experiment with ideas without clutter. Label the whiteboard appropriately if you're collaborating with a team.

3. Activate the Shape Tool

On the toolbar, you'll find the drawing tools and shape tools. Click on the shape tool, which will allow you to draw clean and precise flowchart symbols like rectangles, ovals, diamonds, and arrows.

4. Draw the Start Point (Oval)

Begin by selecting or drawing an oval to represent the start of your process. Inside the oval, write "Start" or describe the event that triggers the process. If you're hand-drawing the oval, use the shape recognition feature to smooth out the drawing for a professional look.

5. Add Process Steps (Rectangles)

Once the start symbol is placed, use rectangles to represent each step in the process. Each rectangle should contain a description of a task or action that occurs in your workflow. For example, if you are mapping a customer order process, one rectangle might be labeled "Process Order" and another "Prepare Shipment."

6. Include Decision Points (Diamonds)

If your process involves decision-making, such as a yes/no question or conditional branching, use a diamond shape. For example, after "Process Order," you might ask, "Is Payment Confirmed?" The two possible answers, "Yes" and "No," would lead to different steps in the flowchart.

7. Connect the Shapes with Arrows

Arrows are crucial for showing the direction of the process. In Microsoft Whiteboard, use the drawing tool or straight line feature to draw arrows connecting each shape. Ensure that each arrow flows logically from one step to the next. For decision points, arrows should branch to different steps based on the outcome (e.g., Yes or No).

8. Continue Adding Steps

Continue adding rectangles, diamonds, and arrows as necessary to complete the process. Each step should logically follow the previous one, and each decision should lead to distinct branches in the flowchart.

9. Indicate End Points (Ovals)

Once your process has concluded, use another oval to mark the endpoint. Label this with "End" or another description that indicates the process is complete.

3. Optimizing Flowcharts for Clarity

When creating flowcharts, clarity is key. The goal is to make the process easy to understand at a glance. Here are some tips to optimize your flowchart for clarity:

- Keep It Simple: Avoid over-complicating the flowchart with too many branches or details. If a process has too many steps, consider breaking it into smaller, manageable sections or separate flowcharts.

- Use Colors to Differentiate Steps: Microsoft Whiteboard allows you to change the color of shapes and arrows. Use different colors to represent different stages of a process or to highlight key decision points. For example, use red for decision diamonds and blue for process rectangles.

- Label Arrows and Connections: Where appropriate, label the arrows between steps, especially for decision points. Instead of just connecting shapes, you might label one arrow "Yes" and another "No" to make the decision-making process clear.

- Align and Distribute Shapes Evenly: Microsoft Whiteboard allows you to move and align shapes for a clean and professional layout. Try to keep the shapes evenly spaced and aligned to avoid cluttered, hard-to-follow diagrams.

- Limit Text to Essentials: Each shape should contain concise, clear text. Avoid large blocks of text inside shapes; instead, use bullet points or short phrases.

4. Collaborating on Flowcharts in Real-Time

One of the powerful features of Microsoft Whiteboard is its collaboration capabilities. Flowcharts often require input from multiple team members or departments, especially in project management, business process design, or development planning. With real-time collaboration, multiple users can contribute to the same flowchart simultaneously.

Here's how you can effectively collaborate on flowcharts using Microsoft Whiteboard:

1. Invite Collaborators

Once you've started the flowchart, click the share button to invite team members to join the whiteboard. You can send invitations via email or share a link. Make sure to adjust permissions so that collaborators can edit the flowchart.

2. Assign Tasks and Responsibilities

While collaborating, it's helpful to assign different sections of the flowchart to different people. For example, one team member might work on defining the decision points while another focuses on outlining the process steps.

3. Use Sticky Notes for Feedback

Collaborators can use sticky notes to leave comments, suggestions, or questions on the flowchart. This is particularly useful for feedback and revision cycles, allowing everyone to leave thoughts without directly altering the flowchart until decisions are made.

4. Track Changes in Real-Time

As collaborators work on the flowchart, changes will appear instantly on the shared whiteboard. You can see who made which edits, and this transparency helps ensure that everyone is on the same page throughout the process.

5. Practical Applications of Flowcharts

Flowcharts can be used in various fields, making them one of the most versatile tools in your digital whiteboard toolkit. Here are some common applications:

- Business Processes: Flowcharts are ideal for mapping out business processes, such as order fulfillment, customer service protocols, and employee onboarding.

- Software Development: Developers and project managers use flowcharts to visualize algorithms, system workflows, and decision trees.

- Project Management: Use flowcharts to break down projects into tasks, dependencies, and milestones.

- Education: Teachers can use flowcharts to explain complex concepts, such as scientific processes or historical events.

- Problem-Solving: Flowcharts are great for troubleshooting, allowing you to break down potential issues step by step and identify solutions.

6. Using Microsoft Whiteboard Flowcharts for Presentations

Flowcharts created in Microsoft Whiteboard can easily be shared and used for presentations. Here are some ways to make your flowcharts presentation-ready:

- Export as an Image or PDF: After completing the flowchart, export it as a high-quality image or PDF. This is useful if you need to include it in a PowerPoint presentation or share it as a standalone document.

- Use During Live Presentations: Microsoft Whiteboard allows you to use your flowchart interactively during live presentations. You can zoom in on specific sections, add comments, or make live edits based on feedback from your audience.

- Embed in Microsoft Teams Meetings: If you're presenting to a remote team, embed your whiteboard flowchart directly in a Microsoft Teams meeting. This allows participants to see and collaborate on the flowchart in real-time.

4.3.2 Mind Mapping with Whiteboard

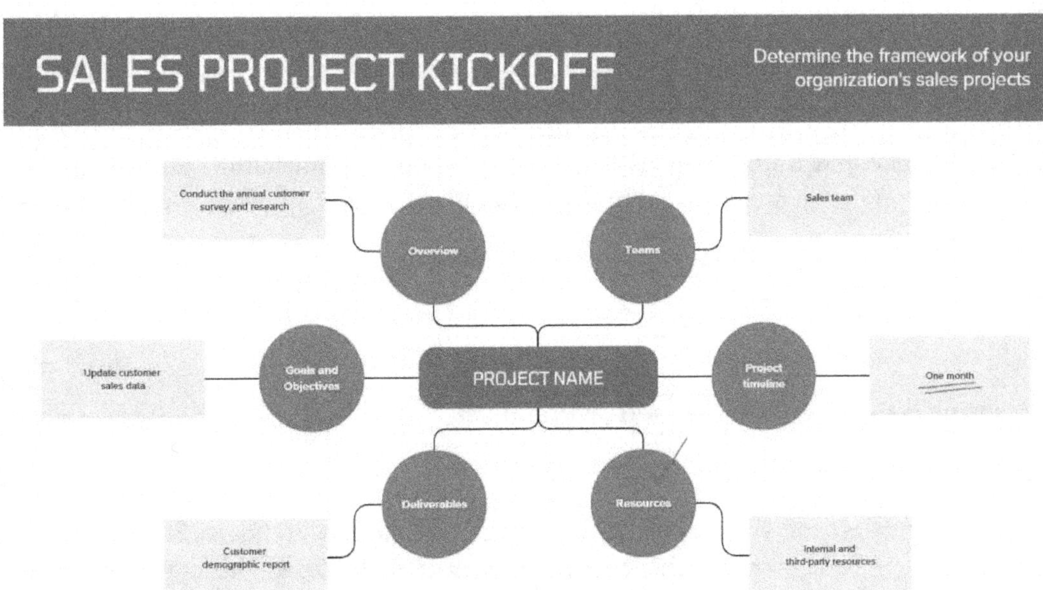

Introduction to Mind Mapping with Microsoft Whiteboard

Mind mapping is a powerful visual tool used for brainstorming, organizing information, and exploring ideas in a structured, yet creative, way. The process typically involves a central concept or idea, with branching nodes representing related subtopics or thoughts. Microsoft Whiteboard provides an excellent platform for mind mapping due to its flexible and user-friendly drawing tools, its ability to add and customize shapes, and its collaborative features.

In this section, we will explore how to use Microsoft Whiteboard to create effective mind maps for both individual use and team collaboration. Whether you're outlining a new project, planning a strategy, or simply brainstorming ideas, mind mapping in Whiteboard can help you visualize complex thoughts in an organized, clear format.

1. Why Use Mind Maps?

Before diving into the practical aspects of creating a mind map with Microsoft Whiteboard, it's essential to understand why mind maps are beneficial:

- Encourage Creativity: Mind maps allow ideas to flow freely without the constraints of linear thinking. You can branch off thoughts and make connections between them, fostering creativity and innovation.

- Simplify Complex Information: With mind maps, you can break down complex concepts into smaller, digestible parts, making it easier to understand relationships between ideas.

- Boost Memory and Retention: Visual representation of information often helps with retention, making mind maps a great tool for studying, planning, or presenting information.

- Facilitate Collaboration: Mind maps created in Microsoft Whiteboard can be shared with team members, encouraging real-time collaboration and brainstorming.

2. Creating a Mind Map in Microsoft Whiteboard

Step 1: Setting Up Your Whiteboard for Mind Mapping

To begin, open Microsoft Whiteboard and create a new blank whiteboard. Start by defining the primary topic or central idea for your mind map. In many cases, this could be a project title, a problem you're trying to solve, or a concept you're exploring.

- Create the Central Idea: Use the Text Tool or the Shape Tool to insert a circle or another shape in the center of the board. This will represent the main idea or concept you want to explore. Type the primary topic inside this shape.

- Choosing the Right Format: Decide how you want your mind map to look. A traditional mind map uses radial branching from a central point, but you can adapt it to suit your specific needs.

Step 2: Adding Branches and Subtopics

Next, start branching out from your central idea. Each branch should represent a subtopic or related idea. These branches should connect the central idea with the additional thoughts or concepts you're exploring.

- Drawing Branches: Use the Pen Tool or Line Tool to draw lines extending from the central idea. These lines should represent the main categories or subtopics related to the central concept.

- Inserting Subtopics: At the end of each branch, use the Text Tool to insert text boxes, shapes, or sticky notes that contain the subtopics. You can change the color of these text boxes or shapes to differentiate them from one another visually. For instance, you could use different colors for different categories or use a gradient effect to show progression from general to specific.

Step 3: Expanding with Additional Layers

Once you've established your primary subtopics, continue expanding the mind map by adding more layers of detail. Each subtopic can branch out further into smaller, more specific ideas.

- Creating Sub-branches: From each subtopic, draw additional branches that lead to smaller categories, details, or ideas. Continue this process until you've fully explored the concept.

- Using Visual Hierarchies: Use varying sizes of text and shapes to establish visual hierarchies, where more critical or overarching ideas are larger and bolder, and more minor, supporting ideas are smaller and less prominent.

Step 4: Enhancing the Mind Map with Visuals and Colors

A significant advantage of using Microsoft Whiteboard for mind mapping is its ability to integrate visual elements like images, icons, and symbols to represent ideas.

- Adding Icons and Symbols: Click on the Image Tool to add icons or symbols that represent specific ideas. For instance, if a branch represents a financial aspect of your project, you could add a dollar sign icon to make it visually distinct. Symbols can act as shorthand for larger ideas, making the map easier to navigate.

- Incorporating Images and Media: If your mind map includes concepts that can be represented by images (like products or design ideas), you can add relevant images directly to the whiteboard. This is particularly useful for presentations or creative brainstorming.

- Using Color Coding: Assign colors to different branches and nodes to visually group related ideas. Microsoft Whiteboard allows you to change the color of shapes, text, and lines, making it easier to organize and differentiate between ideas.

Step 5: Organizing and Refining the Mind Map

As your mind map expands, it's crucial to keep it organized and easy to understand. You can adjust and refine the structure by rearranging branches, changing colors, and ensuring the map remains clear and concise.

- Rearranging Nodes: If the mind map starts to feel cluttered or unorganized, you can move branches and nodes around by dragging them to new locations. Whiteboard's infinite canvas gives you plenty of room to spread out your ideas without running out of space.

- Creating Groups and Clusters: To further organize your ideas, group related branches into clusters. For instance, you could group all branches related to "Marketing" in one area of the board and those related to "Product Development" in another. This will help you focus on specific aspects of the project without feeling overwhelmed by the entire mind map.

- Refining and Finalizing: Once you have added all relevant branches and subtopics, take a step back and evaluate the structure. Make sure that the ideas flow logically and that the map is easy to follow. You can refine the mind map by adjusting branch positions, adding final touches like arrows or labels, or rearranging the hierarchy of ideas.

3. Collaborating on a Mind Map in Real-Time

One of the most powerful aspects of using Microsoft Whiteboard for mind mapping is its real-time collaboration features. You can invite team members to contribute ideas, refine the map, and collaborate on the whiteboard, making it an ideal tool for group brainstorming sessions.

Step 1: Sharing the Whiteboard

To invite others to your mind mapping session, click on the Share button in Microsoft Whiteboard. You can send an invitation via email or generate a shareable link.

- Setting Permissions: Decide whether your collaborators can only view the mind map or if they have editing permissions to add, remove, and modify branches and subtopics. This is particularly useful for managing large teams where only certain individuals need editing access.

Step 2: Real-Time Collaboration Features

As collaborators join the whiteboard, they can see the mind map in real time and add their own ideas or comments. Microsoft Whiteboard allows multiple users to work simultaneously, meaning you and your team can brainstorm and develop the map collaboratively.

- Track Changes: You can see who made each contribution, allowing you to track changes or modifications made by other team members. This feature is particularly useful for reviewing contributions and revising ideas.

Step 3: Communicating in Whiteboard

Use the built-in Comment feature to add notes, questions, or feedback to specific branches or nodes. This can help guide the conversation during brainstorming sessions or leave reminders for the team.

- Tagging Ideas: You can tag team members to specific ideas or tasks on the mind map. For instance, if one branch represents a marketing campaign, you could tag your marketing team to take ownership of that area, ensuring everyone knows their role.

4. Exporting and Using Your Mind Map

After completing your mind map, you may want to export it for use in presentations, documents, or meetings. Microsoft Whiteboard allows you to export your mind map in various formats.

- Exporting as Image or PDF: To share your mind map outside of Microsoft Whiteboard, export it as an image (JPG or PNG) or PDF. This is useful for incorporating the mind map into PowerPoint presentations, documents, or reports.

- Embedding in Other Microsoft Tools: You can embed your mind map in other Microsoft 365 applications, like OneNote, PowerPoint, or Teams. This makes it easy to reference or present the mind map in meetings or collaborative sessions.

5. Best Practices for Mind Mapping in Microsoft Whiteboard

Here are a few tips to maximize your productivity when creating mind maps in Microsoft Whiteboard:

- Start Simple: Begin with a clear central concept and only add branches as necessary. Avoid cluttering the map with too many ideas at the start. Instead, let it grow organically.

- Use Visuals Strategically: Incorporate icons, symbols, and images where appropriate, but don't overwhelm the map with too many visuals. Use them to emphasize important points and ideas.

- Encourage Collaboration: Invite team members to contribute early and often. Mind mapping is most effective when multiple perspectives and ideas are considered.

- Review and Refine: Periodically review and refine your mind map to ensure it remains clear, organized, and aligned with your goals.

By following these steps and best practices, you can create dynamic and effective mind maps in Microsoft Whiteboard that help organize and visualize complex ideas, making them easier to understand and communicate to others.

4.3.3 Using Icons and Symbols for Clarity

Icons and symbols are powerful visual elements that can enhance understanding, streamline communication, and improve the efficiency of your Whiteboard projects. Whether you are brainstorming, planning, or working on complex diagrams, integrating these visual elements can significantly enhance your workflow and the way your content is perceived.

Icons and symbols are not just decorative; they serve as visual cues that can condense information into easily understandable formats. In a collaborative environment, especially when dealing with remote teams or diverse participants, using these visual tools can minimize misunderstandings, highlight key areas, and make complex information digestible.

Why Use Icons and Symbols?

Icons and symbols in a digital whiteboard environment like Microsoft Whiteboard can be used for various purposes, including:

- Simplification of complex ideas: Icons can condense large amounts of information into simple, easy-to-understand visuals.

- Highlighting key points: They can draw attention to important information, ensuring critical details aren't missed during discussions or presentations.

- Organization: Symbols can act as organizational tools, helping users group similar items or ideas together visually.

- Enhancing collaboration: In a shared whiteboard space, icons can help collaborators quickly understand contributions from different team members without needing to wade through large blocks of text.

- Universal communication: Since icons are often universally recognized, they can bridge language gaps and aid in communication with international teams.

Types of Icons and Symbols

When using Microsoft Whiteboard, you'll find a range of icons and symbols available that can be easily integrated into your projects. Here are some categories and types of icons that are commonly used:

- Arrows and directional icons: Perfect for showing the flow of processes in diagrams, such as in flowcharts or mind maps. They can indicate transitions, steps, and directions in a clear, visual way.

- Shapes: Basic shapes (like circles, squares, and triangles) are commonly used in diagrams and flowcharts to represent various steps or concepts. These shapes can be annotated or used in conjunction with text and other visual elements.

- Information symbols: Symbols like question marks, exclamation points, or lightbulbs can serve to highlight questions, ideas, or important points.

- People icons: These can be used to represent participants in discussions, team members in collaborations, or customers in a business workflow.

- Workflow icons: Specific symbols such as gears, graphs, and charts are useful for illustrating business processes or project workflows.

How to Use Icons and Symbols Effectively

1. Incorporating Icons for Visual Communication

The key to effectively using icons and symbols is knowing when and where to place them. When working on a whiteboard, you can strategically place icons near text boxes or sticky notes to provide additional context. For example, if you are creating a workflow and want to highlight a decision-making step, you can use a question mark icon to signify that a decision needs to be made at that point.

Here's how to add icons in Microsoft Whiteboard:

- Access the icon library: While Microsoft Whiteboard doesn't have a built-in, extensive icon library like some other diagramming tools, you can draw icons manually, or copy and paste icons from external sources (e.g., an icon website or PowerPoint).

- Use shapes as icons: The shape tool in Whiteboard is versatile, allowing you to quickly create basic icons that can represent different elements in your diagram. Circles, squares, arrows, and other shapes can be used to create process diagrams, decision points, or directional flows.

- Annotate icons: Once you've inserted an icon, adding a short text label can further enhance its clarity. This is particularly useful when using abstract symbols like stars or exclamation points to ensure everyone understands what they represent.

2. Grouping Information with Symbols

When working with large amounts of data or ideas on a whiteboard, it can quickly become overwhelming. Symbols can act as organizational tools, grouping related information together visually. For example, you can use a specific shape (e.g., squares) to surround ideas related to budget constraints, while a different shape (e.g., circles) can surround ideas related to customer feedback.

This simple visual technique ensures that during collaboration, everyone can easily see how ideas are grouped without needing to read through every piece of content in detail.

3. Creating Visual Hierarchies

Icons and symbols can also help establish a visual hierarchy, allowing you to prioritize information effectively. By using different colors, sizes, or types of icons, you can indicate the importance or urgency of certain items. For example:

- Red exclamation marks can signify urgent tasks or critical issues.

- Green checkmarks can indicate tasks that have been completed or approved.

- Yellow question marks can represent areas that need further clarification or discussion.

Using color and size strategically can help ensure that your audience focuses on the most important information first. Additionally, if your whiteboard becomes crowded with information, icons can prevent important ideas from getting lost in the shuffle.

4. Using Icons for Workflow and Task Management

In business settings, Microsoft Whiteboard is often used for project management and task tracking. By integrating icons and symbols, you can streamline this process, ensuring that tasks are visually represented in a clear and concise way. For example:

- Use arrows to indicate the flow of tasks or dependencies between them.

- Use checkmarks to denote completed tasks.

- Use stars or flags to highlight priority tasks or milestones.

By combining these icons with other whiteboard elements, like sticky notes or text, you can create a highly visual task management system that everyone on the team can understand at a glance.

Customizing and Importing Icons

While Microsoft Whiteboard comes with a limited set of built-in shapes and symbols, you can expand your options by importing custom icons. This can be particularly useful if you're working with specific branding elements or require specialized icons for industry-specific tasks.

Here's how you can do it:

- Importing images as icons: You can easily drag and drop images from your computer into Microsoft Whiteboard. If you have custom icon sets or images that you use frequently, this can save time and improve the consistency of your diagrams.

- Using third-party tools: You can also create custom icons using graphic design tools like Adobe Illustrator or even PowerPoint. Once created, you can save these icons as PNG or SVG files and import them into Whiteboard.

Once you've imported your custom icons, you can manipulate them just like any other object on the whiteboard. Resize, move, and annotate them to suit your needs.

Best Practices for Using Icons and Symbols

To ensure that your use of icons and symbols remains effective, keep the following best practices in mind:

- Avoid overusing icons: While icons can enhance understanding, overloading your whiteboard with too many symbols can have the opposite effect. Use icons sparingly, and ensure that each one serves a specific purpose.

- Ensure consistency: Stick to a consistent set of icons and symbols throughout your whiteboard. This ensures that your audience doesn't get confused by different visual cues representing the same concept.

- Keep it simple: The purpose of icons and symbols is to simplify communication, not complicate it. Stick to basic, universally recognized symbols that everyone can understand at a glance.

Examples of Icon Use in Different Scenarios

1. Educational Settings

In a classroom setting, teachers can use icons to create interactive lessons on a whiteboard. For instance, question marks can be placed next to questions or problems, while lightbulb icons can denote key concepts or moments of insight. These simple cues can help students follow the lesson more effectively and encourage participation in discussions.

2. Business Workshops

During brainstorming or strategy sessions, business teams can use icons to signify different elements in their discussions. For example, a dollar sign icon could represent financial ideas, while a person icon could represent customer-related topics. By visually categorizing ideas, the team can stay focused and ensure that all aspects of a project are addressed.

3. Remote Collaboration

In remote collaboration environments, teams often struggle with miscommunication. By using clear icons, teams can visually highlight key discussion points, mark important decisions, and ensure everyone stays on the same page. For example, arrows can guide the discussion flow, while checkmarks can confirm decisions made during the meeting.

In conclusion, using icons and symbols within Microsoft Whiteboard is a highly effective way to clarify complex ideas, highlight key points, and improve overall collaboration. When used correctly, they can transform a cluttered or confusing whiteboard into an organized and visually engaging workspace that supports efficient communication and problem-solving. Whether you are working on a flowchart, brainstorming session, or project management board, integrating these advanced drawing techniques will help you maximize the potential of Microsoft Whiteboard and ensure that your ideas are clearly communicated to your team.

CHAPTER V
Microsoft Whiteboard for Education and Business

5.1 Using Whiteboard in Educational Settings

The increasing reliance on digital tools in the educational landscape has driven the need for intuitive, collaborative platforms that enhance learning. Microsoft Whiteboard has emerged as an effective tool for facilitating interaction, creativity, and shared problem-solving in classrooms, both in person and online. With its visually driven, flexible design, Whiteboard helps educators move beyond traditional chalkboards and whiteboards, offering a more dynamic, engaging space for both teachers and students.

In this section, we will explore how Whiteboard can be used effectively in various educational settings, from K-12 classrooms to higher education, and how it fosters a collaborative learning environment that supports active engagement, peer learning, and creative thinking.

5.1.1 Collaborative Learning Activities

Collaborative learning is a method of education where students work together to solve problems, complete tasks, or create projects, encouraging peer interaction, deeper learning, and critical thinking. Microsoft Whiteboard, with its multi-user interface and real-time collaboration features, is perfectly suited for this kind of learning. Below, we'll examine specific collaborative learning activities that can be enhanced using Microsoft Whiteboard, offering students and educators a way to engage more meaningfully with their subjects and with each other.

1. Brainstorming Sessions

Brainstorming is one of the most effective ways to gather a variety of ideas and insights from students, encouraging creativity and critical thinking. Microsoft Whiteboard's freeform canvas allows students to contribute their thoughts visually, either by writing, drawing, or adding images and sticky notes.

- How to Set it Up: Teachers can start a blank whiteboard, invite the class to join, and set a clear goal for the brainstorming session. For example, in a literature class, students could brainstorm themes or character motivations for a novel they are reading.

- Collaborative Benefits: Each student can contribute in real-time, building off of one another's ideas. The ability to color-code thoughts, group similar ideas, and move them around the board makes it easier to see patterns and connections.

- Outcomes: Once the brainstorming session is complete, the teacher can guide the class in organizing the ideas into clusters or categories, helping to develop a cohesive framework that can be used in subsequent lessons or projects.

2. Group Problem Solving

Collaborative problem-solving is a key part of modern education, helping students apply knowledge in real-world scenarios. Microsoft Whiteboard facilitates this by providing an interactive space where students can work together on solving math problems, designing science experiments, or tackling complex historical analysis.

- How to Set it Up: Teachers can divide the class into small groups, each working on a different section of the whiteboard. For example, in a math class, each group can be assigned a set of problems to solve. The teacher can observe each group's progress and provide real-time feedback or guidance.

- Collaborative Benefits: Students can see and respond to each other's approaches to problem-solving, learning from different methods and perspectives. The digital tools available—like rulers for geometry problems or the ability to upload diagrams—make it easier to visualize the problems and solutions.

- Outcomes: Each group's section of the whiteboard can be saved and revisited later, allowing for reflection and further discussion about the problem-solving process.

3. Peer-to-Peer Teaching

Peer-to-peer teaching is a powerful way to enhance learning, as students are often able to explain concepts to each other in relatable ways. Microsoft Whiteboard provides a platform for students to demonstrate their understanding of a topic by "teaching" their classmates, using visual aids and collaborative interaction.

- How to Set it Up: Teachers can assign students specific topics to teach. For example, in a biology class, students can be asked to explain different parts of the human body. Using Whiteboard, students can draw diagrams, add text, and include multimedia elements like images or videos to support their explanations.

- Collaborative Benefits: As students present their topics on the whiteboard, their classmates can ask questions, add comments, and even provide supplementary information or suggestions. This active participation deepens engagement and understanding.

- Outcomes: The whiteboard created during the peer-teaching session can be saved as a study resource, accessible to the entire class for review and revision.

4. Concept Mapping

Concept mapping is a great way to visually organize information, helping students understand how different concepts are connected. Microsoft Whiteboard is perfect for creating and manipulating these maps, allowing students to build complex visual representations of their knowledge.

- How to Set it Up: For a history class studying World War II, for example, students can create a concept map linking key events, figures, and consequences. Each node on the map can be customized with drawings, images, or notes.

- Collaborative Benefits: As the concept map evolves, students can suggest new connections or rearrange nodes to reflect their evolving understanding of the material. This collaborative process helps refine the map into a shared resource that represents the collective knowledge of the class.

- Outcomes: The completed concept map can be saved and revisited throughout the course, serving as a living document that grows alongside the students' knowledge.

5. Digital Storytelling

Storytelling is a critical part of education, helping students develop narrative skills and creativity. Microsoft Whiteboard's multimedia capabilities allow students to collaboratively create digital stories, combining text, images, and drawings into a cohesive narrative.

- How to Set it Up: Teachers can assign small groups to create a story based on a specific theme or lesson. For example, in an English class, students could write and illustrate their own short stories. Using Whiteboard, they can collaboratively write the text, add drawings, and even include images or videos to bring their stories to life.

- Collaborative Benefits: Each student can contribute different elements to the story, working together to refine the narrative, suggest new plot twists, or illustrate key scenes. The whiteboard format allows for seamless integration of all these elements, creating an interactive and visually engaging storytelling experience.

- Outcomes: Once completed, the digital stories can be shared with the class, offering opportunities for feedback and discussion. Additionally, these stories can be saved and presented as part of larger projects or exhibitions.

6. Collaborative Research and Presentation

Collaborative research projects are common in education, and Microsoft Whiteboard can help students organize their research findings visually, working together to prepare presentations. This method encourages teamwork, critical thinking, and effective communication.

- How to Set it Up: Teachers can assign research topics, and each group can use Microsoft Whiteboard to collect and organize their findings. For example, in a social studies class, students researching different countries can add maps, facts, and notes to their section of the whiteboard.

- Collaborative Benefits: The group can work together in real-time to develop their presentation, organizing their research into sections, adding multimedia, and rehearsing their presentation. Microsoft Whiteboard's integration with Microsoft 365 tools also makes it easy to bring in content from Word, PowerPoint, or Excel.

- Outcomes: The collaborative whiteboard created during the research phase can be used during the presentation itself, offering a dynamic, interactive way to present information. The board can be saved and shared with the class afterward for further review.

7. Visualizing Science Experiments

Science classes often involve complex concepts that are best understood through visualization. Microsoft Whiteboard can help students design and document science experiments collaboratively, offering a space where they can sketch diagrams, annotate results, and share their hypotheses.

- How to Set it Up: For a physics experiment on forces, students can use Whiteboard to sketch out their experimental setup, label variables, and make predictions. As they conduct the experiment, they can use the whiteboard to record observations and adjust their designs.

- Collaborative Benefits: Students can work together to refine their experimental design, discuss observations, and share findings in real-time. The digital format of Whiteboard makes it easy to incorporate multimedia elements like videos of the experiment or data charts.

- Outcomes: The whiteboard can serve as a comprehensive record of the experiment, which can be saved and submitted as part of a larger lab report or science project.

Conclusion

Collaborative learning activities are crucial for modern education, and Microsoft Whiteboard provides the perfect platform to facilitate these activities in a digital environment. From brainstorming and problem-solving to storytelling and science experiments, Whiteboard's interactive and flexible design enables students to engage deeply with the material, work together creatively, and learn from one another in real-time. Through the use of Microsoft Whiteboard, educators can foster a more dynamic, collaborative classroom experience that prepares students for the complexities of the modern world.

5.1.2 Managing Group Projects

In today's educational landscape, fostering collaboration among students is an essential part of the learning process. Group projects not only encourage teamwork but also develop problem-solving, communication, and time management skills. Microsoft Whiteboard is a powerful tool for managing group projects in an educational setting, enabling students to work together in real-time, whether they are in the same classroom or collaborating remotely. This section will explore how Microsoft Whiteboard can be leveraged to enhance group project management, from initial brainstorming to final presentations.

1. Brainstorming and Ideation

The first step of any group project is often the brainstorming phase, where students are tasked with generating ideas, sharing perspectives, and outlining their approach. Microsoft Whiteboard provides an intuitive, visual platform for this process, allowing all group members to contribute simultaneously. Here are some effective ways to use Whiteboard for brainstorming and ideation during group projects:

- Freeform Brainstorming: Group members can use digital pens to jot down ideas or draw sketches directly on the Whiteboard, simulating the feel of traditional brainstorming on a physical board. This encourages a free flow of ideas without the constraints of structure. With Whiteboard's collaborative nature, everyone can see what others are adding in real-time, sparking further creativity.

- Organizing Ideas with Sticky Notes: Sticky notes in Microsoft Whiteboard are a great tool for categorizing ideas. For example, each student can add their suggestions on individual sticky notes, which can then be grouped by theme or category. This helps the group stay organized while still encouraging creativity.

- Mind Mapping for Clarity: Using Whiteboard's drawing and shape tools, students can create a mind map that visually organizes their ideas. This allows the group to see connections between concepts and identify the most promising avenues for their project. They can also use the ruler tool to ensure their diagram is neatly organized, aiding in comprehension.

2. Assigning Roles and Tasks

Once the group has solidified their project concept, the next step is assigning roles and tasks to individual members. Clear communication and division of responsibilities are key to a successful group project. Microsoft Whiteboard offers several features to help facilitate this stage:

- Creating a Project Plan: Using the text and shape tools, the group can create a visual project plan on the Whiteboard. For example, they could create a timeline with key milestones or break the project down into smaller tasks, each assigned to a specific student. The visual aspect of Whiteboard makes it easy to understand who is responsible for each part of the project.

- Task Assignment with Sticky Notes: Sticky notes can also be used to assign tasks. Each group member can add a sticky note with their assigned task, color-coded for easy reference. For example, one color might represent research tasks, another color for design tasks, and so on. This system helps ensure that all group members are clear on their responsibilities.

- Collaboration on Task Details: As the group progresses, they can use Whiteboard to collaborate on task details. For instance, if one student is responsible for research, they can share their findings directly on the Whiteboard for feedback from the group. Others can add notes or suggestions, fostering a more collaborative and iterative approach.

3. Tracking Progress

Keeping track of progress is crucial in ensuring that a group project stays on track and meets deadlines. Microsoft Whiteboard provides a visual way for students to monitor their work and ensure that everyone is making progress toward the group's goals.

- Creating Progress Charts: Students can use Whiteboard to create charts or visual trackers that show the status of each task. For example, they could create a simple table or a Kanban-style board with columns for "To Do," "In Progress," and "Completed." As tasks are finished, they can be moved across the board, giving everyone a clear sense of what has been done and what still needs attention.

- Visual Timelines: Whiteboard's drawing tools can also be used to create project timelines, allowing students to visually represent their project schedule. They can mark key deadlines and milestones, ensuring that the project stays on track. Students can regularly update the timeline as tasks are completed.

- Collaborative Feedback: Microsoft Whiteboard is ideal for providing and receiving feedback during the project. Group members can leave notes or suggestions on specific tasks or ideas, and others can respond in real-time. This continuous loop of feedback helps the group improve their work and ensures that everyone is aligned with the project's goals.

4. Presenting the Final Project

Once the project is completed, the group will often need to present their work to their peers or teachers. Microsoft Whiteboard provides several tools that make it easy to create a polished, collaborative presentation.

- Designing the Presentation on Whiteboard: Group members can use Whiteboard to collaboratively design their presentation. They can create slides or visual aids directly on the Whiteboard, using its shape and text tools to make their content visually appealing. They can also import images or other media to enhance their presentation.

- Rehearsing the Presentation: One of the benefits of using Microsoft Whiteboard for group projects is that it allows students to rehearse their presentations together, even if they are not in the same physical location. Group members can use Whiteboard as a shared visual aid while they practice their speaking parts. This ensures that everyone is well-prepared for the final presentation.

- Delivering the Presentation Remotely: In today's digital age, many presentations are delivered remotely, and Microsoft Whiteboard is well-suited for this. Students can share their Whiteboard with their teacher or classmates, allowing them to present their ideas visually, even in a virtual setting. They can also collaborate in real-time if their presentation requires interactive elements, such as answering questions or adjusting their content based on feedback.

5. Overcoming Common Challenges in Group Projects

Group projects often come with their own set of challenges, such as communication difficulties or uneven workload distribution. Microsoft Whiteboard can help address some of these challenges, making group work more efficient and productive.

- Improving Communication: One common issue in group projects is a lack of communication between members. Whiteboard helps solve this by providing a shared space where everyone can contribute and stay updated on the project's progress. Group members can leave notes for each other or ask questions directly on the Whiteboard, reducing the need for constant emails or messages.

- Balancing Workloads: Another challenge in group projects is ensuring that all members contribute equally. With Microsoft Whiteboard, it's easy to see who is responsible for each task and whether those tasks are being completed on time. This transparency helps prevent situations where one or two members end up doing most of the work.

- Collaborating Across Time Zones: In a world where remote learning and international collaboration are increasingly common, group projects often involve students working in different time zones. Whiteboard's real-time collaboration features make it easy for students to work together, no matter where they are located. They can leave updates or notes for their group members to see when they log in, ensuring that progress continues even if they are not all working at the same time.

6. Case Studies: Real-World Examples of Group Projects Using Microsoft Whiteboard

To illustrate the benefits of Microsoft Whiteboard for managing group projects, let's explore a couple of real-world examples from both high school and university settings:

- *Case Study 1: High School Science Project*

A group of high school students was assigned a project to research and present on renewable energy sources. Using Microsoft Whiteboard, the students brainstormed their ideas, dividing their research into categories such as solar, wind, and hydro energy. They used sticky notes to assign specific tasks to each member and created a timeline for completing their work. Throughout the project, they used the Whiteboard to share research and collaborate on their presentation. In the end, they delivered a well-organized and engaging presentation using the Whiteboard as their visual aid.

- *Case Study 2: University Marketing Project*

A group of university students was tasked with creating a marketing plan for a local business. Despite being located in different cities, the group used Microsoft Whiteboard to collaborate effectively. They started by brainstorming ideas for their marketing strategy, using sticky notes to organize their thoughts. They then created a detailed project plan with tasks assigned to each member, tracking their progress using a visual Kanban board on the Whiteboard. The group members frequently left comments and feedback on each other's work, ensuring that the project was cohesive and well-organized. Their final presentation, designed collaboratively on the Whiteboard, was a success.

In conclusion, Microsoft Whiteboard is a highly effective tool for managing group projects in educational settings. Its visual, collaborative features make it easy for students to brainstorm ideas, assign tasks, track progress, and present their final work. By using Whiteboard, students can overcome many of the challenges associated with group projects, such as communication difficulties and uneven workload distribution. As technology continues to play an increasing role in education, tools like Microsoft Whiteboard will become even more essential in helping students work together, whether they are in the same room or on opposite sides of the world.

5.2 Microsoft Whiteboard in Business Settings

Microsoft Whiteboard is a powerful tool for business environments, offering a versatile platform for collaboration, brainstorming, and project management. In today's increasingly remote and hybrid workplaces, the ability to ideate and visually represent concepts with colleagues in real-time or asynchronously is vital. Microsoft Whiteboard provides businesses with an easy-to-use, digital solution for fostering creativity, improving project planning, and enhancing communication within teams.

5.2.1 Brainstorming and Ideation Sessions

In business settings, brainstorming is an essential activity for generating fresh ideas, solving complex problems, and exploring innovative approaches. Microsoft Whiteboard offers a rich, flexible space for ideation sessions, allowing teams to share, iterate, and refine ideas in a collaborative digital environment. Let's explore how businesses can maximize the potential of brainstorming sessions using Microsoft Whiteboard.

1. Setting Up a Productive Brainstorming Session

Before diving into brainstorming, it's essential to prepare your Microsoft Whiteboard space effectively to ensure a productive session. A well-organized whiteboard promotes clarity, focus, and creativity.

Creating a Dedicated Brainstorming Template:

One of the features Microsoft Whiteboard offers is its range of built-in templates, which can significantly streamline the brainstorming process. For a typical ideation session, start by selecting or creating a template that fits the objective of the meeting. For example, you can design a simple grid or chart to categorize ideas or use mind-mapping templates to explore relationships between different concepts.

Organizing Key Questions and Goals:

To guide your brainstorming session, it's crucial to define key questions or objectives at the top of your whiteboard. This provides a clear direction for your team. For instance, you might ask: What are the primary pain points our customers are facing? or How can we enhance our product's user experience? These prompts will serve as focal points for the session and help steer participants towards meaningful contributions.

Incorporating Visual Prompts and Examples:

The visual nature of Microsoft Whiteboard makes it easy to introduce prompts, such as images, charts, or text that can spark creative thinking. For example, in a marketing brainstorming session, you could upload an image of your product or customer feedback to ignite discussions about possible improvements or new features. Using visuals to prompt ideas helps create a more dynamic and engaging session.

2. Collaborative Ideation in Real-Time

Once your whiteboard is set up and goals have been established, the real-time collaboration features of Microsoft Whiteboard come into play. Whether participants are in the same room or spread across different time zones, everyone can contribute simultaneously, making it an ideal tool for both in-person and virtual brainstorming.

Encouraging Participation with Digital Sticky Notes:

One of the most commonly used tools during brainstorming is the sticky note feature. Participants can use sticky notes to jot down their ideas, which are then placed on the board for everyone to see. This not only simulates the experience of a traditional in-person brainstorming session but also provides an organized, color-coded way to categorize ideas. For instance, you could assign each team member a specific color, making it easy to track contributions.

Building on Ideas with Ink and Drawing Tools:

In a fast-paced ideation session, one idea often leads to another. The ink and drawing tools in Microsoft Whiteboard allow participants to sketch, diagram, and link concepts fluidly. If someone presents an idea for a new product feature, for example, others can quickly sketch out how it might work, annotate it, or visually connect it to other related ideas. This dynamic back-and-forth interaction encourages deeper exploration of each suggestion.

Using Infinite Canvas for Expansive Thinking:

Microsoft Whiteboard's infinite canvas enables brainstorming sessions to expand without limitations. As ideas grow and evolve, you can easily pan across the canvas to add new ideas, without feeling confined to a small space. This encourages expansive thinking and allows participants to develop multiple ideas simultaneously. For example, different parts of the whiteboard could be used to explore different aspects of a challenge — such as customer needs, potential solutions, and potential obstacles.

3. Structuring and Refining Ideas

Once a large volume of ideas has been generated, the next step is to organize, prioritize, and refine those ideas. Microsoft Whiteboard offers several features that help teams transition from free-form brainstorming to structured decision-making.

Grouping Ideas for Clarity:

After a brainstorm, ideas may be scattered across the whiteboard. One useful technique is to group similar ideas together. You can drag and drop sticky notes, text boxes, and shapes to create clusters of related ideas. For example, during a product development session, you could group ideas based on categories like Features, User Interface, or Marketing Strategy. Grouping allows the team to identify trends and patterns that might not be apparent when ideas are scattered.

Using Connectors for Visual Structure:

Connectors, arrows, and lines are valuable for creating a visual flow of ideas. These tools allow participants to link concepts and show the relationships between different elements. For instance, in a brainstorming session for process improvement, you might connect ideas about specific tasks to broader process stages, creating a visual map of potential workflow changes.

Voting and Prioritizing Ideas:

To facilitate decision-making, you can use visual markers, such as checkmarks or icons, to have team members vote on the best ideas. Another option is to create a simple matrix to evaluate each idea based on criteria like Impact and Feasibility. This can be particularly useful in business settings, where teams need to focus on ideas that provide the most value with the least effort. For example, during a marketing strategy session, ideas can be placed in a grid where one axis represents the potential impact on customer engagement and the other represents the ease of implementation.

4. Asynchronous Brainstorming and Idea Generation

One of the unique advantages of Microsoft Whiteboard is its ability to support asynchronous collaboration. In today's global business landscape, teams are often spread across different time zones, making it difficult to gather everyone in one place for live brainstorming. Microsoft Whiteboard addresses this challenge by allowing users to contribute to the whiteboard at different times.

Inviting Team Members to Contribute Asynchronously:

After an initial brainstorming session, or even as an alternative to a live session, you can invite team members to add their thoughts and ideas asynchronously. Participants can open the shared whiteboard, view existing ideas, and contribute new ones at their convenience. This approach is particularly beneficial for fostering diverse perspectives, as it allows individuals who may not be able to attend the live session to share their insights.

Using Comments for Discussion and Feedback:

As ideas are added asynchronously, team members can use the comment feature to discuss and provide feedback on specific ideas. This facilitates an ongoing conversation and ensures that the brainstorming session remains dynamic and inclusive. For example, during a product design brainstorming session, a team member in one time zone might propose a feature, and another team member in a different time zone could leave a comment suggesting a refinement or an alternative approach.

Tracking Changes and Iterations:

Because Microsoft Whiteboard automatically saves all changes, you can easily track the evolution of ideas over time. This is particularly useful for extended brainstorming sessions that occur over several days or weeks. Participants can see how ideas have developed, what new suggestions have been added, and how the conversation has progressed.

5. Incorporating External Resources for Inspiration

Brainstorming doesn't have to happen in a vacuum. Microsoft Whiteboard allows you to pull in external resources that can serve as inspiration or context for ideation sessions. This feature is especially useful in business settings where brainstorming needs to be grounded in data, customer feedback, or market research.

Uploading Documents and Reports:

If your brainstorming session is focused on solving a specific business challenge, you can upload relevant documents, such as market research reports, customer surveys, or financial data. These resources can provide valuable context and help guide the team's thinking. For instance, during a product brainstorming session, having access to a customer satisfaction report directly on the whiteboard can help the team focus on areas that need improvement.

Using Images and Visual References:

In creative brainstorming sessions, such as those for branding or marketing campaigns, visual inspiration is key. Microsoft Whiteboard allows you to upload images, logos, or designs that can spark new ideas. For example, if you're brainstorming a new logo, you can upload examples of competitor logos or design elements you find inspiring.

Incorporating Web Links and External Content:

For more information-rich sessions, Microsoft Whiteboard supports the addition of web links. This is particularly useful when you want to reference external resources like articles, industry reports, or trend forecasts during a session. For example, a team brainstorming new product ideas could link to articles about emerging technology trends to stay informed and inspired.

In summary, Microsoft Whiteboard provides businesses with an innovative, flexible platform for brainstorming and ideation. Whether used in real-time or asynchronously, its range of tools—from sticky notes and drawing capabilities to connectors and external resource integration—makes it an invaluable tool for fostering creativity, collaboration, and problem-solving in the business environment. Through well-organized and facilitated brainstorming sessions, businesses can generate fresh ideas, streamline decision-making, and ultimately drive innovation.

5.2.2 Project Planning and Management

Introduction to Project Planning and Management

In today's fast-paced business environment, effective project planning and management are critical to the success of any organization. Whether you are working on a small internal project or managing large-scale initiatives across multiple teams, clear communication, well-defined objectives, and organized tasks are essential. Microsoft Whiteboard offers a dynamic and collaborative environment that helps streamline the project management process. It allows teams to map out projects visually, collaborate in real-time, and ensure that everyone is on the same page throughout the entire project lifecycle.

This section explores how to use Microsoft Whiteboard for project planning and management, including the essential features that can help you plan tasks, manage resources, and monitor progress. From creating project timelines to assigning responsibilities, you will learn how to make the most of Whiteboard's intuitive tools to lead successful projects.

Visualizing Project Goals and Objectives

Before diving into the detailed planning, it's essential to start with a clear understanding of the project's goals and objectives. Microsoft Whiteboard provides an open, flexible space where you can brainstorm with your team, listing and categorizing the key goals for your project.

Steps to Visualizing Goals:

1. Create a New Whiteboard: Begin by creating a new whiteboard specifically dedicated to the project.

2. Use Sticky Notes: Use sticky notes to jot down each goal or objective. You can assign different colors to represent different categories (e.g., short-term goals in green, long-term goals in blue).

3. Group Similar Goals: After listing all the objectives, use the lasso tool to group related goals. You can create clusters of goals related to different aspects of the project, such as financial targets, technical requirements, or customer satisfaction objectives.

4. Create a Vision Board: With the visual nature of Whiteboard, you can also upload images, charts, and reference documents to create a comprehensive vision board that gives context to the project's goals.

Building a Project Timeline

One of the most critical aspects of project management is tracking time. A project timeline ensures that everyone is aware of key milestones, deadlines, and deliverables, which is crucial for maintaining productivity and accountability.

Steps to Creating a Project Timeline:

1. Draw a Horizontal Line: Using the pen tool, draw a horizontal line across the whiteboard. This will serve as the base for your project timeline.

2. Mark Key Dates and Milestones: Add text boxes along the line to indicate significant dates, such as project kickoff, key review points, and final deadlines.

3. Add Milestones: Create symbols or shapes (e.g., circles or stars) to highlight major milestones along the timeline. Label each milestone with a brief description.

4. Color-Coding for Clarity: You can use different colors to represent various phases of the project. For instance, planning activities might be in red, development phases in blue, and testing in green.

5. Link Tasks to Milestones: Use connectors or arrows to visually represent the relationship between tasks and their corresponding milestones, making it easier to understand how each activity fits into the larger timeline.

The timeline provides a high-level overview of the project's progress, helping team members stay aligned on important deadlines. Microsoft Whiteboard's real-time editing capabilities allow for easy adjustments to the timeline if deadlines shift or priorities change.

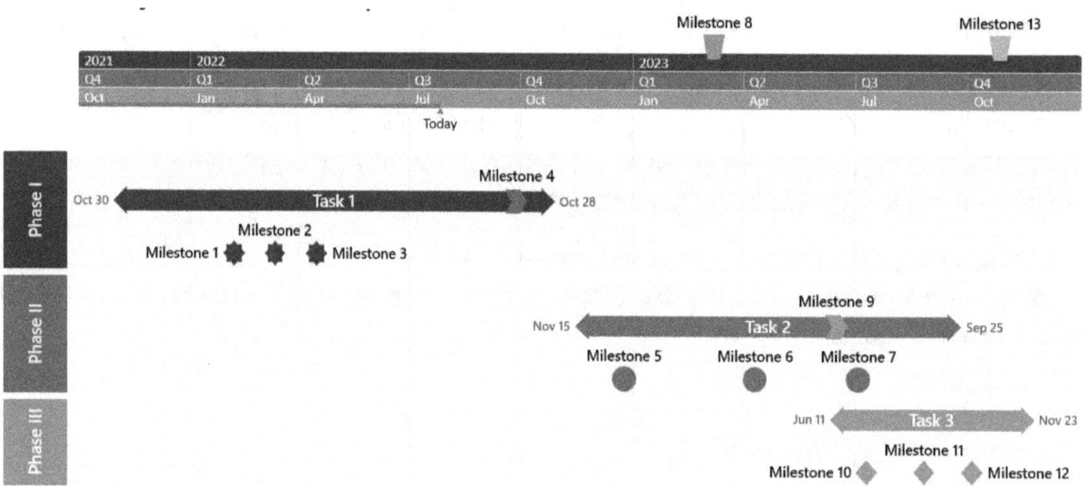

Assigning Tasks and Responsibilities

Once the project's goals and timeline have been defined, the next step is to assign specific tasks to team members. Assigning clear responsibilities is essential for ensuring that each team member knows what is expected of them and that the workload is distributed evenly across the group.

Steps to Assigning Tasks:

1. Create a Task List: Using sticky notes or text boxes, create a list of all the tasks that need to be completed during the project. You can categorize tasks by phase or department (e.g., "Development," "Design," "Marketing").

2. Assign Team Members: Write the name or initials of the person responsible for each task next to the task description. This can be done using either text boxes or sticky notes.

3. Track Task Progress: As the project progresses, you can use color codes or symbols to indicate the status of each task (e.g., green for completed tasks, yellow for in progress, and red for delayed).

4. Use Tags for Priority: Whiteboard allows you to use symbols or tags (e.g., stars, flags) to indicate high-priority tasks that require immediate attention.

Having all tasks visually mapped out in one place helps prevent confusion about who is responsible for what and provides a quick reference for team leaders to check the status of different project components.

Collaborating in Real-Time on Project Plans

Effective project management often requires collaboration between various stakeholders, each bringing different perspectives and expertise to the table. Microsoft Whiteboard's real-time collaboration capabilities enable team members to contribute to the project plan, regardless of their physical location.

Real-Time Collaboration Features:

1. Invite Team Members: Send invitations to other team members by sharing the Whiteboard link or using email invitations. Ensure that permissions are set so that everyone can contribute equally.

2. Simultaneous Editing: As team members work on the whiteboard simultaneously, they can add tasks, provide input, and make adjustments in real-time. This allows for more dynamic discussions and brainstorming sessions.

3. Adding Comments and Annotations: Use the sticky notes or text tool to leave comments or suggestions on different parts of the project plan. This can be particularly helpful when reviewing the plan during virtual meetings.

4. Version Control: Whiteboard automatically saves your work to the cloud, so all team members have access to the latest version of the project plan. If needed, you can revert to earlier versions of the whiteboard or review the changes made by others.

Tracking Project Progress and Deliverables

Keeping track of progress is key to ensuring that your project stays on schedule and that any roadblocks are addressed before they become bigger issues. Microsoft Whiteboard allows you to visualize the status of various tasks and deliverables throughout the project.

Steps to Tracking Progress:

1. Create a Progress Dashboard: Set up a section of the whiteboard as a progress dashboard where you can track the completion of tasks. Use color-coded sticky notes or status bars to represent tasks in different stages of completion.

2. Milestone Checkpoints: At each milestone, use the whiteboard to review progress and update the timeline or task list accordingly. Milestones should be treated as checkpoints to ensure that the project is still on track.

3. Monitor Task Status: Update the status of individual tasks regularly, either by marking them as complete, in progress, or delayed. This visual representation makes it easy to see which areas need attention.

4. Integrate with Other Tools: If your team is using other project management tools like Microsoft Planner or Trello, you can integrate those platforms with Microsoft Whiteboard. Upload screenshots or export task lists to keep everything in one place for easy reference.

Problem Solving and Risk Management

No project goes entirely according to plan. When issues arise, it's essential to have a method for identifying and resolving problems quickly. Microsoft Whiteboard can be used to facilitate problem-solving sessions and help teams brainstorm solutions collaboratively.

Using Whiteboard for Problem Solving:

1. Brainstorming Solutions: Use a section of the whiteboard for brainstorming potential solutions to project roadblocks. Encourage team members to add their ideas using sticky notes or text boxes.

2. Evaluating Risks: Create a risk assessment area where you can list potential risks to the project. Categorize risks by severity and likelihood, and use visual symbols to highlight high-risk areas.

3. Assigning Risk Mitigation Tasks: For each identified risk, assign tasks to team members responsible for mitigating the risk. Track the progress of these tasks alongside the main project plan to ensure that risks are managed proactively.

Finalizing the Project and Reviewing Outcomes

As the project nears completion, it's important to review the outcomes and reflect on the lessons learned. Microsoft Whiteboard can serve as a visual reference for the entire project, from initial planning to final deliverables.

Project Wrap-Up:

1. Conducting a Post-Project Review: Use the whiteboard to facilitate a post-project review meeting. Team members can add notes on what went well, what could have been improved, and any challenges that were encountered.

2. Summarizing Deliverables: Create a final section on the whiteboard that lists all completed deliverables, along with a summary of the project's overall success.

3. Archiving the Whiteboard: Once the project is complete, you can archive the whiteboard for future reference or share it with stakeholders as a visual record of the project's lifecycle.

Conclusion

Using Microsoft Whiteboard for project planning and management offers a flexible, visual, and collaborative approach that enhances communication and keeps teams organized. By combining brainstorming, task assignment, real-time collaboration, and progress tracking in one platform, Microsoft Whiteboard simplifies the complex process of managing projects and ensures that everyone involved has a clear understanding of their roles and responsibilities.

5.2.3 Visualizing Data and Reports

In the world of business, data is king. Making sense of large amounts of information is crucial for making informed decisions, tracking performance, and presenting findings to stakeholders. Microsoft Whiteboard offers a unique and dynamic way to visualize data and reports, enabling teams to collaborate effectively, brainstorm, and present data-driven insights with clarity and creativity. In this section, we'll explore the various ways Microsoft Whiteboard can be utilized to visualize complex data and reports, transforming them into actionable intelligence that is easy to understand.

1. Organizing Data on the Whiteboard

One of the greatest challenges in data visualization is organizing large datasets in a manner that tells a coherent story. Microsoft Whiteboard allows you to visually organize and structure information in real-time. You can start by laying out key data points, figures, or statistics in a way that makes them digestible for the team. Whether you're dealing with sales figures, project metrics, or user engagement data, you can group related data sets and create clear sections within your Whiteboard to help streamline the flow of information.

By using sticky notes, text boxes, and containers within the Whiteboard, you can label and categorize different pieces of data. This helps in simplifying complex reports by breaking them down into smaller, more manageable sections. For example, if you're presenting a quarterly sales report, you can dedicate one part of the Whiteboard to revenue, another to expenses, and another to customer acquisition metrics. This segmentation makes it easier to focus on specific areas of the report during discussions.

Additionally, Microsoft Whiteboard offers the flexibility to modify your visualization as the discussion evolves. As new insights are discovered or new data is presented, you can move, group, or annotate elements of the Whiteboard in real-time, allowing for a dynamic and interactive data exploration experience.

2. Creating Graphs and Charts

Graphs and charts are integral tools for presenting data visually. Microsoft Whiteboard doesn't have built-in chart creation tools like Excel, but it allows you to import graphs and charts from other applications like Excel or PowerPoint, making it easy to integrate existing visualizations into your Whiteboard session.

To get started, you can create the necessary graphs, such as bar charts, line charts, or pie charts, in Excel or PowerPoint and then copy and paste them into your Whiteboard. Once imported, these charts can be resized, annotated, and moved around as needed to fit within the overall context of your discussion. For instance, you can place a sales trend line chart next to a series of annotations explaining the key factors that influenced the results. This helps the team focus on the most important insights, rather than getting lost in numbers.

Moreover, Microsoft Whiteboard allows for freehand drawing, which can be helpful if you need to sketch out additional graphs or provide quick visual comparisons. For example, if you're discussing sales projections for the next quarter, you can quickly draw out a line graph, highlight potential growth areas, and use different colors to indicate various scenarios.

3. Importing and Annotating Reports

Microsoft Whiteboard supports the import of various file types, including PDFs and images. This feature is particularly useful when working with business reports that are already prepared in external applications. For example, if you have a financial report or a PowerPoint presentation summarizing key performance indicators, you can import these files into the Whiteboard to serve as the foundation for further discussion and analysis.

Once a report is imported, the team can annotate directly on the document, adding comments, suggestions, or highlighting key data points. Annotations can help clarify sections of the report that require further attention, mark areas for revision, or suggest actionable insights based on the data. For example, a report might show that sales have plateaued over the last two quarters. Team members can use the annotation tools to highlight this trend, add sticky notes with potential explanations, and brainstorm solutions in real time.

Annotations also allow for a deeper level of collaboration. If you're running a remote meeting, team members can simultaneously contribute to the report by adding their insights, comments, or suggestions directly on the Whiteboard. This feature enables everyone to participate equally, regardless of location, and ensures that all contributions are captured in the final version of the Whiteboard.

4. Data Storytelling and Presentations

Data visualization is not just about displaying numbers; it's about telling a story. Microsoft Whiteboard enables businesses to present data in a way that tells a cohesive, compelling narrative. With the flexibility of a digital canvas, you can create a visual journey that takes stakeholders from the initial data points through to the insights and recommendations.

Start by structuring your Whiteboard with an introduction, the core data, and the final takeaways. For instance, if you're reporting on the success of a marketing campaign, you can first outline the campaign goals, followed by the key performance metrics, and finally a conclusion based on the analysis of those metrics.

As you move through the presentation, you can use various Whiteboard tools, such as drawing arrows, circling important figures, or underlining key terms, to emphasize critical points. This level of interaction not only makes the presentation more engaging but also helps clarify complex data sets. You can involve the audience in the presentation by inviting them to contribute their thoughts or ask questions, further promoting a collaborative approach to data storytelling.

5. Collaborating on Data Insights in Real-Time

Microsoft Whiteboard shines as a collaborative tool, especially when analyzing data and generating insights. Real-time collaboration allows multiple users to work on the same Whiteboard simultaneously, meaning team members can collectively assess data, suggest improvements, and provide feedback during meetings.

For instance, if your team is analyzing a customer satisfaction report, different individuals can focus on different aspects of the report. One person might highlight customer feedback trends, while another focuses on the performance of specific product lines. This real-time interaction ensures that every angle is explored, leading to richer insights.

Teams can also use the brainstorming capabilities of Whiteboard to generate ideas based on the data. For example, after reviewing sales performance, the team might brainstorm strategies to improve the next quarter's results. Sticky notes can be used to jot down potential ideas, and those ideas can be grouped or prioritized directly on the Whiteboard.

6. Whiteboarding for Data-Driven Decision Making

Data-driven decision making is crucial in today's business environment, and Microsoft Whiteboard serves as a powerful tool to facilitate this process. Once your data is visualized and insights have been generated, the team can use the Whiteboard to discuss and vote on possible courses of action. Features like sticky notes, drawing tools, and templates for decision-making matrices can aid in structuring this discussion.

For example, after analyzing a report on product performance, you can create a decision-making matrix to evaluate the potential risks and benefits of launching a new product feature. Using sticky notes, team members can add their thoughts on each axis, and the group can collectively determine the best path forward.

This process ensures that decisions are based on well-organized data, thoughtful discussion, and the input of multiple team members, all of which is captured visually on the Whiteboard. This visual approach helps to eliminate confusion and ensures that everyone is aligned on the final decision.

7. Creating Dashboards with Microsoft Whiteboard

Another way to visualize data and reports is by creating dashboards on Microsoft Whiteboard. While the Whiteboard itself doesn't have dashboarding capabilities like Power BI, it can act as a collaborative dashboard space where multiple data sources are brought together for discussion. You can pull in visualizations from other tools and arrange them on the Whiteboard to create a comprehensive overview of business performance.

For example, you can import key graphs, charts, and KPIs from tools like Excel, Power BI, or other reporting platforms, and organize them in one section of your Whiteboard. Then, using sticky notes or text boxes, you can provide commentary, outline insights, and even assign action items based on the data. This approach creates an interactive, real-time dashboard that the entire team can reference and contribute to during meetings.

8. Using Templates for Reporting and Data Analysis

Microsoft Whiteboard includes a variety of templates that can be used to structure your reporting and data analysis activities. Whether you're conducting a SWOT analysis, a sales pipeline review, or a project post-mortem, templates can help standardize the process and ensure all important elements are covered.

You can customize these templates to fit your specific business needs. For example, if you're analyzing a sales report, you can use a pre-designed chart template and fill it in with your data points. This saves time and provides a clear framework for analyzing performance.

Templates also promote consistency across teams, ensuring that reports are structured similarly and that all important data points are considered in every discussion.

By using Microsoft Whiteboard effectively in business settings for visualizing data and reports, you can foster a more interactive, collaborative, and insightful data-driven environment. It empowers teams to organize and explore complex information, make informed decisions, and present compelling narratives in a visual format that is both engaging and accessible.

5.3 Whiteboard for Remote Work and Virtual Teams

The rise of remote work and virtual teams has transformed the way we collaborate and communicate. As physical presence is no longer necessary for meetings or brainstorming sessions, tools like Microsoft Whiteboard have become invaluable. In remote work settings, Microsoft Whiteboard facilitates real-time collaboration, visual communication, and brainstorming in a way that bridges the gap between geographically dispersed team members. This section explores the many ways in which Microsoft Whiteboard can enhance remote work and support virtual teams in maintaining productivity, creativity, and effective communication.

5.3.1 Enhancing Remote Meetings

Remote meetings can be challenging due to the lack of physical interaction and the inherent limitations of video conferencing tools. However, Microsoft Whiteboard introduces a new dimension to remote meetings by providing a shared digital space where team members can collaborate visually in real-time. Whether you're hosting a brainstorming session, planning a project, or working on a presentation, Microsoft Whiteboard enhances the remote meeting experience by allowing participants to contribute actively and creatively. Let's explore how Microsoft Whiteboard improves remote meetings and some best practices for maximizing its potential.

1. Real-Time Collaboration and Interaction

One of the biggest challenges in remote meetings is maintaining engagement and interaction among participants. Without physical presence, it's easy for team members to lose focus or feel disconnected from the conversation. Microsoft Whiteboard addresses this by offering real-time collaboration, allowing all participants to contribute simultaneously. Team members can draw, add sticky notes, annotate on existing content, and interact with the whiteboard, making meetings more dynamic and engaging.

For example, during a brainstorming session, everyone can contribute their ideas directly on the whiteboard using different colors or shapes. This not only keeps participants engaged but also allows everyone to visualize the flow of ideas. Moreover, the ability to interact in real time helps create a sense of unity, as if everyone were physically present in the same room.

Best Practice: To enhance real-time collaboration, encourage team members to use the drawing tools or sticky notes feature to jot down ideas. Use the color-coding option to distinguish between different participants' inputs.

2. Structured and Organized Discussions

Remote meetings can easily become disorganized, especially when multiple people are sharing ideas or discussing different aspects of a project. Microsoft Whiteboard helps bring structure to remote meetings by allowing organizers to create pre-defined sections on the board. You can divide the whiteboard into different areas for specific topics or agenda points, ensuring that discussions stay on track.

For instance, in a project planning meeting, you can allocate different sections of the whiteboard for tasks, timelines, and resource allocation. As the meeting progresses, team members can add their contributions in the relevant sections, keeping everything organized and easy to follow. This structured approach reduces confusion and makes remote meetings more efficient.

Best Practice: Before the meeting, prepare the whiteboard with sections dedicated to specific agenda items or discussion topics. This helps participants stay focused and ensures that no critical topics are overlooked.

3. Visualizing Complex Concepts

One of the challenges in remote work is explaining complex ideas or processes without being able to use physical whiteboards or hand gestures. Microsoft Whiteboard helps overcome this by allowing users to visualize complex concepts in real-time. You can create flowcharts, diagrams, or sketches to represent ideas clearly and concisely.

For example, during a product design meeting, you can use Microsoft Whiteboard to sketch out the initial design concepts, draw connections between different components, and get feedback from the team. The ability to visualize ideas makes it easier for team members to grasp complicated concepts and provide meaningful input.

Best Practice: Use the shapes and diagramming tools in Microsoft Whiteboard to create clear visual representations of processes, workflows, or ideas. This is particularly useful when discussing technical concepts or developing project plans.

4. Centralized Knowledge Sharing

In remote teams, sharing knowledge and resources is crucial to ensuring everyone stays on the same page. Microsoft Whiteboard serves as a centralized hub for meeting notes, diagrams, and ideas. Once the meeting concludes, the whiteboard can be saved, shared, and accessed by all team members for future reference.

For instance, if you're conducting a sprint planning session for an agile team, the whiteboard can be used to visualize the sprint goals, tasks, and timelines. After the meeting, you can save the whiteboard and share it with the team, ensuring that everyone has access to the same information and can refer back to it throughout the sprint.

Best Practice: Always save and share the whiteboard after each meeting. This ensures that any key takeaways, decisions, or action items are documented and accessible to everyone. Use Microsoft OneDrive or Teams to store and organize whiteboard files for easy access.

5. Enhancing Brainstorming Sessions

Remote brainstorming sessions can sometimes feel less spontaneous or productive compared to in-person sessions. However, Microsoft Whiteboard's flexibility makes it a powerful tool for virtual brainstorming. Team members can freely contribute ideas using drawing tools, sticky notes, or text, and ideas can be grouped, reorganized, or expanded upon in real-time.

Moreover, Microsoft Whiteboard offers templates that can help guide brainstorming sessions. Templates for mind maps, SWOT analysis, and flowcharts provide a starting point for teams to structure their brainstorming sessions more effectively.

For example, in a marketing brainstorming session, team members can use a mind map template to expand on a central campaign idea, adding branches for different strategies, target audiences, and content ideas. This collaborative process sparks creativity and helps generate more ideas in a remote environment.

Best Practice: Utilize the pre-built templates in Microsoft Whiteboard to guide brainstorming sessions. This provides structure while still allowing for free-flowing ideas. Encourage participants to use sticky notes for quick idea generation, then group related ideas together for further discussion.

6. Seamless Integration with Microsoft Teams

One of the standout features of Microsoft Whiteboard is its seamless integration with Microsoft Teams, making it an ideal tool for remote meetings. When hosting a meeting in Teams, you can easily launch a shared whiteboard, allowing all participants to interact with it during the meeting. This integration streamlines the process and eliminates the need for switching between multiple apps or platforms.

Additionally, the whiteboard remains accessible even after the meeting ends, ensuring that team members can revisit the content or continue collaborating on it asynchronously. This is particularly useful for teams spread across different time zones, as it allows collaboration to continue even outside of scheduled meeting times.

Best Practice: Use Microsoft Whiteboard within Teams to streamline remote meetings and collaboration. After meetings, encourage team members to continue adding to or refining the whiteboard content asynchronously. This is especially effective for ongoing projects or discussions.

7. Supporting Asynchronous Collaboration

In remote work environments, not all team members may be able to participate in meetings at the same time, especially when working across different time zones. Microsoft Whiteboard supports asynchronous collaboration, meaning that team members can contribute to the whiteboard at different times.

For example, if you're working on a global product launch plan, team members from different regions can add their inputs, suggestions, and updates to the whiteboard at their own convenience. The whiteboard serves as a living document that evolves as team members contribute over time.

Best Practice: Encourage asynchronous collaboration by allowing team members to contribute to the whiteboard outside of formal meetings. This ensures that everyone's input is captured, regardless of their time zone or availability. Use the "ink together" feature to highlight key contributions made asynchronously.

8. Enhancing Communication Across Teams

In remote teams, communication can often be less clear than in face-to-face interactions. Microsoft Whiteboard helps bridge this communication gap by providing a visual platform for teams to express their ideas. Instead of relying solely on verbal or written communication, team members can use diagrams, sketches, and notes to communicate more effectively.

For example, in a technical team meeting, developers can use the whiteboard to diagram system architectures or workflows, making it easier to explain complex systems to non-technical stakeholders. The combination of visual and verbal communication ensures that everyone has a clear understanding of the discussion.

Best Practice: Use Microsoft Whiteboard to complement verbal communication with visual elements. This is particularly useful for explaining complex ideas or when working with cross-functional teams where different areas of expertise are involved.

Conclusion

Microsoft Whiteboard is an indispensable tool for enhancing remote meetings and facilitating collaboration within virtual teams. Its real-time interaction features, combined with the ability to organize discussions, visualize ideas, and share knowledge, make it a powerful asset for remote work. By integrating Whiteboard into your remote meetings, you can increase engagement, improve communication, and foster a more collaborative team environment, no matter where your team members are located.

5.3.2 Collaborating Across Time Zones

In today's globalized business environment, teams are often spread across multiple time zones, making effective collaboration a challenge. Microsoft Whiteboard provides a unique solution to this issue by enabling real-time collaboration and asynchronous work. The platform is designed to bridge the gap between team members who may be hours apart, providing a shared space where ideas can be visually communicated, refined, and tracked, regardless of location or time zone.

The Importance of Time Zone Management

Collaboration across time zones brings both opportunities and challenges. On one hand, a geographically distributed team allows companies to have a round-the-clock workforce. On the other hand, coordinating efforts between individuals who may be working while others are sleeping can lead to delays, miscommunication, and a lack of real-time feedback. This is where Microsoft Whiteboard shines, as it offers flexible collaboration features that make time zone differences much easier to manage.

Whiteboard's ability to facilitate both synchronous and asynchronous work means that a team member can contribute to the whiteboard during their working hours, leave notes, drawings, or ideas, and then another team member in a different time zone can pick up where they left off. This can significantly enhance productivity and allow for smoother transitions between team members.

Real-Time Collaboration

One of Microsoft Whiteboard's core strengths is its real-time collaboration feature, allowing multiple users to work on the same whiteboard at once, regardless of their location. When team members are working across time zones but have some overlap in working hours, this feature becomes invaluable. The entire team can see updates made in real-time, including drawings, text, sticky notes, and other elements added to the board.

For example, a team in New York may start a brainstorming session in the morning. Colleagues in London can then join the session in the afternoon, view the ideas already presented, and build upon them. This shared whiteboard ensures everyone is on the same page, literally and figuratively, reducing the chances of miscommunication. Since Microsoft Whiteboard is cloud-based, the latest updates are always visible to everyone, making collaboration seamless even across vast time differences.

Asynchronous Collaboration

Microsoft Whiteboard's ability to support asynchronous collaboration is critical when working across different time zones, especially when there is little or no overlap in working hours. Team members can leave comments, annotations, or drawings that others can access and respond to later. This ensures that work can continue even when one part of the team is offline, eliminating the downtime that traditionally comes with time zone differences.

Imagine a design team spread between Tokyo, San Francisco, and Paris. The team in Tokyo could work on a project, leave detailed annotations on the whiteboard, and then the San Francisco team could pick up where they left off. Later, the Paris team could refine the work, adding new ideas and providing feedback on the previous contributions. Each team can contribute to the project during their local workday, yet the project continues to move forward around the clock.

Integrating Other Tools for Time Zone Collaboration

To maximize the potential of Microsoft Whiteboard for remote collaboration, it's beneficial to integrate other tools within the Microsoft 365 ecosystem. For example, Microsoft Teams can be used alongside Whiteboard for better communication and scheduling. Microsoft Teams provides features like shared calendars, time zone conversions, and scheduled meetings, which can be crucial for organizing team collaboration across time zones.

By embedding Microsoft Whiteboard into a Microsoft Teams meeting, you allow everyone to contribute to a live session, regardless of their location. This also ensures that all meeting participants, whether attending live or reviewing the recorded meeting later, can see the visual elements that were discussed during the session. Whiteboard's integration with OneNote and Outlook can also provide additional organizational features for managing tasks and keeping track of ongoing projects.

Overcoming Communication Barriers

One of the key challenges when collaborating across time zones is maintaining effective communication. In traditional work environments, team members can have face-to-face conversations or quickly clarify points via a phone call or meeting. In distributed teams, communication often relies on written messages or recorded video calls, which can lead to misinterpretation or delays in response time. Microsoft Whiteboard helps mitigate these issues by providing a visual platform where ideas can be expressed more clearly.

The use of visual elements such as drawings, diagrams, flowcharts, and sticky notes can help explain concepts that might be difficult to convey through text alone. This visual approach minimizes the risk of miscommunication and allows team members to quickly grasp complex ideas. Additionally, when working asynchronously, team members can use the Whiteboard to leave detailed explanations and visual cues, ensuring that their contributions are clear and easy to understand.

Managing Project Handovers Across Time Zones

Another common challenge when collaborating across time zones is managing project handovers. When one team finishes their workday, they need to pass their progress to another team in a different time zone to ensure continuity. Microsoft Whiteboard provides an ideal platform for these handovers by allowing team members to visually document their progress, leave instructions, and highlight areas that need further attention.

For example, a software development team in India might document their progress on a whiteboard, leaving detailed notes and diagrams for the team in the United States to review when they begin their day. The U.S. team can then pick up where the Indian team left off, ensuring that work continues smoothly without unnecessary delays. By using a shared visual space, teams can reduce the friction often associated with time zone handovers, improving overall productivity.

Best Practices for Whiteboard Use in Time Zone Collaboration

To maximize the effectiveness of Microsoft Whiteboard when working across time zones, consider implementing the following best practices:

1. Set Clear Guidelines for Asynchronous Collaboration

Ensure that all team members understand how and when to contribute to the whiteboard. Encourage team members to leave detailed annotations and instructions when they finish their work so that others can easily pick up where they left off.

2. Use Visual Cues to Highlight Key Areas

When leaving work for others to continue, use visual elements like arrows, highlighted text, or sticky notes to draw attention to important sections. This ensures that key points are not overlooked.

3. Incorporate Regular Check-Ins and Updates

Even in asynchronous collaborations, it's essential to have regular check-ins to ensure that everyone is aligned. Use Microsoft Teams or email to provide updates on the whiteboard's progress and clarify any potential issues.

4. Use Templates for Standardized Workflows

Microsoft Whiteboard allows for the creation of custom templates. If your team regularly collaborates across time zones, creating standardized templates for project handovers or brainstorming sessions can help streamline the process.

5. Leverage Microsoft Whiteboard's History Feature

The ability to see previous versions of the whiteboard can be useful when team members need to review earlier work or track changes. Encourage your team to take advantage of this feature to ensure nothing gets lost in the shuffle.

Leveraging Time Zone Differences to Your Advantage

Rather than viewing time zone differences as a barrier, teams can use tools like Microsoft Whiteboard to turn them into an advantage. By setting up an efficient asynchronous workflow, you can create a continuous cycle of work, where progress is made 24 hours a day. While one team finishes their workday, another begins, ensuring that projects move forward without interruption.

For instance, a product development team with members in Asia, Europe, and North America can operate in such a way that there's always someone working on a project. Using Microsoft Whiteboard as a central hub for collaboration ensures that everyone has access to the latest information and can contribute meaningfully to the project, regardless of time zone.

Conclusion

Microsoft Whiteboard's combination of real-time and asynchronous collaboration features makes it a powerful tool for remote teams working across time zones. Its cloud-based platform ensures that all team members have access to the same information, and its integration with other Microsoft 365 tools further enhances its utility for global collaboration. By implementing best practices and leveraging the platform's visual and collaborative capabilities, teams can overcome the challenges posed by time zone differences and work together effectively, no matter where they are in the world.

5.3.3 Effective Communication with Virtual Whiteboards

In today's fast-paced digital work environments, effective communication is critical for success, especially for remote teams. Virtual whiteboards, like Microsoft Whiteboard, offer an innovative platform for teams spread across different locations to collaborate in real time. This not only facilitates communication but also enhances productivity, enabling teams to brainstorm, plan, and solve problems more effectively.

In this section, we will explore how Microsoft Whiteboard can be utilized for clearer, more efficient communication in virtual workspaces, as well as best practices for maximizing its potential in a remote setting.

The Role of Visual Communication in Remote Work

One of the biggest challenges remote teams face is the lack of face-to-face interaction, which can lead to miscommunication or misunderstandings. While video calls and chats are helpful, they cannot fully replicate the immediacy and clarity of a live, in-person conversation. This is where visual communication tools like Microsoft Whiteboard come into play.

Visual communication bridges the gap between written and spoken language, allowing teams to express ideas and concepts through drawings, diagrams, and visual aids. Research shows that people process visual information more quickly than text, making tools like Whiteboard essential for remote teams needing to convey complex ideas succinctly.

For instance, instead of writing lengthy emails to explain a process, a team leader can simply draw a flowchart or diagram on Microsoft Whiteboard. This way, the entire team can visualize the workflow in real time, ask questions, and suggest modifications. This collaborative, visual method makes communication not only more effective but also more engaging for team members.

Key Features for Effective Communication with Microsoft Whiteboard

Microsoft Whiteboard offers a range of features designed to support and improve communication for remote teams. Here are some of the most useful ones for fostering collaboration and ensuring clarity in virtual meetings and projects.

1. Real-Time Collaboration

One of the most powerful features of Microsoft Whiteboard is its real-time collaboration functionality. This allows multiple users to access and work on the same whiteboard simultaneously, no matter where they are located. As team members draw, type, or add content, others can see these updates in real time, leading to a dynamic and interactive exchange of ideas.

Real-time collaboration enables immediate feedback. For instance, if a team member sketches a design or proposes a solution, other participants can quickly chime in, either by adding their own sketches, comments, or modifying the content on the board. This helps keep discussions fluid and ensures everyone is on the same page.

2. Sticky Notes for Feedback and Comments

Feedback is an essential aspect of effective communication, and Microsoft Whiteboard's sticky notes feature makes it easy to leave comments or suggestions without interrupting the flow of a meeting. During a brainstorming session, team members can use sticky notes to jot down their thoughts or highlight points they want to revisit.

Sticky notes are particularly helpful in remote teams as they allow asynchronous communication. Team members in different time zones can leave feedback or contribute to discussions without the need for immediate responses. When others come online, they can review the notes and add their input. This makes collaboration more inclusive and flexible.

3. Text and Drawing Tools for Clarity

Microsoft Whiteboard offers an array of text and drawing tools that help team members convey their ideas clearly and concisely. The text tool allows users to type content, ideal for labeling diagrams or providing additional context for visuals. Meanwhile, the drawing tools (pens, pencils, highlighters) let users express themselves in a more freeform way, perfect for sketching out concepts, diagrams, or even casual notes.

To make communication even more precise, team members can use the highlighter tool to emphasize key points, or the eraser tool to clean up and adjust their work as needed. The simplicity and flexibility of these tools help remote teams communicate without unnecessary distractions.

4. Shapes and Templates for Structured Communication

In addition to freehand drawing, Microsoft Whiteboard provides various shapes and templates to help organize information and facilitate structured communication. Shapes such as rectangles, circles, arrows, and lines can be used to create flowcharts, diagrams, and other visual aids that communicate complex processes or structures.

Templates, on the other hand, provide a pre-built framework for teams to use in meetings or brainstorming sessions. Templates for project planning, SWOT analysis, and problem-solving offer a clear path for communication, ensuring that conversations stay focused and organized.

Using templates is especially valuable in remote meetings where time is limited. They provide a clear starting point, enabling teams to jump into discussions without needing to set up structures manually. This helps streamline communication and ensures that everyone can follow along easily.

5. Integrating with Microsoft Teams

For remote work, Microsoft Whiteboard's integration with Microsoft Teams enhances communication even further. Teams is already a widely used platform for virtual meetings, and embedding Whiteboard into Teams meetings makes collaboration smoother.

During a video call, team members can open Microsoft Whiteboard and share it with participants in real time. This enables them to brainstorm together or illustrate concepts visually, even while having a face-to-face conversation over video. This integration breaks down the barrier between verbal and visual communication, making it easier for teams to express and share ideas.

The Teams integration also facilitates seamless sharing of whiteboards after meetings. Once a whiteboard is created, it can be saved and shared with the team, allowing members to revisit the content and add more notes or modifications even after the meeting ends.

Best Practices for Using Microsoft Whiteboard in Remote Teams

To get the most out of Microsoft Whiteboard and enhance communication in remote teams, it's important to follow certain best practices. These tips will help ensure that the whiteboard remains an effective tool rather than a source of confusion.

1. Establish Clear Objectives for the Whiteboard Session

Before starting a whiteboard session, it's important to establish clear objectives. Whether the goal is to brainstorm ideas, plan a project, or solve a specific problem, having a well-defined purpose helps keep the session focused. Without this clarity, whiteboard sessions can easily become disorganized, with too many unrelated ideas crowding the workspace.

Start the session by clearly communicating the objectives to all participants, and ensure that everyone is aligned on what the outcome should be. This not only streamlines communication but also helps ensure that the whiteboard is being used efficiently.

2. Create a Collaborative Environment

Fostering a sense of collaboration is key to making the most of Microsoft Whiteboard. Encourage all team members to contribute to the board, whether by adding ideas, giving feedback, or making adjustments to existing content. This inclusion helps create a sense of ownership and ensures that everyone's perspectives are considered.

As a team leader or facilitator, make sure to prompt quieter members to contribute by asking for their input directly or assigning them specific sections of the whiteboard to work on. This helps avoid situations where only a few team members dominate the conversation.

3. Use Color Coding and Labels for Clarity

To avoid confusion and keep the whiteboard organized, it's a good idea to use color coding and labels. Assign different colors to different team members or topics. For example, one color could represent ideas, another color could represent feedback, and a third color could represent action items.

Similarly, use labels to clearly mark different sections of the board or to categorize content. This is especially important in larger whiteboards with multiple ideas or diagrams. Labels make it easier to follow along, even if team members join the session later or review the whiteboard asynchronously.

4. Facilitate Asynchronous Collaboration

In a global work environment, team members often operate in different time zones. Microsoft Whiteboard supports asynchronous collaboration, meaning that team members can contribute at their own pace and time. Encourage asynchronous participation by leaving clear instructions and questions on the whiteboard for others to address later.

Make use of sticky notes or text boxes to leave comments or requests for feedback. When team members come online, they can review the notes, make changes, or add their ideas without needing to be in the same meeting at the same time. This flexibility ensures that communication continues smoothly across time zones.

5. Review and Consolidate Ideas After the Session

Once the whiteboard session is complete, it's important to review and consolidate the ideas discussed. Assign one person to clean up the board, ensuring that key takeaways, action points, and important ideas are organized and easy to find. This helps prevent the whiteboard from becoming too cluttered and ensures that the team has a clear understanding of the next steps.

You can also save the whiteboard and distribute it to the team via Microsoft Teams or other channels. This serves as a reference point for future discussions and keeps everyone aligned on the progress made during the session.

Conclusion

Effective communication is the foundation of successful remote teams, and Microsoft Whiteboard is a powerful tool for facilitating this communication. By leveraging its real-time collaboration features, visual tools, and seamless integration with Microsoft Teams, remote teams can communicate more clearly, engage more actively, and work more efficiently.

Incorporating best practices such as setting clear objectives, encouraging collaboration, using color coding, and facilitating asynchronous participation can further enhance the effectiveness of Microsoft Whiteboard in virtual settings. As remote work continues to evolve, tools like Microsoft Whiteboard will play an increasingly important role in how teams communicate, collaborate, and achieve their goals.

CHAPTER VI Troubleshooting and Tips for Success

6.1 Common Issues and How to Fix Them

6.1.1 Syncing Problems

One of the most common issues users face when working with Microsoft Whiteboard, particularly in a cloud-based environment, is syncing problems. Since Microsoft Whiteboard operates largely as a collaborative tool, relying on cloud storage and real-time updates, syncing is crucial for seamless performance. Syncing ensures that any changes made to a whiteboard—whether it's text, images, drawings, or annotations—are reflected in real-time across all devices and for all participants. However, when syncing issues arise, it can disrupt the collaborative flow, cause data loss, or prevent the most up-to-date version of the whiteboard from being accessed.

In this section, we'll explore the various causes of syncing problems, the steps to troubleshoot them, and how to prevent future syncing issues from occurring. We'll cover:

- Causes of Syncing Problems
- Verifying Network Connectivity
- Ensuring Proper Login Credentials
- Managing Cloud Storage Issues
- Troubleshooting Mobile Device Syncing

- Fixing Sync Problems on Desktop

- Advanced Syncing Solutions

- Preventing Syncing Issues in the Future

Causes of Syncing Problems

Syncing issues can stem from a variety of factors. Common causes include poor or unstable internet connections, issues with Microsoft's cloud servers, device storage limitations, or errors in user authentication. To effectively troubleshoot, it's essential to first identify the root cause. Some frequent sources of syncing problems are:

- Internet Connectivity: Poor or intermittent internet connection can disrupt syncing. Since Whiteboard depends on a stable online connection to sync with the cloud, any fluctuations can result in data not updating in real time.

- Cloud Storage Problems: Microsoft Whiteboard syncs its data through OneDrive or other cloud services, depending on your setup. If there is a storage issue (e.g., your OneDrive is full), Whiteboard may not be able to sync correctly.

- Login and Account Problems: Syncing is tied to the user's Microsoft account. If there's an issue with logging into your Microsoft account, such as incorrect credentials or account permissions, it can prevent syncing.

- Device-Specific Errors: Syncing problems can also be caused by device-specific issues such as software bugs, outdated apps, or device settings that interfere with proper syncing.

- Server-Side Problems: Occasionally, the issue may lie with Microsoft's cloud servers, which can experience downtime or technical glitches that hinder syncing.

Understanding these causes is the first step to troubleshooting.

Verifying Network Connectivity

The most fundamental requirement for syncing is a stable internet connection. If Microsoft Whiteboard cannot connect to the internet, it cannot sync changes with the cloud, resulting in discrepancies between devices. Here's how you can check and address network issues:

1. Check Internet Speed: Use an internet speed test tool to check if your connection is stable and fast enough. Microsoft Whiteboard requires a consistent connection, so a slow or frequently interrupted network can cause syncing delays or failures.

2. Switch Network Connections: If you're experiencing connectivity issues, try switching from Wi-Fi to a wired Ethernet connection or another Wi-Fi network. Sometimes, local network issues, such as interference or bandwidth congestion, can disrupt syncing.

3. Disable VPNs or Firewalls: Virtual Private Networks (VPNs) or firewalls can sometimes interfere with the syncing process. Temporarily disable these services to see if it resolves the issue. Ensure your firewall is not blocking Microsoft Whiteboard's communication with the internet.

4. Reconnect to the Network: Disconnecting and reconnecting to your network can resolve minor glitches. If possible, restart your router to refresh your connection.

5. Check for Offline Mode: Make sure Microsoft Whiteboard is not in offline mode, as this will prevent syncing. In offline mode, changes will only sync once you reconnect to the internet.

Ensuring Proper Login Credentials

Another frequent cause of syncing problems is user authentication issues. Since Microsoft Whiteboard requires you to be signed into a Microsoft account to sync, any login-related problems can affect syncing. Here are the steps to resolve authentication issues:

1. Verify Your Login Information: Double-check that you are logged into the correct Microsoft account. If you have multiple accounts (e.g., personal, work, school), ensure you are signed into the correct one that is linked to the Whiteboard you are trying to sync.

2. Sign Out and Sign Back In: Sometimes, signing out of Microsoft Whiteboard and signing back in can refresh your account permissions and fix syncing problems. To do this:

- Open the Microsoft Whiteboard app.
- Go to your account settings.
- Select "Sign Out" and then "Sign In" again using the correct credentials.

3. Check Account Permissions: If you're using a work or school account, make sure your account has the necessary permissions to sync with OneDrive or the organization's cloud storage. Contact your IT administrator if you believe your account is restricted.

4. Check for Account Lockouts: In some cases, your Microsoft account might be temporarily locked due to security reasons (e.g., too many failed login attempts). If this happens, follow the instructions provided by Microsoft to unlock your account.

Managing Cloud Storage Issues

Microsoft Whiteboard saves its data on OneDrive or another cloud service, depending on your account type. If there's an issue with your cloud storage, syncing will not work correctly. Here are ways to troubleshoot cloud storage problems:

1. Check Available Storage: Ensure that you have enough storage space on your OneDrive or cloud service. If your storage is full, Whiteboard will be unable to sync new data. You can free up space by:

- Deleting old files.
- Upgrading your storage plan with Microsoft.

2. Sync with the Correct Cloud Service: If your organization uses a different cloud service (such as SharePoint), ensure that your Whiteboard is syncing with the right cloud provider. Check your account settings to confirm the correct service is selected.

3. Monitor Cloud Service Status: Occasionally, cloud services may experience outages. If you suspect this is the case, check Microsoft's service status page to see if there are any ongoing issues. You can also monitor OneDrive or SharePoint to ensure they're fully operational.

Troubleshooting Mobile Device Syncing

If you're using Microsoft Whiteboard on a mobile device (e.g., phone or tablet), there are additional factors to consider that could cause syncing problems. Here are troubleshooting steps specific to mobile devices:

1. Update the App: Make sure you're using the latest version of Microsoft Whiteboard. Syncing problems can occur if the app is outdated. Visit the App Store (iOS) or Google Play (Android) to check for updates.

2. Check Mobile Data Permissions: If you're using a mobile device, ensure that Microsoft Whiteboard has the proper permissions to use cellular data. Go to your device's settings and enable mobile data for the app if needed.

3. Switch Between Wi-Fi and Cellular Data: If syncing isn't working on Wi-Fi, try switching to mobile data to see if the issue persists. Sometimes, network-specific settings on mobile can disrupt syncing.

4. Clear App Cache: On mobile devices, app cache data can sometimes interfere with syncing. Clear the cache for Microsoft Whiteboard by going to your device settings and finding the Whiteboard app in the "Apps" or "Storage" section. After clearing the cache, restart the app and check if the issue is resolved.

Fixing Sync Problems on Desktop

For desktop or laptop users, there are several specific troubleshooting steps to resolve syncing issues:

1. Check for Software Updates: Ensure that both your operating system and the Microsoft Whiteboard app are up-to-date. Outdated software can often cause syncing problems. If updates are available, install them and restart your device.

2. Reset the Whiteboard App: If the syncing problem persists, consider resetting the app. Here's how to do it on Windows:

- Open Settings > Apps > Apps & features.
- Scroll down to find Microsoft Whiteboard.
- Select Advanced options and click Reset.
- After resetting, log back in and check if syncing works.

3. Use the Web Version of Microsoft Whiteboard: If the desktop app is having trouble syncing, try accessing the Whiteboard via the web at whiteboard.microsoft.com. Sometimes, the web version may sync properly even when the app doesn't.

Advanced Syncing Solutions

If basic troubleshooting steps don't solve the problem, you may need to explore more advanced solutions:

1. Check for Corrupt Files: In rare cases, a corrupt file or element within the Whiteboard may prevent syncing. If you suspect this is the case, create a new Whiteboard and gradually copy over the elements from the old one. This can help isolate the problematic component.

2. Reinstall the App: If all else fails, uninstall Microsoft Whiteboard and reinstall it. This process can resolve deep-rooted syncing issues that may be caused by corrupted installation files.

Preventing Syncing Issues in the Future

While syncing problems can be frustrating, there are proactive steps you can take to prevent them from occurring again:

1. Maintain a Stable Internet Connection: Whenever possible, use a reliable, high-speed internet connection to avoid interruptions during syncing.

2. Regularly Update Software: Keeping your apps and operating systems up-to-date can prevent compatibility issues and bugs that may interfere with syncing.

3. Monitor Cloud Storage Usage: Periodically check your OneDrive or cloud storage to ensure you have enough available space.

This helps prevent issues caused by full storage.

4. Backup Your Whiteboards: Although Microsoft Whiteboard automatically saves your data in the cloud, it's good practice to periodically export important whiteboards as images or PDFs. This ensures you have a backup in case of sync failures.

In conclusion, syncing problems with Microsoft Whiteboard can often be resolved by addressing internet connectivity, login credentials, cloud storage issues, or device-specific factors. By following the steps outlined above, users can troubleshoot and resolve these issues, ensuring a smooth and seamless experience with Microsoft Whiteboard.

6.1.2 Performance and Speed Issues

Microsoft Whiteboard is a powerful tool designed for seamless collaboration and creativity. However, as with any software, users may occasionally experience performance and speed issues. These problems can be frustrating, especially when they disrupt collaborative efforts or cause delays in real-time sessions. This section explores the common performance and speed issues that users encounter and provides detailed solutions to resolve them, ensuring smoother operation and improved efficiency when using Microsoft Whiteboard.

Causes of Performance and Speed Issues

Before diving into the solutions, it's essential to understand the potential causes of performance and speed issues in Microsoft Whiteboard. Identifying the root causes can help target the problem more effectively. Some common causes include:

1. Network Connectivity: Microsoft Whiteboard is a cloud-based tool, meaning its performance is heavily dependent on a stable internet connection. Weak or unstable connections can result in slow loading times, delays in syncing, and lag during real-time collaboration.

2. Device Specifications: The performance of Microsoft Whiteboard can vary depending on the device's specifications. Low-end devices with limited RAM, CPU power, or older operating systems may struggle to run Whiteboard efficiently, leading to slower response times.

3. Whiteboard Complexity: The more complex a whiteboard becomes, with multiple drawings, images, and objects, the more processing power is required. Large and content-heavy whiteboards can cause the application to slow down, particularly on lower-spec devices or under suboptimal network conditions.

4. Browser or Application Issues: Users accessing Microsoft Whiteboard through a browser may experience performance problems due to browser compatibility issues, outdated browser versions, or an overloaded browser cache. Additionally, using multiple tabs with other resource-heavy applications can affect the overall performance.

5. Background Processes: Other applications running in the background can consume significant system resources, affecting the performance of Microsoft Whiteboard. For instance, applications such as video conferencing tools, virtual private networks (VPNs), or cloud backup services can strain bandwidth and computing resources.

6. Outdated Software: Running an outdated version of Microsoft Whiteboard or the operating system can introduce performance issues. Microsoft regularly releases updates

to improve the app's efficiency, security, and features, and failing to keep up with these updates can result in poor performance.

Solutions to Performance and Speed Issues

Here are some practical solutions to address performance and speed issues in Microsoft Whiteboard. These troubleshooting steps can help mitigate any problems and ensure optimal performance, whether you are working on a simple personal project or managing a collaborative whiteboard with a team.

1. Check and Optimize Internet Connection

As Microsoft Whiteboard relies on cloud-based functionality, a stable and high-speed internet connection is crucial. Follow these steps to check and improve your connection:

- Run a Speed Test: Use a speed test tool to verify your internet connection's speed and stability. Look for download and upload speeds of at least 5 Mbps for basic functionality and 10+ Mbps for real-time collaboration.

- Connect to a Wired Network: If you are using Wi-Fi, switching to a wired connection can reduce latency and improve speed. Ethernet connections provide a more stable and consistent connection than Wi-Fi, especially in environments with multiple users sharing the same wireless network.

- Limit Bandwidth Consumption: If you are working in an environment with other devices connected to the same network, limit bandwidth-hogging activities like video streaming, file downloads, or cloud backups.

- Restart Router: Restarting your router or modem can sometimes resolve connectivity issues. If your router is old, consider upgrading to a newer model with better bandwidth management capabilities.

- Use a VPN with Caution: If you are using a VPN, be aware that it may slow down your internet connection. Consider temporarily disabling it when working on Microsoft Whiteboard if your connection is lagging.

2. Upgrade Device Specifications

If performance issues persist, it could be due to the limitations of your device's hardware. Consider upgrading or optimizing your system:

- Upgrade RAM: If your computer has limited RAM, consider upgrading to at least 8 GB for improved performance. Additional RAM allows for smoother multitasking, especially when dealing with large whiteboards with complex elements.

- Upgrade to SSD: Switching from a traditional hard drive (HDD) to a solid-state drive (SSD) can significantly improve your device's overall performance, including faster loading times for applications and files.

- Close Unnecessary Applications: When working with Microsoft Whiteboard, close unnecessary background applications that might be consuming system resources. Video conferencing tools, virtual machines, and large file transfers are common culprits.

- Ensure Your Device Meets Minimum Requirements: Ensure your device meets the minimum system requirements for Microsoft Whiteboard. If your device is outdated or underpowered, it may struggle to run the application efficiently. If upgrading the hardware is not an option, consider using a less resource-intensive device for Whiteboard tasks, such as a newer tablet or laptop.

3. Optimize Whiteboard Complexity

If the whiteboard itself is the source of performance issues, try simplifying the content to reduce strain on the application:

- Limit the Number of Objects: Excessive objects, such as images, text boxes, and shapes, can cause the whiteboard to slow down. Try to limit the number of objects or consolidate them whenever possible. For example, instead of adding individual shapes, consider grouping them together to reduce complexity.

- Resize or Compress Images: Large image files can significantly slow down Microsoft Whiteboard. Before uploading images, resize or compress them to reduce their file size without sacrificing too much quality. Many free online tools can help with this process.

- Organize Content into Multiple Whiteboards: Instead of packing everything into a single whiteboard, break up your content into multiple smaller whiteboards. This approach can reduce load times and make it easier to navigate through the information. For instance, if you're conducting a brainstorming session, create separate whiteboards for each category or idea.

- Utilize Templates Wisely: While templates are an excellent feature for organizing information, overloading a template with too much content can affect performance. Use templates strategically and avoid overloading them with excessive text, images, or complex designs.

4. Optimize Browser or Application Settings

If you are accessing Microsoft Whiteboard through a browser, consider optimizing browser settings to improve performance:

- Clear Browser Cache: Over time, cached files can build up in your browser, causing it to slow down. Regularly clearing your browser cache can improve performance. In most browsers, you can find this option in the settings under "Privacy and Security."

- Update Your Browser: Make sure you are using the latest version of your browser. Outdated versions may have performance issues or compatibility problems with Microsoft Whiteboard. Most browsers will automatically update, but it's worth checking manually to ensure you're running the latest version.

- Limit Browser Extensions: Browser extensions and add-ons can slow down performance. Try disabling unnecessary extensions while using Microsoft Whiteboard. If you are using resource-heavy extensions like ad blockers, consider turning them off temporarily.

- Use Dedicated Desktop App: Microsoft Whiteboard also has a dedicated desktop app. If you are experiencing performance issues in the browser version, try switching to the desktop app, which may offer better stability and performance.

5. Manage Background Processes

Background processes running on your device can consume valuable system resources, affecting the performance of Microsoft Whiteboard. Here's how to manage background tasks more effectively:

- Use Task Manager (Windows) or Activity Monitor (Mac): Use these tools to monitor the resources your device is using. You can identify which applications are consuming the most memory, CPU, or disk resources. Once identified, close any unnecessary applications or processes.

- Pause Cloud Sync Services: Cloud services like OneDrive, Google Drive, or Dropbox often run in the background, syncing files and consuming bandwidth. Consider pausing these services temporarily when using Microsoft Whiteboard to free up resources.

- Close Unused Browser Tabs: If you have multiple browser tabs open, each one is using system resources. Close any unused tabs to help improve performance.

- Optimize Power Settings: If you are using a laptop, switch to "High Performance" mode in your device's power settings. This setting ensures your device is using its full processing power, although it may reduce battery life.

6. Update Software Regularly

Running outdated software can result in performance issues and security vulnerabilities. It's essential to keep your software up to date:

- Update Microsoft Whiteboard: Ensure you are running the latest version of Microsoft Whiteboard. Updates often include performance improvements, bug fixes, and new features. If you are using the app on a desktop, check for updates through the Microsoft Store or directly within the app. For browser users, Microsoft automatically rolls out updates to the online version.

- Update Your Operating System: Keeping your operating system updated ensures compatibility with the latest versions of Microsoft Whiteboard. Both Windows and macOS regularly release updates that improve system performance and security.

- Check for Driver Updates: Ensure that your graphics drivers, network adapters, and other essential components are updated. Outdated drivers can lead to performance bottlenecks and crashes when using resource-intensive applications like Microsoft Whiteboard.

By following these steps, you can significantly reduce performance and speed issues when using Microsoft Whiteboard, allowing for a more seamless and efficient experience. Whether you're using Whiteboard for personal brainstorming or team collaboration, ensuring optimal performance will enhance your productivity and overall satisfaction with the tool.

6.1.3 Connectivity Troubleshooting

Microsoft Whiteboard, like any cloud-based application, relies heavily on stable internet connectivity to function effectively. When users face connectivity issues, it can disrupt collaborative workflows, cause loss of data, or prevent real-time updates from being shared between team members. Connectivity problems can stem from various factors including poor network conditions, firewall restrictions, or even issues within the Microsoft ecosystem itself.

This section addresses the common causes of connectivity problems with Microsoft Whiteboard and offers practical solutions to resolve these issues.

1. Identifying the Issue

Before diving into solutions, it's important to first understand the exact nature of the connectivity issue. Some common signs of connectivity problems in Microsoft Whiteboard include:

- Delayed synchronization: Whiteboard content takes too long to sync across devices.

- Missing updates: Changes made by collaborators aren't visible in real-time.

- Intermittent disconnections: The user is frequently disconnected and reconnected to the Whiteboard session.

- Failure to load: Microsoft Whiteboard may not load, or users may be unable to access specific whiteboards.

The first step is identifying whether the problem is due to local network issues, system restrictions, or an issue with Microsoft's services.

2. Checking Network Connectivity

Start by verifying your internet connection. A slow or unstable network can result in poor performance or connection failures in Microsoft Whiteboard. Follow these steps to ensure your network connection is reliable:

- Test your internet speed: Use an online speed test tool to check if your internet connection is delivering the expected speed. A slow connection may not support the data transfer needs of real-time collaboration tools.

- Switch networks if possible: If you're using a Wi-Fi network that appears unreliable, consider switching to a different network or using a wired Ethernet connection, which typically provides more stable and faster internet access.

- Restart your router/modem: Sometimes, connectivity issues can be resolved by simply rebooting your router or modem to reset the connection.

- Use a network diagnostic tool: Many operating systems come with built-in network diagnostic tools that can help identify issues with your connection.

3. Firewall and Proxy Settings

Firewalls or network security settings can sometimes block Microsoft Whiteboard's ability to connect to Microsoft's servers. This can result in a failure to load whiteboards, sync issues, or connection drops during sessions.

- Check firewall settings: If your organization uses a firewall, make sure that Microsoft Whiteboard is allowed through. You might need to consult with your IT administrator if you're unsure how to adjust firewall settings.

- Whitelisting Microsoft services: To ensure seamless connectivity, ensure that all Microsoft Whiteboard-related URLs and services (such as those related to Microsoft 365) are whitelisted in your firewall and network security software.

- Adjust proxy settings: If your organization uses a proxy server, ensure that it is configured to allow Microsoft Whiteboard traffic. You may need to update the proxy settings in your device's network settings or consult with your network administrator.

4. Checking Microsoft 365 Status

At times, the issue may not be on your end but with Microsoft's own cloud services. Microsoft Whiteboard is integrated with the broader Microsoft 365 ecosystem, and connectivity issues can arise if Microsoft's servers are experiencing problems.

- Check the Microsoft 365 Service Health Dashboard: This tool can help determine whether Microsoft Whiteboard or other Microsoft services are experiencing outages or performance issues. If the issue is on Microsoft's side, you may need to wait until the problem is resolved by their support team.

- Follow Microsoft Support Channels: In case of widespread connectivity issues, Microsoft often provides real-time updates through its official support channels, including Twitter, forums, and the Office 365 Admin Center.

5. Restarting Microsoft Whiteboard

If the above solutions do not resolve the issue, you may need to restart the Microsoft Whiteboard application to refresh the connection. Sometimes, cached data or a minor bug within the app can disrupt connectivity, and a simple restart can resolve the problem.

- Close and reopen the Whiteboard app: Whether you're using Microsoft Whiteboard on Windows, iOS, or via the web, close the application completely and then reopen it. This can reset the connection and allow the app to reconnect to Microsoft's servers.

- Sign out and sign back in: If restarting the app doesn't work, try signing out of your Microsoft account and then signing back in. This can refresh your session and clear any temporary issues with your account's connection to the Whiteboard service.

6. Clearing Cache and Temporary Files

Over time, cache files and temporary data can build up and cause issues with Microsoft Whiteboard, including connectivity problems. Clearing the cache can help resolve these issues by forcing the app to reload data from the cloud rather than relying on outdated local files.

- On Windows: Open the Settings menu, go to "Apps," find Microsoft Whiteboard, and select "Advanced Options." Here, you can clear the app's cache or reset the app entirely.

- On iOS: You can clear the cache by uninstalling and reinstalling the app, which forces the app to download fresh data when you log in again.

- On Web: Clear your browser's cache if you're using the web version of Microsoft Whiteboard. You can do this by going to your browser's settings and choosing the option to clear cache and cookies.

7. Software and Firmware Updates

Sometimes connectivity issues arise because of outdated software or firmware. It's essential to keep both your device's operating system and the Microsoft Whiteboard app updated to the latest version to avoid compatibility problems.

- Update the Microsoft Whiteboard app: Make sure you are using the latest version of the app by checking for updates in your device's app store or Microsoft Store.

- Update your operating system: Ensure that your operating system (Windows, iOS, etc.) is fully updated, as system updates often include important fixes for networking and connectivity issues.

- Update your network drivers and firmware: If you are experiencing persistent network issues, check that your device's network drivers are up-to-date. For users on Wi-Fi, ensuring that your router's firmware is updated can also help resolve connectivity issues.

8. Checking Device Compatibility

Ensure that your device meets the minimum requirements for running Microsoft Whiteboard smoothly. Older devices or devices with insufficient hardware specifications may struggle to maintain a stable connection, especially during heavy collaboration sessions.

- Device requirements: Ensure that your device has adequate memory (RAM), processing power (CPU), and storage to run the Whiteboard app without issues.

- Optimize your device for performance: Closing other apps and processes that may be consuming network or system resources can help free up capacity for Microsoft Whiteboard.

9. Reinstalling Microsoft Whiteboard

If none of the above solutions resolve the connectivity issue, it may be necessary to uninstall and reinstall Microsoft Whiteboard. This ensures that any corrupted files or settings are cleared, and a fresh installation may resolve any underlying issues.

- Uninstall the app: Follow your device's instructions to uninstall Microsoft Whiteboard.

- Reinstall the app: Download and install the latest version of the app from the official app store or Microsoft website.

- Sign in again: After reinstalling, sign in with your Microsoft account and check if the connectivity issue is resolved.

10. Contacting Microsoft Support

If all else fails, and you continue to experience connectivity problems, the issue may be more complex and require professional assistance. Contact Microsoft Support for further guidance, providing as much detail as possible about the issue you're facing, including error messages, screenshots, and steps you've already taken to resolve the problem.

- Use the Microsoft Whiteboard Help Center: Visit the official Microsoft Whiteboard help page for detailed guides and troubleshooting steps.

- Submit a support ticket: Through the Microsoft 365 admin center or Microsoft support website, you can open a support ticket for more personalized help.

- Check online forums: Microsoft support forums and communities often provide solutions for specific issues that may not be covered in the official documentation.

By following the steps outlined above, most users should be able to resolve common connectivity issues in Microsoft Whiteboard. Whether it's a network configuration problem or a local app issue, these troubleshooting tips provide a comprehensive approach to identifying and fixing the root cause of the problem. Maintaining stable connectivity ensures that you can fully leverage Microsoft Whiteboard's collaboration and productivity features, keeping your workflow smooth and uninterrupted.

6.2 Best Practices for Efficient Use

Efficient use of Microsoft Whiteboard can significantly improve productivity, collaboration, and organization in both personal and professional environments. Understanding best practices will ensure that users are not only comfortable with the platform but are also maximizing its potential. This section delves into methods and strategies that will help users organize their whiteboards, enhance collaboration, and streamline workflow.

6.2.1 Organizing Your Whiteboards

Organization is key to making the most of Microsoft Whiteboard. As the number of whiteboards increases—whether for personal projects, professional meetings, or educational lessons—it can become challenging to keep track of ideas and tasks without a clear organizational structure. In this section, we will explore how to efficiently manage, structure, and access your whiteboards.

The Importance of Whiteboard Organization

A cluttered workspace, whether physical or digital, can negatively affect productivity. When working with multiple whiteboards, it's easy to create a chaotic digital environment that slows down workflows and makes it difficult to locate specific information. The more organized your whiteboards are, the easier it will be to navigate between projects and tasks, saving time and reducing frustration. Organizing your whiteboards ensures that your content is accessible, structured, and easy to manage.

Naming Conventions

One of the simplest yet most effective ways to keep whiteboards organized is by adopting a consistent naming convention. Just like with folders and files on your computer, naming whiteboards based on their purpose or content makes them easier to identify at a glance. It's recommended to use clear, descriptive names that provide context for the whiteboard's purpose. For example:

- "Marketing Team Meeting - September 2024"

- "Brainstorming Session - Product Development"

- "Classroom Lesson - Biology Unit 3"

By adopting a standardized naming system, you can avoid confusion when searching through multiple boards. Additionally, it is helpful to include dates, version numbers, or project names in the title to further categorize and differentiate whiteboards.

Creating and Managing Folders

Microsoft Whiteboard integrates with OneDrive and Microsoft Teams, allowing users to create folders for storing and managing multiple whiteboards. Folders are essential for grouping related boards together, such as those used for a particular project, department, or academic course. Consider creating folders with the following structure:

- Work Projects: Group whiteboards based on projects you're working on with different teams.

- Education: Group whiteboards for different courses, lessons, or subjects.

- Personal: Separate personal boards from professional or educational ones for clarity.

Inside each folder, you can organize the boards chronologically or by category, ensuring you can easily find the board you're looking for when needed. Regularly review and update your folders to maintain order and remove outdated or irrelevant whiteboards. This will ensure that your digital workspace stays clutter-free and organized.

Using Templates for Standardization

For repeated processes, such as weekly meetings or brainstorming sessions, consider using templates to maintain consistency. Microsoft Whiteboard offers built-in templates for various purposes, including project management, brainstorming, and lesson planning. Using these templates can streamline your workflow by reducing the amount of time spent setting up a new board.

For example, a template for weekly team meetings might include sections for "Agenda," "Notes," "Tasks," and "Follow-Up." This ensures that each meeting follows the same structure and makes it easier to review and retrieve relevant information later on.

Color-Coding for Quick Reference

Microsoft Whiteboard allows users to color-code sticky notes, shapes, and sections of the board. Leveraging color as a visual organizational tool can greatly enhance clarity and make navigating whiteboards more intuitive. Here are a few examples of how to use color coding effectively:

- Task Management: Assign colors to different types of tasks. For example, use red for urgent tasks, yellow for pending tasks, and green for completed tasks.

- Project Phases: For a project whiteboard, use different colors to represent each phase of the project, such as planning, execution, and review.

- Team Members: If collaborating with multiple people, assign each participant a unique color for their contributions to easily differentiate inputs.

The consistent use of color can provide instant visual cues, making it easier to scan a board and locate relevant information. It also creates a structured and visually appealing whiteboard, reducing clutter and improving overall readability.

Sectioning and Grouping

One of the strengths of Microsoft Whiteboard is its infinite canvas, allowing you to expand your board as much as needed. However, this flexibility can lead to sprawling, disorganized boards if not managed properly. To avoid this, it's important to section and group content logically.

- Use Frames: Just as you would group related notes or images on a physical board, group similar elements together on your digital whiteboard. For instance, in a brainstorming session, you might group all ideas related to marketing in one section and those related to product development in another.

- Create Visual Dividers: Use shapes or lines as dividers between different sections of the board. This will help create clear boundaries and make it easier to separate content, especially when collaborating with multiple people on the same board.

- Hierarchy of Information: When presenting information, establish a hierarchy with the most important information prominently displayed. For example, create larger or bolder sections for key ideas and smaller areas for secondary information. This helps ensure that the focus remains on the main points of the board.

By keeping your whiteboard organized into distinct sections, you can prevent information overload and maintain a clear focus on the task at hand.

Pinning Frequently Used Whiteboards

In Microsoft Whiteboard, you can pin important or frequently accessed boards to the top of your dashboard, ensuring quick access. This feature is particularly useful if you're juggling multiple projects or tasks, as it allows you to prioritize key boards without scrolling through a long list.

- Project Boards: If you're working on a long-term project, pin the related whiteboard(s) for easy access during meetings or brainstorming sessions.

- Templates: Pinning commonly used templates will save time when creating new whiteboards for recurring tasks.

- Ongoing Collaborations: Pin boards shared with teams for ongoing collaborations, making it easy to jump back into projects.

Once a board is no longer needed frequently, you can unpin it to declutter your dashboard while still retaining access to it through the main whiteboard list.

Regular Maintenance and Cleanup

Over time, whiteboards can become cluttered, just like physical workspaces. To maintain efficiency, it's important to regularly review and clean up your boards. Dedicate time at the end of each week or month to go through your whiteboards and:

- Delete or Archive: Remove boards that are no longer relevant, or move them to an archive folder if you might need them later.

- Consolidate Information: Combine multiple whiteboards if they contain overlapping or related content to reduce redundancy.

- Update Information: Ensure that each board's content is current, and remove outdated notes or ideas.

By conducting regular maintenance, you ensure that your workspace remains clean, organized, and efficient, allowing you to focus on the tasks that matter most.

Access and Security Considerations

If you are working with sensitive or confidential information, it's important to consider the security settings of your whiteboards. Microsoft Whiteboard allows users to control access and permissions for each board. Some best practices include:

- Restrict Access: Limit access to specific team members or collaborators who need to be involved. This prevents unnecessary edits or visibility by those not associated with the project.

- Set Permissions: Assign roles, such as viewer or editor, depending on the involvement level of each collaborator. Viewers can observe the content without making changes, while editors can actively contribute.

- Monitor Activity: Regularly review the activity logs to track any changes made to the whiteboard. This ensures that all edits are intentional and made by authorized users.

In collaborative environments, especially those involving sensitive data, maintaining control over access and permissions is critical for protecting your work and ensuring smooth collaboration.

By implementing these best practices for organizing your whiteboards, you can streamline your workflow, improve efficiency, and maintain clarity within your projects. A well-organized whiteboard not only enhances your own productivity but also creates a more collaborative and cohesive environment for teams working together.

6.2.2 Optimizing for Collaboration

Microsoft Whiteboard is a powerful tool for teamwork, allowing multiple users to engage simultaneously in brainstorming sessions, planning, and visual collaboration. Whether you're using Whiteboard in an office environment, for educational purposes, or in remote work settings, optimizing it for effective collaboration is crucial. Here, we'll explore best practices and strategies to maximize the collaborative potential of Microsoft Whiteboard, ensuring that teams work efficiently and in harmony.

1. Set Clear Objectives for Each Whiteboard Session

Before diving into the collaborative process, it's important to define the purpose of the session. Whether the goal is brainstorming new ideas, planning a project, or conducting a meeting, having a clear objective ensures that everyone is on the same page. Start by asking the following questions:

- What is the outcome we want from this session?

- What key points or topics need to be addressed?

- How will each team member contribute?

Once you've established these goals, communicate them clearly with the team. This helps avoid confusion, keeps the whiteboard focused, and streamlines the collaboration process.

2. Leverage Templates for Structured Collaboration

Microsoft Whiteboard offers a variety of templates, such as brainstorming grids, SWOT analysis charts, project management templates, and flowcharts. These templates are excellent for providing structure to the collaborative process. Using templates ensures that everyone knows where to contribute their ideas and helps guide the flow of the discussion.

For example, during a brainstorming session, a team can use a mind map template. Each participant can add their thoughts to different branches, allowing ideas to flow naturally while keeping them organized. Using pre-built templates also saves time and prevents team members from working on a blank canvas without direction.

3. Enable Real-Time Collaboration with Seamless Communication

Microsoft Whiteboard allows multiple users to work on the same board simultaneously, making it ideal for real-time collaboration. However, real-time collaboration can be chaotic without clear communication channels. Here are some tips to enhance communication while collaborating on Whiteboard:

- Use Microsoft Teams Integration: Microsoft Whiteboard is integrated with Microsoft Teams, making it easy to collaborate while video conferencing or chatting with your team. Ensure that the Whiteboard session is shared in the Teams meeting and that all participants can contribute while discussing ideas in real-time.

- Utilize Commenting and Sticky Notes: Not all collaboration happens at the same moment. If team members work asynchronously, adding comments or sticky notes to key areas of the whiteboard can help provide feedback or suggestions without interrupting the workflow of others.

- Tagging and Assigning Tasks: If your whiteboard session involves assigning responsibilities or tasks, use tags to identify who is responsible for specific elements on the whiteboard. Assign tasks with clear labels so that each team member knows what is expected of them.

4. Use Visual Cues for Better Organization

When collaborating with a large team, the whiteboard can quickly become cluttered. Visual cues such as color-coding, symbols, and distinct shapes can help keep things organized. By assigning different colors to specific themes, categories, or users, team members can easily navigate the whiteboard and focus on the parts that are relevant to them.

For example:

- Use green sticky notes for ideas that are already agreed upon.

- Red notes can highlight points that require further discussion.

- Blue notes may represent tasks assigned to specific team members.

By creating a visual hierarchy, teams can manage information more efficiently and ensure the whiteboard remains structured, even during complex collaboration sessions.

5. Manage Permissions and Access Levels

Not all team members may need full editing rights during a whiteboard session. Sometimes, restricting editing access to certain users while allowing others to view or comment can streamline the process and avoid potential confusion or accidental deletions.

When setting up the whiteboard, use Microsoft Whiteboard's permission settings to:

- Grant Full Access to Core Contributors: Only users directly involved in shaping the content should have full editing access.

- Allow View-Only Access to Stakeholders: If external partners, clients, or stakeholders need to monitor the session without contributing, granting them view-only access prevents unintentional interference with the collaborative process.

- Assign Commenting Rights: Some users may only need to provide feedback rather than directly modify the content. In such cases, granting them commenting rights can allow for valuable input without disrupting the whiteboard's organization.

6. Asynchronous Collaboration: Keeping the Momentum

Collaboration on Microsoft Whiteboard doesn't always need to happen in real-time. In today's fast-paced world, team members may be working across different time zones or schedules. Asynchronous collaboration on Whiteboard can be just as effective with the right approach.

Here's how to facilitate asynchronous collaboration:

- Set Clear Deadlines: If your team is collaborating asynchronously, make sure deadlines are in place for each part of the project. This helps ensure that tasks are completed in a timely manner and that the project moves forward smoothly.

- Encourage Regular Updates: Team members should regularly update the board with their progress, even if they are not contributing in real-time. This ensures that everyone is kept in the loop and can respond or add to the board when it's their turn.

- Annotate and Leave Feedback: If you're reviewing others' contributions outside of the live session, make use of comments, sticky notes, or annotations to leave feedback. This enables other team members to address or respond to your suggestions at their convenience.

7. Optimize Whiteboard for Remote Work and Hybrid Teams

In remote work or hybrid teams, the need for efficient collaboration is even greater. Microsoft Whiteboard's cloud-based platform allows remote users to contribute from anywhere. To optimize Whiteboard for remote collaboration:

- Use High-Quality Audio and Video: Pair Whiteboard sessions with clear communication tools, like Microsoft Teams. Ensure that participants have good-quality audio and video to make discussions smoother and minimize misunderstandings during remote meetings.

- Set Collaboration Guidelines: Establish guidelines for collaboration that outline how team members should interact on the whiteboard. For instance, encourage team members to announce when they are making major changes or additions, ensuring that no one's work is overwritten unintentionally.

- Foster Inclusivity in Sessions: Make sure everyone's voice is heard, especially in remote settings. Encourage quieter team members to use Whiteboard's features, like comments or sticky notes, to share their input if they're not comfortable speaking up during a meeting.

8. Whiteboard Hygiene: Keep Your Board Clean

Just like physical whiteboards, digital whiteboards can become cluttered over time. A messy whiteboard can make it difficult for teams to find important information or contribute effectively. Keeping your whiteboard clean and organized is essential for maintaining productivity.

Here are some tips to keep your whiteboard tidy:

- Periodically Archive Old Information: If parts of the whiteboard are no longer relevant, move them to a separate area or delete them altogether. Whiteboard offers the ability to save snapshots or export your work, so you don't have to lose important data, but it's crucial to keep the active board free of distractions.

- Use Sections for Different Themes: Organize the whiteboard into clear sections for different themes, tasks, or stages of the project. This prevents overlap and makes it easier for team members to locate the parts they need to work on.

- Appoint a Whiteboard Moderator: For large collaborative projects, assigning someone as the whiteboard moderator can help maintain order. This person can ensure the board stays organized, clear redundant information, and guide the collaborative session.

9. Review and Reflect: Continuous Improvement

After each collaborative session, take time to review how the session went and identify areas for improvement. Reflecting on what worked well and what didn't allows the team to fine-tune their collaboration process.

Key questions to consider in post-session reviews:

- Did the team achieve the session's objectives?

- Was the whiteboard easy to navigate, or did it become cluttered?

- How effective was communication during the collaboration?

By addressing these questions, teams can continuously optimize their use of Microsoft Whiteboard and make future sessions even more productive.

Conclusion

Optimizing Microsoft Whiteboard for collaboration is key to ensuring successful teamwork, whether working in real-time or asynchronously. By setting clear objectives, using templates, leveraging visual cues, and maintaining good whiteboard hygiene, teams can maximize the platform's potential. Additionally, proper management of permissions and fostering inclusivity can streamline the process and make Microsoft Whiteboard an indispensable tool for collaborative efforts.

6.2.3 Streamlining Workflow with Keyboard Shortcuts

In today's fast-paced digital environment, efficiency is key, and mastering keyboard shortcuts can significantly speed up your workflow in Microsoft Whiteboard. While the Whiteboard interface is designed to be user-friendly, relying solely on the graphical interface can slow you down, especially when performing repetitive tasks. By incorporating keyboard shortcuts into your routine, you can streamline your process, allowing for quicker navigation and manipulation of content. In this section, we'll explore the essential keyboard shortcuts that every Microsoft Whiteboard user should know, how they can boost your productivity, and tips for customizing your workflow for maximum efficiency.

The Importance of Keyboard Shortcuts

Keyboard shortcuts are more than just a convenient alternative to using a mouse or trackpad. They allow you to:

- Save Time: Shortcuts eliminate the need to navigate through menus and toolbars, reducing the time spent switching between tools.

- Improve Focus: With fewer distractions, you can stay focused on the task at hand instead of hunting for options in the interface.

- Enhance Accessibility: Shortcuts make navigation easier for users who may struggle with precise mouse movements, ensuring that everyone can use Whiteboard efficiently.

- Boost Productivity: By automating repetitive actions, such as undoing mistakes or switching between tools, shortcuts allow you to focus more on the content rather than the mechanics of the software.

Essential Microsoft Whiteboard Keyboard Shortcuts

Below is a list of some of the most useful keyboard shortcuts that can help streamline your workflow. These shortcuts cover basic navigation, drawing, formatting, and collaboration features in Microsoft Whiteboard.

Action	Windows Shortcut	Mac Shortcut

Undo	Ctrl + Z	Command + Z
Redo	Ctrl + Y	Command + Y
Select All	Ctrl + A	Command + A
Copy	Ctrl + C	Command + C
Paste	Ctrl + V	Command + V
Cut	Ctrl + X	Command + X
Delete	Delete	Delete
Zoom In	Ctrl + +	Command + +
Zoom Out	Ctrl + -	Command + -
Reset Zoom	Ctrl + 0	Command + 0
Pan (Hand Tool)	Spacebar + drag mouse	Spacebar + drag mouse
Draw (Pen)	P	P
Toggle Eraser	E	E
Open Color Picker	C	C
Toggle Ruler	R	R
Move Ruler	Arrow keys	Arrow keys
Rotate Ruler	Shift + Arrow keys	Shift + Arrow keys
Add Sticky Note	N	N
Insert Image	Ctrl + Shift + I	Command + Shift + I
Start Ink-to-Shape Mode	Shift + P	Shift + P
Full-Screen Mode	F11	Command + F
Exit Full-Screen Mode	Esc	Esc
Switch Between Open Whiteboards	Ctrl + Tab	Command + Tab

How to Effectively Use Keyboard Shortcuts

While the table above covers the basic shortcuts, knowing when and how to use them effectively is crucial for streamlining your workflow. Let's dive into practical scenarios where these shortcuts can make a big difference.

1. Navigating the Whiteboard with Speed

Navigating around the Whiteboard can sometimes be cumbersome, especially when you're working on a large canvas. Instead of using the mouse to zoom in and out, simply use `Ctrl +` or `Ctrl -` to quickly adjust your view. Similarly, resetting your zoom level with `Ctrl + 0` lets you return to a default view instantly. Combining these with the `Spacebar + drag` command allows for seamless movement across the canvas without having to manually switch to the hand tool.

2. Managing Objects and Layers Efficiently

Working with multiple objects—whether they are drawings, sticky notes, or images—can quickly become overwhelming. The `Ctrl + A` shortcut selects all items on the board, which is useful for mass actions like moving or resizing. Once selected, use `Ctrl + C` and `Ctrl + V` to quickly copy and paste objects. These shortcuts can also be used for duplicating sticky notes or shapes when brainstorming, allowing for rapid content creation.

In collaborative environments, it's common to delete or rearrange content. Using `Delete` to remove unwanted elements or `Ctrl + X` to cut and move them elsewhere saves you from having to right-click or find delete options in menus. These shortcuts ensure you maintain momentum while organizing your whiteboard content.

3. Correcting Mistakes Instantly

No matter how experienced you are with Whiteboard, mistakes happen. Instead of navigating to the toolbar for the undo button, pressing `Ctrl + Z` for undo and `Ctrl + Y` for redo becomes second nature after a while. These shortcuts are indispensable for quickly correcting errors or reverting changes without disrupting your flow.

4. Drawing and Sketching with Precision

If you use Microsoft Whiteboard for brainstorming or sketching, drawing tools are essential. Switching between the pen tool (`P`), eraser (`E`), and ruler (`R`) via shortcuts ensures smooth transitions while sketching diagrams or annotations. For example, you can toggle the ruler to draw straight lines and then rotate it using `Shift + Arrow keys` to create angled lines. This combination of drawing tools and shortcuts helps you create precise visual representations without slowing down your creative process.

The `Shift + P` shortcut activates Ink-to-Shape mode, which automatically converts hand-drawn shapes into perfect circles, squares, and other geometric figures. This is particularly useful in project planning or educational settings where visual clarity is essential.

5. Customizing Your Workflow

While Microsoft Whiteboard offers a default set of keyboard shortcuts, customization options may become available over time through Microsoft updates. Keeping an eye on these developments allows you to tailor your workflow even further, adapting Whiteboard to your specific use cases. In the meantime, learning to combine existing shortcuts creatively—such as zooming, selecting, and copying objects—can drastically improve your overall efficiency.

Case Study: Streamlining Collaboration with Shortcuts

To illustrate the impact of keyboard shortcuts on workflow efficiency, let's explore a scenario where you're working on a collaborative project with your team.

Scenario: You're leading a virtual brainstorming session using Microsoft Whiteboard. Your goal is to organize ideas into categories, sketch out a basic project roadmap, and finalize a draft for team review.

- Step 1: Brainstorming Session – As the team begins sharing ideas, you create multiple sticky notes by pressing `N` for each new idea. After a few minutes, the board is filled with notes. You quickly switch to the selection tool (`Ctrl + A`) to gather all the notes and group them into clusters based on themes.

- Step 2: Organizing and Categorizing – You use the ruler tool (`R`) to create dividing lines between categories and adjust the angle of the lines with `Shift + Arrow keys` to ensure they're aligned perfectly. For each category, you insert images and icons (`Ctrl + Shift + I`) to visually represent the ideas.

- Step 3: Sketching the Project Roadmap – You switch to the pen tool (`P`) and begin sketching the roadmap. With the Ink-to-Shape mode activated (`Shift + P`), your rough sketches are automatically converted into perfect shapes, making the roadmap look professional and easy to follow.

- Step 4: Finalizing the Draft – Once the roadmap is complete, you use `Ctrl + Z` to undo minor mistakes made during the drawing phase. You zoom out (`Ctrl -`) to view the entire whiteboard and make sure all elements are in place. After a final review, you save and export the whiteboard as a PDF, ensuring the project is ready for team review.

In this case study, keyboard shortcuts significantly reduced the time spent on repetitive tasks and allowed for smoother transitions between brainstorming, organizing, and finalizing content. These small, quick actions accumulate over time, leading to a more streamlined and productive workflow.

Tips for Mastering Keyboard Shortcuts

1. Start Small – Don't overwhelm yourself by trying to learn all the shortcuts at once. Start with the most frequently used shortcuts like `Ctrl + Z` (Undo) and `Ctrl + C` (Copy), and gradually build up your shortcut repertoire over time.

2. Create a Cheat Sheet – Keep a printed or digital list of shortcuts nearby as you get accustomed to them. Eventually, you'll internalize them, and your workflow will become much faster.

3. Practice Regularly – Consistency is key to mastery. The more you use shortcuts in your day-to-day work, the more intuitive they will become.

4. Customize Where Possible – Keep an eye on future Whiteboard updates, as customization features for shortcuts may be added. Tailoring shortcuts to your specific workflow can further improve efficiency.

Conclusion: The Power of Shortcuts in Enhancing Productivity

Keyboard shortcuts are an integral part of any efficient digital workspace, and Microsoft Whiteboard is no exception. By mastering shortcuts, you can focus less on the mechanics of the software and more on the ideas and collaboration that drive your projects. Whether you're brainstorming with your team, sketching complex diagrams, or managing project boards, shortcuts offer a faster, more intuitive way to interact with Whiteboard. As you continue using these time-saving techniques, you'll find your workflow becoming more streamlined, enabling you to accomplish more in less time.

6.3 Maximizing Productivity with Microsoft Whiteboard

Microsoft Whiteboard is a powerful tool that can revolutionize the way individuals and teams collaborate, brainstorm, and visualize ideas. However, like any tool, its true potential is unlocked when users understand how to use it efficiently. In this section, we'll explore how to maximize productivity using Whiteboard by focusing on key time-saving tips that will enhance your workflow and streamline your processes.

6.3.1 Time-Saving Tips

One of the most valuable aspects of Microsoft Whiteboard is its ability to simplify complex tasks and make collaboration seamless. To truly harness the efficiency of this tool, you need to understand the shortcuts, features, and strategies that save time while boosting effectiveness. Below are several key time-saving tips to help you get the most out of Microsoft Whiteboard.

1. Use Keyboard Shortcuts

Keyboard shortcuts are a simple yet effective way to speed up your work within Microsoft Whiteboard. Instead of manually clicking through menus, you can use shortcuts to perform actions faster. Here are a few essential shortcuts that can drastically improve your workflow:

- Ctrl + Z: Undo the last action.

- Ctrl + Y: Redo an action.

- Ctrl + C: Copy selected content.

- Ctrl + V: Paste copied content.

- Ctrl + X: Cut selected content.

- Ctrl + A: Select all elements on the whiteboard.

- Ctrl + D: Duplicate the selected object.

- Ctrl + G: Group selected items together.

By memorizing and using these shortcuts, you can perform common tasks much faster, leaving you more time to focus on brainstorming and collaboration rather than repetitive actions.

2. Create and Save Templates

If you find yourself repeatedly setting up similar structures or layouts, consider creating and saving templates within Microsoft Whiteboard. Templates can serve as starting points for your projects, saving you from recreating the same elements every time. For instance, if you often use flowcharts, brainstorming grids, or project planning boards, you can create a template with these features prearranged.

To save a whiteboard as a template:

1. Set up the elements you need.

2. Save the whiteboard with a clear template name.

3. Reopen and reuse the template for future projects by duplicating it.

Templates can also help maintain consistency across team projects, as everyone will be working from the same structure. This not only saves time but also ensures a unified approach to different projects.

3. Utilize the 'Ink to Shape' Feature

Drawing precise shapes with a mouse or stylus can be difficult and time-consuming. Microsoft Whiteboard includes an Ink to Shape feature that automatically recognizes hand-drawn shapes and converts them into perfect circles, squares, triangles, and more. This can save you time when creating diagrams, flowcharts, or visual aids by allowing you to draw naturally without worrying about perfection.

To use this feature:

1. Draw any rough shape, such as a circle or rectangle.

2. Watch as Microsoft Whiteboard automatically converts it into a clean, precise shape.

This feature is particularly useful in brainstorming sessions or meetings where speed is of the essence, but you still want to maintain a clean and professional look on your whiteboard.

4. Leverage Sticky Notes for Quick Organization

One of the quickest ways to organize thoughts or ideas on Microsoft Whiteboard is by using Sticky Notes. These can act as placeholders for text or ideas, allowing you to quickly jot down information without needing to format it. Sticky Notes are ideal for brainstorming, project planning, and collaborative sessions where participants need to contribute their thoughts rapidly.

Here are a few tips for using Sticky Notes efficiently:

- Color-code your notes: Assign different colors to categorize ideas, making it easier to differentiate between them at a glance.

- Use keyboard shortcuts: Press Ctrl + Enter to quickly insert a new Sticky Note.

- Bulk manage notes: Group similar notes together by dragging and dropping them into clusters.

By incorporating Sticky Notes into your workflow, you can structure your whiteboard more fluidly and dynamically, allowing for faster brainstorming sessions and easier navigation through ideas.

5. Group and Organize Content

When working on a whiteboard with multiple elements—whether they are drawings, shapes, Sticky Notes, or images—it can become overwhelming to manage and move everything around. Microsoft Whiteboard allows you to group items together, so you can treat them as a single unit. This is a massive time-saver, especially when reorganizing your whiteboard or shifting large sections around.

To group items:

1. Select multiple elements on the whiteboard by clicking and dragging.

2. Right-click and choose Group from the menu.

3. You can now move, resize, or manipulate the entire group as a single object.

Additionally, naming groups of elements can be helpful when working on large whiteboards. It allows you to quickly identify and access relevant sections without spending time searching through different parts of the board.

6. Import Existing Content

Microsoft Whiteboard allows you to import documents, images, and PDFs directly into your whiteboard. This is a fantastic way to save time, especially if you're collaborating on a project that already has pre-existing documents. Instead of manually recreating content or referencing external files, you can upload them to the whiteboard and continue working directly on the imported materials.

To import content:

1. Click on the Insert button.

2. Choose the type of content you want to upload (image, PDF, etc.).

3. Position and resize the file as needed on the whiteboard.

This is particularly useful for presentations, as you can bring in charts, graphs, or reports, and annotate them in real-time during meetings. It eliminates the need for switching between multiple applications, thus streamlining the entire process.

7. Collaborate in Real-Time with Clear Roles

When working on a collaborative whiteboard, it can save significant time if team members are assigned clear roles or responsibilities. Microsoft Whiteboard supports multi-user collaboration, meaning multiple people can work on the same board simultaneously. However, without clear coordination, it's easy to lose track of progress or create confusion.

Here's how to streamline real-time collaboration:

- Assign tasks or areas: Before starting a collaborative session, assign each participant a specific part of the whiteboard to work on. This prevents overlap and ensures that everyone is contributing efficiently.

- Use colors to differentiate work: Ask each participant to use a specific color when adding Sticky Notes, drawings, or text. This will make it easier to track contributions and assign follow-up tasks.

This kind of pre-planning saves time in the long run and ensures that the whiteboard remains organized, even when multiple people are working on it simultaneously.

8. Pin Frequently Used Tools to the Toolbar

By customizing the toolbar, you can access your most-used tools without having to search for them repeatedly. Pinning frequently used tools—such as the pen, Sticky Notes, or ruler—directly to the toolbar will streamline your workflow and reduce time spent navigating the interface.

To customize your toolbar:

1. Click on the toolbar settings.

2. Select Pin Tool next to the tools you use most frequently.

3. They will remain pinned for quick access.

Having quick access to your essential tools ensures that you can maintain momentum during your whiteboarding sessions, rather than pausing to search through menus.

9. Automate with Power Automate and Other Integrations

For advanced users, integrating Microsoft Whiteboard with tools like Power Automate or Microsoft Teams can further enhance productivity. Power Automate allows you to set up workflows that can trigger actions based on your whiteboard usage. For example, when a whiteboard is updated, you can automatically send notifications to relevant team members or update linked tasks in Microsoft Planner.

This automation not only saves time but also ensures that nothing falls through the cracks in terms of project management and communication.

Conclusion

Incorporating these time-saving tips into your daily Microsoft Whiteboard usage can significantly boost your productivity. By utilizing keyboard shortcuts, creating reusable templates, leveraging collaboration tools effectively, and automating tasks, you'll find that your workflow becomes more streamlined and efficient. These strategies not only save time but also make working within Microsoft Whiteboard more enjoyable and intuitive.

6.3.2 Keeping Your Whiteboard Organized

Maintaining organization in Microsoft Whiteboard is crucial for maximizing productivity, especially when dealing with large-scale projects, collaborative work, or multi-step tasks. An organized whiteboard ensures that ideas are easy to find, tasks are clear, and team members can quickly locate information without confusion. This section will dive deep into techniques and best practices for keeping your whiteboard space clean, structured, and optimized for efficiency.

1. Group Related Elements Together

One of the simplest ways to keep your whiteboard organized is to group related elements. Whether you're working with text, shapes, images, or sticky notes, grouping relevant items helps create a visual flow that is easier to follow. For example, if you're using the whiteboard for a project planning session, consider grouping tasks under categories like "To Do," "In Progress," and "Completed." This not only makes the whiteboard more visually appealing but also helps provide structure, which is key for quick navigation.

How to group items:

- Select the objects you want to group by dragging your cursor across them.

- Use the alignment and arrangement tools to keep things in line.

- Make use of different colors or shapes for specific categories of information to further differentiate sections of your board.

Grouping also applies to collaborating with a team. Ensure each team member's contributions are clearly defined and organized. For example, assign a specific area of the whiteboard for each contributor to prevent clutter and overlap.

2. Use Color-Coding for Clarity

Colors are powerful visual tools, and using them effectively in your whiteboard can significantly improve clarity and organization. Color-coding different elements, such as tasks, categories, or ideas, helps differentiate items and makes the whiteboard easier to navigate at a glance.

Best practices for color-coding:

- Assign specific colors to specific categories (e.g., red for urgent tasks, green for completed ones, yellow for notes, etc.).

- Use consistent color schemes across all your whiteboards to create a sense of familiarity and structure.

- Avoid using too many different colors. Stick to a palette of four to five colors for simplicity and avoid overwhelming the viewer.

The use of color can also extend to collaborative work. If several people are contributing to the whiteboard, assigning each individual a color for their contributions can make it easier to track who has added what content.

3. Utilize Sections and Labels

Breaking your whiteboard into distinct sections is another highly effective organizational strategy. If you're working on multiple tasks or themes within one whiteboard, having clearly defined sections will help ensure information doesn't overlap and become confusing. Each section can represent a different part of the project or meeting, making it easier to move between topics without losing focus.

How to create sections:

- Use the "Insert Text" or sticky note feature to label different areas.

- Separate sections with visual dividers or by drawing lines between topics.

- Maintain consistent labeling conventions across different whiteboards for coherence.

For example, in a project planning whiteboard, you could have sections like "Milestones," "Goals," "Challenges," and "Next Steps." These clearly defined sections allow you to organize your thoughts and ensure nothing is overlooked. Sections also work well for educational use cases, where different subjects or topics are organized into designated spaces on the board.

4. Leverage Templates for Repeated Processes

If you regularly use Microsoft Whiteboard for specific purposes, such as project planning or brainstorming sessions, you can save time and keep things organized by creating templates. A template helps maintain a consistent structure and reduces the time needed to arrange and organize your whiteboard for each new session. Microsoft Whiteboard offers several built-in templates, or you can design your own custom templates to suit your needs.

Tips for using templates:

- Pre-create layouts for common activities, such as brainstorming, project management, and meeting agendas.

- Ensure the template is simple and flexible enough to be reused across different projects or sessions.

- Share templates with team members so that everyone can quickly adapt to the whiteboard structure, keeping collaboration streamlined and efficient.

Templates can include pre-labeled sections, color-coded areas, and suggested content that makes starting a new project on Microsoft Whiteboard faster and more organized. This feature is especially helpful for recurring team meetings, where consistency is key to productivity.

5. Organize Sticky Notes by Priority and Category

Sticky notes are one of the most frequently used tools in Microsoft Whiteboard, particularly in brainstorming sessions, meetings, and project planning. However, without organization, they can quickly clutter your whiteboard and become overwhelming. To avoid this, make sure that your sticky notes are arranged in a clear and intentional way.

Best practices for organizing sticky notes:

- Sort sticky notes by priority, using a visual hierarchy where high-priority tasks are placed at the top.

- Group related notes together based on their category or function (e.g., tasks, questions, ideas, etc.).

- Use colors to differentiate between types of sticky notes, such as green for completed tasks, blue for pending tasks, and yellow for notes.

You can also create a dedicated section on your whiteboard for sticky notes, which makes it easier to manage and prevent clutter. Use this section to collect ideas and action items, keeping them separate from other whiteboard content like drawings, diagrams, or text blocks.

6. Regularly Review and Clean Up the Board

One key aspect of maintaining an organized whiteboard is regularly reviewing and cleaning it up. Over time, whiteboards can become cluttered with old or irrelevant information, which makes it harder to find what's important. By periodically revisiting your whiteboard, you can remove outdated content, reorganize sections, and update the board with fresh information.

Tips for reviewing and cleaning up your whiteboard:

- Set aside time at the end of each session to tidy up the board.

- Archive or save copies of important content before deleting it.

- Remove duplicate or outdated elements to prevent unnecessary clutter.

- Consolidate related content into groups or sections for easier navigation.

If your whiteboard is used for ongoing collaboration, regular cleanup becomes even more important. Each team member should take responsibility for maintaining their contributions and ensuring that the overall board remains clean and focused on the current task or project.

7. Take Advantage of the Locking Feature

When you have certain elements on your whiteboard that you don't want accidentally moved or altered, such as diagrams, templates, or important notes, use the "Lock" feature to keep them in place. This prevents unintended modifications and ensures that your layout remains intact even during collaborative sessions with multiple contributors.

How to use the locking feature:

- Select the item or group of items you wish to lock.

- Right-click and choose the "Lock" option to fix the object in place.

- To unlock, repeat the process and select "Unlock."

Locking is particularly useful when working with large or complex whiteboards, where even a small change to the layout can result in disorganization. It is also helpful for templates or static elements that are referenced repeatedly but don't need to be altered.

8. Use Zoom and Pan for Better Navigation

Microsoft Whiteboard offers the ability to zoom in and out, as well as pan across the board, which can greatly enhance your organization and navigation experience. If you're working on a large whiteboard, zooming out allows you to see the big picture, while zooming in lets you focus on specific details. The pan feature helps you move easily across different sections of your board.

Best practices for zoom and pan:

- Zoom out periodically to ensure your board is organized and that no elements are misplaced.

- Use zoom to concentrate on specific sections when working on detailed tasks.

- Pan across the board to maintain a continuous flow of work, especially when collaborating with others.

Efficient use of the zoom and pan tools also allows you to manage large amounts of information on a single whiteboard without sacrificing clarity or organization.

9. Archive Completed Whiteboards

As your work on a whiteboard is completed, it's important to archive or export it rather than leaving it active. Archiving finished boards keeps your workspace clean and helps you focus on current tasks, while also ensuring that past work is preserved for future reference.

How to archive or export whiteboards:

- Use the export feature to save your whiteboard as an image or PDF.

- Move completed boards to an "Archived" folder in your Microsoft Whiteboard account.

- Keep backups of important whiteboards to prevent data loss.

Archiving ensures that your Microsoft Whiteboard account doesn't become cluttered with old, irrelevant content, allowing you to keep your workspace clean and focused.

By implementing these organizational strategies, you can maintain an efficient, clutter-free whiteboard that boosts productivity and collaboration. Keeping your whiteboard organized is key to ensuring that it remains a valuable tool for brainstorming, project management, and communication. With the right approach, your whiteboard can become a streamlined, structured space that enhances your workflow and keeps your ideas and tasks clearly defined.

6.3.3 Utilizing Advanced Features

While Microsoft Whiteboard is commonly viewed as a simple tool for basic brainstorming and collaboration, it offers a wide array of advanced features that can greatly enhance your productivity when fully utilized. These features allow for more sophisticated collaboration, customization, and integration, making the platform not just a tool for sketching ideas, but a comprehensive environment for managing projects, conducting meetings, and fostering creativity.

In this section, we'll explore several advanced features and techniques, offering practical tips on how to integrate them into your workflow.

1. Interactive Content and Real-Time Collaboration

One of Microsoft Whiteboard's most powerful advanced features is its ability to host interactive content and enable seamless real-time collaboration. Unlike traditional whiteboards, Microsoft Whiteboard is not limited to static drawings or notes. Instead, you can insert interactive elements, such as:

- Embedded Content: Whether it's a PDF, Word document, or PowerPoint slide, embedding documents directly into your whiteboard makes collaboration more efficient. This feature is especially useful when conducting group reviews or brainstorming sessions. Users can annotate on top of the documents, highlight critical points, and suggest changes directly on the whiteboard without having to switch between multiple apps.

- Interactive Links: Adding hyperlinks to your whiteboard allows you to link external resources directly. For instance, if your team is brainstorming for a marketing campaign, you can link directly to competitor research, customer feedback surveys, or other resources for reference. This reduces friction in your workflow, allowing team members to access information quickly and stay focused on the task at hand.

- Live Editing: When multiple users are working on the same whiteboard, the updates happen in real-time, providing the sensation of working together in the same room. Live editing reduces delays caused by versioning issues or miscommunication. Whiteboard participants can immediately see annotations, sketches, and content added by others, enhancing overall group productivity and synergy.

Practical Example:

Imagine you're hosting a virtual project kick-off meeting. Using Microsoft Whiteboard, you can upload the project charter, timeline, and risk register directly to the whiteboard. As the meeting progresses, participants can highlight sections, add comments, and insert relevant links—such as a market analysis report—all in real time. This centralizes communication, enabling more fluid discussions and real-time decisions.

2. Advanced Pen Tools and Shape Recognition

While the basic drawing tools are sufficient for sketching quick ideas, advanced pen tools and the automatic shape recognition feature take things a step further. Whether you are creating diagrams, flowcharts, or mind maps, these tools ensure that your visual content is clean, organized, and professional.

- Custom Pen Settings: Microsoft Whiteboard allows you to customize your pen settings with different colors, line thicknesses, and styles. This feature can be used to differentiate between team members' contributions or to structure complex diagrams in a visually organized way. For instance, thicker lines can be used to represent primary concepts, while thinner lines can indicate secondary or tertiary information.

- Shape Recognition: With Microsoft Whiteboard's automatic shape recognition, you can draw freehand shapes like circles, rectangles, and triangles, and the system will automatically refine them into perfect geometrical shapes. This feature is perfect for creating professional-looking diagrams, graphs, or flowcharts, ensuring that your whiteboard looks clean and organized even when quickly sketched.

Practical Example:

In a team planning meeting, you might be drawing a workflow that involves several decision points and actions. As you sketch circles and arrows to represent these, Microsoft Whiteboard automatically converts them into neat, evenly spaced shapes and lines. This improves the clarity of your diagram, making it easier for others to follow the workflow.

3. Templates for Structured Brainstorming and Planning

Microsoft Whiteboard includes a variety of templates designed to streamline specific types of sessions, such as brainstorming, strategic planning, and problem-solving workshops. Instead of starting from scratch, you can choose from pre-built templates that guide the team through structured exercises, ensuring that sessions stay on track and are productive.

- Built-in Templates: Microsoft Whiteboard offers templates for activities like SWOT analysis, project planning, and retrospectives. Using these templates provides structure to your meetings, ensuring that important aspects of the discussion aren't overlooked. For example, a retrospective template will already include sections for "What went well" and "What can be improved," allowing the team to immediately start adding notes rather than worrying about organizing the whiteboard themselves.

- Custom Templates: If you find yourself conducting similar meetings or workshops frequently, creating custom templates in Microsoft Whiteboard can save a lot of time. You can design your whiteboard in a way that's specific to your organization's needs, whether that's a particular project management framework or brainstorming session format.

Practical Example:

During a strategic planning meeting, your team can use the built-in SWOT analysis template. The pre-formatted template divides the board into four sections—Strengths, Weaknesses, Opportunities, and Threats—allowing team members to add their input directly into the appropriate boxes. This keeps the discussion focused and ensures that all key areas are addressed.

4. Using Sticky Notes and Grouping for Effective Idea Management

Sticky notes are a powerful feature that facilitates idea generation and organization in brainstorming sessions. They are great for jotting down quick ideas, to-do lists, or key insights, and can be grouped and organized to find common themes or priorities.

- Sticky Notes for Brainstorming: Sticky notes allow each participant to contribute their thoughts in a concise, visual way. Each idea can be color-coded or labeled to indicate its importance or relevance to different categories.

- Grouping Sticky Notes: Once all ideas are on the whiteboard, you can easily drag and group related sticky notes together. This is particularly useful for identifying themes, organizing ideas for project plans, or creating action items for team members to address after a meeting.

Practical Example:

In a product development brainstorming session, team members can each add their ideas using sticky notes. After everyone has contributed, the facilitator can quickly group the sticky notes into themes such as "Feature Requests," "User Experience Improvements," and "Technical Challenges." This allows the team to identify the most important ideas and focus their efforts on prioritizing the tasks ahead.

5. Real-Time Feedback with Reactions and Annotations

One of the features that makes Microsoft Whiteboard stand out for collaboration is the ability to provide real-time feedback using simple reactions and annotations. This allows team members to quickly communicate their thoughts on specific content without disrupting the flow of the meeting.

- Reactions: Users can add reactions—such as a thumbs-up, heart, or lightbulb icon—directly onto specific parts of the whiteboard. This is an easy and non-intrusive way for participants to agree on ideas, signal their approval, or highlight important concepts without needing to interrupt the meeting for a formal discussion.

- Annotations: In addition to standard drawing tools, the annotation feature allows users to make notes directly on top of images, documents, or diagrams that have been inserted into the whiteboard. This is especially useful in feedback sessions or group reviews, where participants can highlight areas that need improvement or further discussion.

Practical Example:

During a design review, a team member can highlight sections of a proposed UI layout and use a heart reaction to indicate their approval of specific elements. Other members might use the annotation tool to circle areas that need adjustment, leaving detailed comments about what should be changed.

6. Infinite Canvas for Large-Scale Projects

The infinite canvas in Microsoft Whiteboard allows you to create large, sprawling whiteboards without running out of space. This is particularly useful for managing large-scale projects, mind maps, or complex brainstorming sessions that require significant visual space to organize ideas.

- Zooming and Navigation: With the infinite canvas, you can zoom in and out freely, exploring different sections of the whiteboard without losing the overall structure. This is perfect for visualizing the entire project from a high-level perspective, then zooming in to focus on specific details as needed.

- Organizing Complex Workflows: Using the infinite canvas feature, you can create detailed workflows or project maps that include multiple interconnected ideas. By adding sections for each phase of the project or workstream, you can easily navigate between them while keeping all related content in the same workspace.

Practical Example:

In a product roadmap planning session, you can use the infinite canvas to create a detailed map of all product milestones, phases, and tasks. Each section of the roadmap can be worked on independently, with team members contributing content and feedback as the project evolves.

Conclusion

By taking advantage of Microsoft Whiteboard's advanced features, you can significantly enhance your productivity and the effectiveness of your collaboration efforts. Whether you're managing large projects, conducting brainstorming sessions, or facilitating remote meetings, these tools provide the flexibility and functionality needed to streamline your workflow. Utilizing these advanced features not only helps keep your whiteboard organized but also ensures that your collaboration is more dynamic, efficient, and results-driven.

Conclusion

Key Takeaways

As we come to the conclusion of "Microsoft Whiteboard Basics: A Beginner's Guide," it's important to reflect on the key concepts and skills that you've gained throughout this journey. The goal of this book has been to provide you with a strong foundation for using Microsoft Whiteboard effectively, whether you're working alone or collaborating with others. Let's summarize the key takeaways that will empower you to use this tool efficiently and creatively.

1. Understanding the Core Interface

From the outset, you learned how to navigate Microsoft Whiteboard's interface. This is the first critical step in mastering any digital tool, and now you should feel confident moving through the workspace, whether it's adjusting the layout, switching between boards, or locating tools in the toolbar.

The interface's simplicity is designed to enhance creativity, rather than overwhelm the user. By familiarizing yourself with features like the toolbar, workspace, and the various menus, you've gained a deeper understanding of how to set up and access whiteboards quickly and efficiently. Remember, every time you start a new whiteboard, your knowledge of the interface will enable you to dive straight into content creation with minimal setup.

2. Effective Use of Whiteboard Tools

The variety of tools Microsoft Whiteboard offers allows users to express ideas visually. You've mastered key tools such as the pen and pencil, eraser, and ruler, which enable you to create precise and clear diagrams or notes. You've also learned how to customize these tools by changing colors and thickness to suit your needs.

Furthermore, features such as sticky notes, text boxes, and shapes offer a great way to organize and display information in a structured manner. These tools help you manage your ideas and present them clearly, ensuring that any project or brainstorming session is not only engaging but easy to follow.

3. Collaboration and Real-Time Communication

One of the standout features of Microsoft Whiteboard is its real-time collaboration capabilities. Whether you are working on a project within your organization or collaborating with clients remotely, you now know how to invite collaborators, set permissions, and track changes as you work together on a shared whiteboard.

The ability to communicate effectively while co-creating on a whiteboard has become more important than ever in today's remote work environment. Features such as tagging, commenting, and assigning tasks directly within a whiteboard streamline collaboration, allowing teams to stay on the same page and maintain productive workflows. This level of interaction enhances communication and ensures that all participants are engaged in the creative process.

4. Integrating Microsoft Whiteboard with Other Tools

Microsoft Whiteboard doesn't exist in a vacuum. One of the major advantages of the tool is its seamless integration with other Microsoft 365 applications like Teams, OneNote, and PowerPoint. Throughout this guide, you learned how to embed whiteboards into virtual meetings via Teams, share them during presentations, and incorporate them into documents.

This integration empowers you to take your whiteboards beyond the application itself and use them as part of larger projects. Whether you're presenting ideas in a meeting or embedding a whiteboard into a report, knowing how to connect Microsoft Whiteboard with other tools amplifies its usefulness.

5. Creativity and Customization with Templates

You now understand how to use built-in templates for brainstorming, planning, and organizing ideas. Templates provide a structured approach for various tasks, ensuring that your workflow remains organized and focused. More importantly, you've also explored how to customize and save your own templates, which adds a personal touch to your whiteboards.

Custom templates enable you to standardize workflows, especially in repetitive tasks such as project management or classroom activities. The ability to create, modify, and reuse templates allows you to streamline your work and save time, all while maintaining creativity.

6. Whiteboard as a Learning and Business Tool

One of the overarching themes of this guide is the versatility of Microsoft Whiteboard. Whether you are using it as an educational tool to facilitate interactive learning or as a business tool to streamline meetings and visual brainstorming, you've explored how to use Whiteboard in a variety of contexts.

Educators can benefit from the collaborative environment it creates for students, offering visual explanations and fostering group projects. In business settings, Whiteboard can be used to drive innovation, assist in project management, and enhance remote communication. Its adaptability is what makes it a powerful tool for multiple professional and personal applications.

7. Problem-Solving and Troubleshooting

As with any technology, issues may arise, and troubleshooting is an essential skill. From syncing issues to connectivity challenges, you've learned how to address common problems that might disrupt your workflow. By understanding these common issues and having solutions ready, you can quickly resolve problems and keep your focus on the task at hand.

Efficiency in troubleshooting ensures that you won't lose valuable time or work when dealing with minor technical difficulties, further reinforcing your confidence in using Microsoft Whiteboard in a professional setting.

8. Maximizing Efficiency Through Best Practices

Efficiency and productivity were key themes throughout this guide. By mastering organizational techniques, such as naming and categorizing your boards, making use of keyboard shortcuts, and keeping your boards tidy, you've learned how to streamline your workflow. These best practices ensure that your work with Microsoft Whiteboard is both efficient and effective, allowing you to accomplish more in less time.

Moreover, applying advanced features, like mind mapping or diagramming, enables you to use Whiteboard not only for basic visual communication but also as a powerful tool for complex projects and problem-solving.

9. Leveraging Advanced Features

As your skills progress, you can take advantage of the more advanced tools Microsoft Whiteboard offers. This includes using diagrams, flowcharts, and even incorporating media files into your whiteboards. You've learned how to annotate, draw, and import files in ways that enhance your ability to present information clearly.

These advanced tools will be especially useful when tackling larger projects that require a higher level of organization and detail. Whether you're drafting a project plan, creating a roadmap, or visually outlining an argument, advanced features take your Whiteboard skills to the next level.

10. The Role of Microsoft Whiteboard in a Digital Workspace

In conclusion, Microsoft Whiteboard is more than just a digital whiteboard—it's a tool that enhances creativity, promotes collaboration, and brings efficiency to both individual and team workflows. Its place in the broader Microsoft 365 ecosystem ensures that it can be used effectively across various digital environments, making it a powerful tool for modern work and learning settings.

By mastering the basics and exploring advanced features, you are now equipped to use Microsoft Whiteboard to its full potential, whether that's in the classroom, the boardroom, or your home office.

These key takeaways serve as a quick reference and reminder of the comprehensive skill set you have acquired through this guide. Keep these points in mind as you continue your Microsoft Whiteboard journey, and you will be well-prepared to tackle any creative or collaborative task with confidence.

Acknowledgments

First and foremost, I would like to extend my heartfelt thanks to you, the reader, for choosing this book. Your decision to embark on the journey of learning Microsoft Whiteboard is truly appreciated, and it is a privilege to have the opportunity to guide you through this process. Whether you're using Whiteboard for personal creativity, team collaboration, or business purposes, my hope is that this guide will serve as a valuable resource for unlocking the full potential of this powerful tool.

Writing this book has been a rewarding journey, and it wouldn't have been possible without the support and encouragement of many people. To my family and friends, your patience and understanding during the countless hours I spent writing and revising have meant the world to me. I am incredibly grateful for your unwavering belief in this project.

To my colleagues and the larger community of Microsoft Whiteboard users—your insights, questions, and experiences have been a constant source of inspiration. By sharing your stories and challenges, you have shaped the direction of this book, ensuring it speaks to the real needs of its readers. Thank you for your contributions, which have helped make this book both practical and relatable.

I would also like to express my gratitude to the development team behind Microsoft Whiteboard. Your vision in creating a tool that enhances collaboration and creativity has revolutionized the way we work and communicate in both personal and professional settings.

Finally, to you, the reader—thank you for placing your trust in this book. I understand the time and effort it takes to learn something new, and I sincerely hope that this guide serves you well as you explore all that Microsoft Whiteboard has to offer. I am excited to see how you will apply these skills in your projects, teams, and creative endeavors.

Thank you once again, and I wish you much success on your Microsoft Whiteboard journey!

Warmest regards,

www.ingramcontent.com/pod-product-compliance
Lightning Source LLC
LaVergne TN
LVHW081333050326
832903LV00024B/1141

* 9 7 9 8 3 3 9 8 4 5 2 1 8 *